WITNESS
FOR THE
DEFENSE

ELIZABETH LOFTUS, Ph.D. AND KATHERINE KETCHAM

ST. MARTIN'S PRESS | NEW YORK

WITNESS FOR THE DEFENSE

THE ACCUSED, THE EYEWITNESS, AND THE EXPERT WHO PUTS MEMORY ON TRIAL

■

We dedicate this book to the women and men who have been wrong-fully accused, convicted, imprisoned, or have otherwise suffered because of faulty eyewitness testimony.

WITNESS FOR THE DEFENSE: THE ACCUSED, THE EYEWITNESS, AND THE EXPERT WHO PUTS MEMORY ON TRIAL. Copyright © 1991 by Elizabeth Loftus and Katherine Ketcham. All rights reserved. Printed in the United States of America. No part of this book may be used or reproduced in any manner whatsoever without written permission except in the case of brief quotations embodied in critical articles or reviews. For information, address St. Martin's Press, 175 Fifth Avenue, New York, N.Y. 10010.

Design by Chris Welch

Library of Congress Cataloging-in-Publication Data
Loftus, Elizabeth F.
    Witness for the defense : the accused, the eyewitness, and the
    expert who puts memory on trial / Elizabeth Loftus and Katherine
    Ketcham.
        p. cm.
    ISBN 0-312-08455-2 (pbk.)
    1. Witnesses—United States.   2. Evidence, Criminal—United
States.   3. Criminals—United States—Identification.
4. Psychology, Forensic.   I. Ketcham, Katherine.
II. Title.
KF9672.L65   1991
345.73'066—dc20
[347.30566]   90-48523
                                                                        CIP

10 9 8 7 6

Hamlet: Do you see yonder cloud that's almost in shape of a camel?

Polonius: By the mass, and 'tis like a camel, indeed.

Hamlet: Methinks it is like a weasel.

Polonius: It is backed like a weasel.

Hamlet: Or like a whale?

Polonius: Very like a whale.

—William Shakespeare,
Hamlet, Act III, scene ii

CONTENTS

ACKNOWLEDGMENTS

A book of this nature could not have been written without the cooperation of numerous individuals personally involved in the cases described. The authors owe a great debt of thanks to the defendants, their family members, lawyers, investigators, jurors, and others whose lives were caught up in these tragic dramas. We would like to offer special thanks to Richard Hansen, David Allen, Tom Hillier, Les Burns, and Joanne Spencer.

The book weaves basic psychological research into the fabric of these real-life cases involving murder, rape, and other heinous crimes. For supporting the basic research, Elizabeth Loftus is especially grateful to the National Science Foundation and the National Institute of Mental Health.

We express great gratitude to our literary agent, Carole Abel, who helped pull this book out of the dream stage into reality.

Several friends and colleagues commented on chapters and gave us valuable suggestions for revising. Among the hardest-working were Billy Heath, Jean McMenemy, Laurie Becker, Missy Peterson, and Karen Preston. Marcia Gossard provided valuable research assistance.

Finally, we thank our families and close friends. In particular, Geoffrey Loftus and Patrick Spencer provided love and support. And Kathy Ketcham would like to thank her three young children, Robyn, Alison, and Benjamin, for everything and then some.

AUTHORS' NOTE

Witness for the Defense is a collection of true stories based on Dr. Elizabeth Loftus's personal experiences as an expert witness. It is our goal to use these real-life courtroom dramas as a vehicle for conveying information about psychology in general and memory in particular.

Our material is drawn from trial transcripts, police reports, newspaper accounts, and interviews with witnesses, defendants, defense and prosecuting attorneys, jurors, and family members. Certain scenes have been dramatically re-created in order to convey important ideas or to simplify the story, and trial transcripts and testimony were edited in places to make the material more understandable and readable. We chose to change the names and identities of certain individuals to protect their privacy; in those cases, the name is italicized the first time it appears.

In order to tell these stories, we have had to rely on the memories of those involved in the dramas as well as our own personal memories of the events described. Although we have struggled to correct obvious biases and base our accounts on the known and undisputed facts, it is unavoidable that these retrospective interpretations will contain memory flaws.

We know all too well from the psychological research and the experience of writing this book that memory is not always the same thing as the truth.

WITNESS FOR THE DEFENSE

PART ONE

BACKGROUND

TRIALS OF A PSYCHOLOGIST

"I don't think a lot of people realize how important innocence is to innocent people."

—From the movie *A Cry in the Dark*

I walk up the narrow wooden aisle, the silence amplified by the clicking of my heels on the slick polished floor. The court clerk, an ancient, grandmotherly type with pink rouge in perfect circles on her cheeks, is waiting for me. I raise my hand and listen to her recite by heart the litany: "Do you swear to tell the truth, the whole truth and nothing but the truth, so help you God?" Automatically I answer, "I do." The clerk retreats, and I walk the few steps to the wooden box, step up, sit down, facing the courtroom. All eyes are fixed on me.

The defense attorney approaches the witness box, nods his head at me. He is defending a twenty-three-year-old man accused of breaking into a home in the upper-middle-class community of Van Nuys, California, and shooting to death an elderly man.

"Would you state your name, please?"

"My name is Elizabeth Loftus." I know the routine by heart and spell out my last name for the court reporter. "L-O-F-T-U-S."

"Dr. Loftus," the defense attorney says, his deep voice resounding throughout the courtroom like a baritone solo in a church choir, "what, exactly, is your profession or occupation?"

"I'm currently a professor of psychology at the University of Washington in Seattle."

"Could you tell us a little bit about your educational background and teaching experience?"

For the next ten minutes I recite my credentials—the Ph.D. from Stanford, the honorary degrees, memberships in various professional societies, honors, awards, books and articles published. The twelve members of the jury look slightly bored—Okay, okay, she's an expert, let's get on with it.

"Have you ever qualified as an expert witness in eyewitness identification before?" the defense attorney asks me.

"Yes, many times; approximately a hundred times."

"In this state?"

"Yes, and in many other states also. Thirty-five states altogether."

"All right," the defense attorney says. He walks back to the defense table and shuffles some papers. I'm suddenly aware of the sounds of legs being crossed, feet scraping against the wooden floors, throats being cleared. A moment passes and the noise begins to die down.

"Dr. Loftus, let me ask you—is there a generally accepted theory of how memory works?"

"There is a generally accepted theory in our field that memory doesn't work like a videotape recorder. We don't record an event and then play it back later. The process is much more complex . . ."

I talk, then, about the acquisition, retention, and retrieval stages of memory, reciting all the details that I have recited so many times in the past. The prosecutor rolls a pencil between his fingers and watches me, his skepticism evident in the frown creasing his face. He is hoping to find a little hole, a tiny rip in the fabric of my testimony where he can dig in and begin to tear me apart.

I talk for nearly two hours about the way memory works and the way it fails. At 11:00 A.M., the judge calls a fifteen-minute recess. I stand up, step down, and walk across the courtroom, headed out to the hallway for a drink of water and a change of scenery. When I pass the defense table, the defendant raises his eyes and looks directly at me. I see the tiny beads of perspiration on his upper lip and notice how his starched shirt cuts into the soft flesh of his neck. He is a mechanic, twenty-three years old, married, has two children, and is studying in night school to get his high school degree. I've read hundreds of pages in preparation for my testimony, and those are among the few personal facts I encountered about the defendant. Sometimes it is better not to know too much.

He is looking up at me with such hope, his fear palpable in the still air of this stark, windowless courtroom, that I am struck by the incongruity of this face-to-face meeting. What am I doing here? What business does a research psychologist have in a court of law, offering facts taken from countless scientific experiments, hoping to communicate that our memories are sometimes distortions of reality, inaccurate images of the past?

With that question, even as I continue walking down the courtroom aisle and out to the hallway, I think back in time to a polished wood table in a conference room in Ventura Hall at Stanford University.

It is 1969. A graduate student is droning on about "decay rates in picture perception" and I am writing a quick letter to my uncle Joe in Pittsburgh. I'm halfway through my doctoral dissertation—titled "An Analysis of the Structural Variables that Determine Problem-Solving Difficulty on a Computer-Based Teletype"—and to tell the truth, I'm a bit bored with the whole thing. Somewhere, at that very moment, in schools throughout the Santa Clara valley, twelve- and thirteen-year-old kids were sitting down at computers, trying to solve increasingly complex word problems. I'd take the data, tabulate the answers, and make tentative conclusions about how adolescents solve problems, which problems are more difficult to solve, and why.

It was tedious work, no doubt about it. The theoretical model had been set up years earlier by my Ph.D. advisor, and I was just one of several graduate students, each of us plugged into a specific slot, computing our statistical analyses, feeding our results into a common pot. It occurred to me that my particular job was a little like cutting up carrots to put in a soup. To the left and right of me were other students, equally frenzied and meticulous about cutting up their onions, celery, potatoes, chunks of beef, and then tossing them into the same huge pot. And I couldn't help thinking, All I've done is cut up the carrots.

My thesis was in the final draft stage, and I was five weeks into a social psychology course that I needed to fill my distribution requirements when my neat, tidy, slightly boring world began to tilt on its axis. The professor, Jon Freedman, a funny, fiercely intelligent social psychologist, was discussing the topic of attitude change, and during the lecture I asked a question about the role of memory in changing attitudes.

After class, Freedman stopped me and said, "So, you're interested in memory? Well, so am I. If you'd like to do some research, I could use your help on a project. The question I'd like to explore is this: How do people reach into their long-term memory storage vaults and produce appropriate responses to given questions? We know people can do it and that they do it all the time—but how, exactly, does our brain organize, store, and retrieve information from long-term memory?"

With that conversation, my life changed. Freedman and I designed an experiment in which we gave subjects two word cues and then measured how long it took them to search through their memories and come up with a response. I had an informal title for the study—"Give Me an Animal Beginning with the Letter Z." We presented one group of subjects with two cues: Animal/Z, for example, or Fruit/Small, and then we timed their responses. We presented another group of subjects with the two word cues transposed—Z/Animal, Small/Fruit—and timed their responses. When we compared the response times of the two groups, we discovered that the cues beginning with the concept—animal or fruit—elicited a faster response, approximately 250 milliseconds, or one-quarter of a second faster. This led us to hypothesize that the human brain organizes information according to concepts or categories, such as animals or fruits, rather than attributes, such as "small" or "words beginning with the letter Z."

In my last six months of graduate school, I spent every free moment in Freedman's lab, setting up the experimental design, running subjects, tabulating the data, and analyzing the results. As the project took shape and Freedman and his students realized that we were on to something, that we were actually discovering something new about how the brain works, I began to think of myself for the first time as a *research psychologist*. Oh, those were lovely words—I could design an experiment, set it up, and follow it through. I felt for the first time that I was a scientist, and I knew with ultimate clarity that it was exactly what I wanted to be doing with my life.

"Retrieval of Words from Long-term Memory" was published in

6

1971 in the *Journal of Verbal Learning and Verbal Behavior*. A year later Freedman and I published a second paper about long-term memory; this time my name appeared first, as senior author. The study of memory had become my specialty, my passion. In the next few years I wrote dozens of papers about how memory works and how it fails, but unlike most researchers studying memory, my work kept reaching out into the real world—to what extent, I wondered, could a persons's memory be shaped by suggestion? When people witness a serious automobile accident, how accurate is their recollection of the facts? If a witness is questioned by a police officer, will the manner of questioning alter the representation of the memory? Can memories be supplemented with additional, false information? I wanted substance, I needed to end up with more than theoretical hot air. I wanted my work to make a difference in people's lives.

In 1974 I wrote an article that would radically alter the direction of my life. "Reconstructing Memory: The Incredible Eyewitness" appeared in the December 1974 issue of *Psychology Today*. At the end of the article—in which I discussed experiments I'd conducted in my laboratory that showed how leading questions can introduce new information that actually alters a person's memory of an event—I mentioned a case I'd worked on with the Seattle public defender's office. A young woman and her boyfriend had gotten into a violent argument. The woman ran to the bedroom, grabbed a gun, and shot him six times. The prosecutor called it first-degree murder, but her lawyer claimed she acted in self-defense. At the trial, a dispute arose about the time that had elapsed between the grabbing of the gun and the first shot. The defendant and her sister said two seconds, while another witness said five minutes. The exact amount of elapsed time made all the difference in the world to the defense, which insisted that the killing had occurred suddenly, in fear, and without a moment's hesitation. In the end, the jury must have believed the defendant; it acquitted her.

Within days of publication of the *Psychology Today* article, my phone was ringing off the hook. Lawyers wanted my opinion about the eyewitness evidence against their clients, people who had been accused of all manner of heinous crimes, from armed robbery to rape to murder. I offered my advice, and I began to appear in courtrooms as an expert witness on the subject of the fallibility of memory.

In late December 1975, just before Christmas, I received a call from a Utah lawyer by the name of John O'Connell. O'Connell was representing a young law student from Seattle who was accused of kidnapping an eighteen-year-old woman in Salt Lake City. The kidnapping victim identified the man more than eleven months after the incident, after viewing hundreds of mug-shot pictures. The police transcript was replete with leading and suggestive questions by the interviewer and hesitations and uncertainties on the part of the victim.

I decided to take the case, and on February 25, 1976, I testified in Salt Lake City. The defendant was eventually found guilty of aggravated kidnapping and sentenced to one to five years in prison. His name was Ted Bundy.

Ted Bundy was not the last guilty man whose case I worked on. In 1982 I agreed to testify for Angelo Buono, who was eventually convicted of sexually assaulting and strangling nine women in Los Angeles; Buono and his cousin, Kenneth Bianchi, were popularly known as the Hillside Stranglers.

In 1984 I testified for Willie Mak, who was convicted of murdering thirteen people in Seattle's Wah Mee massacre. A cousin of sixty-one-year-old Wai Chin, the sole survivor of the massacre, told a newspaper reporter that he wanted to spit in my face after I discussed in court the impact of the extraordinary trauma of the killings on Wai Chin's memory.

Another unpopular case that I worked on intermittently for many years was the McMartin Preschool case. Raymond Buckey, and his mother, Peggy McMartin Buckey, were charged with sixty-five counts of child molestation at their Manhattan Beach, California, preschool. Children testified that Ray Buckey stuck pencils, silverware, and other stray objects into their vaginas and anuses, that he killed a horse with a baseball bat, and that he took them on field trips to cemeteries.[1] As I reviewed the voluminous transcripts of the first trial, covering twenty-eight months of testimony, I found

1. In January 1990, jurors acquitted Peggy McMartin Buckey, sixty-three, on all charges; Raymond Buckey, thirty-one, was acquitted on all but thirteen charges. (In a second trial, jurors could not reach a verdict on the remaining thirteen charges against Raymond Buckey, and the prosecution decided not to re-try him.) The trials ran nearly three years and cost $15 million. The Buckeys spent two years and five years, respectively, in jail.

several fascinating quotes about memory. The judge proclaimed on February 25, 1988, on page 28,857 of the trial transcript:

> "Knowledge can be conscious or subconscious. In other words, there's a concept, which I think is accurate, that you never forget, that is, lose from your memory anything you've ever seen or heard, but that your ability to call it into your consciousness is quite limited."

I've spent twenty years of my professional career trying to dispel the myth that human memory is infallibile and immune from distortion, and that's why I was consulted in the McMartin case. One child witness was four when the alleged abuse took place, seven when she first mentioned it to a social worker, eight when she told her story to a grand jury, and ten when she testified in court. What could have happened to her memory in those six years? That seemed to me a crucial question for the jury to consider in their weighing of guilt and innocence, and yet few people can regard my testimony in such sensational cases with dispassion. At a recent lunch with a friend who is a kindergarten teacher and the mother of preschool children, I mentioned my involvement in the McMartin case. She turned and looked at me as if I were a fly that had just landed in her soup. "How could you?" she exclaimed. "Do you have no morals, no conscience?"

Several years ago a prosecutor confronted me in the hallway outside the courtroom where I had testified for the defense in a rape case. He walked right up to me and, in a voice heavy with self-righteous fury, said, "You're nothing but a whore." The defense attorney quickly took my arm and led me away.

Judges often view me as an unnecessary complication and only reluctantly accept my testimony; they claim that such expert testimony invades the province of the jury, or that I offer jurors little more than commonsense information.

My fellow psychologists are in bitter disagreement about the appropriateness of expert psychological testimony. My opponents argue that my research is unproven in real-life situations and that my testimony is therefore premature and highly prejudicial.

Victims' rights groups accuse me of tampering with truth and justice by undermining a witness's credibility. They suggest that I should assume personal responsibility for allowing the guilty to go free.

I recently testified about the problematical nature of eyewitness testimony in a rape case. After the rapist was acquitted, I received a long, angry letter from the mother of the victim. By testifying for the defendant, she claimed, I had negated her daughter's testimony and contributed to her suffering. By accepting a fee for my testimony, she insinuated, I had joined hands with the murderers and rapists of the world and turned my back on the innocent victims.

How did that letter make me feel? Rotten, miserable, awful. For days I walked around wondering why I do what I do and thinking that maybe it was time to go back in my windowless lab and stay there for a decade or two. But life is very strange. A week after I received this mother's anguished letter, a call came through from a lawyer with whom I'd been working on an appeal for a juvenile convicted of sexual assault. "I just came back from a hearing," he told me. "We're trying to get the case dismissed because it turns out that the prosecution hid a witness, a woman who was apparently assaulted by the same man and who insisted that it couldn't have been my client who attacked her. The prosecution lied to us, distorted the evidence, and threw every obstacle he could find at us in an attempt to nail my client. An innocent man has been accused, convicted, and locked up in prison because the system has gone rotten. At this moment, to tell you the truth, I'm ashamed to call myself a lawyer."

This was not the first time a defense lawyer told me that the police and prosecutors had gone too far in trying to make a case against a defendant. The problem, in most cases, isn't malice; it isn't even incompetence. When police and prosecutors withhold evidence, twist the facts, or pressure their witnesses, they do so because they believe with full confidence and assurance that they have the right person in custody, and that it is their duty to see justice done. Once they say to themselves "we've got the right person, we have to get this person off the streets," they may not even perceive that withholding evidence or slightly distorting the facts is the wrong thing to do. But the problem doesn't end there, for misinformation can be communicated to the witnesses, who may ignore their doubts and misgivings, and testify confidently in court that they are absolutely convinced that the defendant is, indeed, the real criminal. In such circumstances, there is an increased risk that an innocent person will be convicted.

As Francis Bacon said in the sixteenth century: "For when once the court goes on the side of injustice, the law becomes a public robber, and one man really a wolf to another." I remember the words of the great nineteenth-century jurist William Blackstone, who insisted that it is better to let ten guilty men go free than to convict one innocent man. And I remember the simple, anguished words of Philip Caruso, falsely convicted of armed robbery in 1938: "When you're guilty and in prison, you're okay. You can get a good night's sleep. But I was innocent, and I kept thinking about that, and I didn't sleep so good."

Our criminal justice system is not foolproof; it fails more often than it is comfortable to contemplate. It failed, for example, in the case of Isadore Zimmerman. The prison guards gave him his last meal, allowed him to smoke a cigarette, cut his hair, and made a slit in his pants' leg for the electrodes that would be attached to the electric chair. Then they left him alone with his family to cry, to pray, and to try to find the strength to face the final event of his life. Just moments before his scheduled execution, the guard told him his death sentence had been commuted to life imprisonment.

Zimmerman had been accused, tried, and convicted of murdering a New York City patrolman during a robbery on April 10, 1937. In prison Zimmerman was beaten by guards, lost his right eye in a fight with another prisoner, and once tried to commit suicide by banging his head against the wall of his cell. Throughout his quarter-century ordeal, he steadfastly insisted that he was innocent and had been railroaded by the district attorney. After he had been in prison for more than twenty-four years, laboratory techniques that were not available when he was convicted proved that Zimmerman could not have committed the crime.

In 1983, forty-four years after he was scheduled to die in the electric chair, the New York State's Court of Claims awarded the retired doorman $1 million, one of the largest awards ever received in U.S. history for wrongful imprisonment. But Zimmerman remains bitter. "I missed watching my family grow up, my nieces and nephews," he told a reporter after learning of the court's decision. "I missed the great love of my mother and father. I desperately would have loved to be a father. I don't have an income. I'm a cripple. I'm highly destitute. The nightmare will stay with me for the rest of my life. No amount could compensate for the things that I have lost that can never be replaced."

The justice system failed, too, for Francis Hemauer, who was identified by a victim in 1971 as the man who raped her three years earlier. After eight years in prison, Hemauer was released when blood tests showed that the attacker had blood type B; Hemauer had type A blood.

It failed in the case of Nathaniel Walker, a thirty-three-year-old factory worker who was picked out of a police lineup by a rape victim and imprisoned for nearly ten years before a laboratory report showed that he could not have committed the crime.

It failed for Randall Adams, Robert Dillen, Larry Smith, Frank McCann, Kim Bock . . . I could go on and on, but you won't recognize these names, they won't mean anything to you. For the innocent people whose lives have been shattered by a pointing finger of blame, we have selectively short memories. These people are considered an aberration, a necessary loss. "No system is perfect," people say to me. "We have to expect mistakes." I look at them, speechless. If it were *your* life, I want to ask, the words building in rage, would you be content to call it a mistake?

Suddenly I am brought back to the present, as the bailiff swings open the doors to the courtroom and the spectators begin to file back in. I follow them, walking down the aisle and through the waist-high door, up the steps and into my wooden box. Facing the courtroom, listening to the hollow rap of the judge's gavel, I quickly put away my personal memories and reach into the other areas, the storage places where my training and expertise about memory and perception reside. The prosecutor was standing up, studying the questions he would be asking me. I straightened my back, took a deep breath. I needed to be alert, wholly in the present moment. A man's future depended on it.

I stole one last look at the defendant sitting in his place at the defense table. Was he innocent or guilty? A defense attorney once told me that he never lets himself think about that question, for it would influence the way he represents his clients. They're almost all guilty, he said. And yet this was the lawyer who represented Steve Titus, a tragic victim of mistaken identification. I remember a line from the movie *True Believer*, when actor James Wood is interviewing an idealistic lawyer. "So you want to be a defense attorney?" he asks, his tone bitterly sarcastic. "Then know this going in—they're all guilty." But true to Hollywood tradition, the cynic encounters a man who has been locked up in prison for crimes he did not commit and, in the subsequent fight for justice, the lawyer rediscovers his passion for his profession.

I know that innocence does, in fact, come into the courtroom and sits, like this defendant in this courtroom sits, helpless, without hope, eyes wide, fear turning into panic. Innocence comes into the courtroom, but it is not surrounded by a halo and white cloud. It comes in disguised as guilt, looking like guilt, smelling like guilt; and when the eyewitness points at the defense table and says, "He did it! He's the one!" you can almost hear the nails being pounded into the coffin.

Eyewitness identification is the most damning of all evidence that can be used against a defendant. When an eyewitness points a finger at a defendant and says, "I saw him do it," the case is "cast-iron, brass-bound, copper-riveted, and airtight" as one prosecutor proclaimed. For how can we disbelieve the sworn testimony of eyewitnesses to a crime when the witnesses are absolutely convinced that they are telling the truth? Why, after all, would they lie?

Ah, there's the word—*lie*. That's the word that gets us off the track. You see, eyewitnesses who point their finger at innocent defendants are not liars, for they genuinely believe in the truth of their testimony. The face that they see before them *is* the face of the attacker. The face of innocence has become the face of guilt. That's the frightening part—the truly horrifying idea that our memories can be changed, inextricably altered, and that what we think we know, what we believe with all our hearts, is not necessarily the truth.

THE MAGIC OF THE MIND

"Think about it. Three pounds of wet tissue packed with billions of tiny information processors connected in networks, driven by chemistry and electricity to produce the magic of the mind."
—Roger Bingham, producer, *Memory: Fabric of the Mind*

August, 1979. The prosecutor's case against the balding sharp-featured, fifty-three-year-old Roman Catholic priest was apparently ironclad. Seven eyewitnesses swore under oath that Father Bernard Pagano was the well-dressed man who had pointed a small silver gun at them and, in a series of armed robberies, politely demanded that they empty their cash registers.

Father Pagano insisted that he was a victim of mistaken identity. But one question tormented every member of the jury: "How could seven eyewitnesses be wrong?"

The prosecutor had just wrapped up his case when the judge stunned the courtroom with the news that another man had confessed to the robberies. Robert Clouser told the police that he had not confessed sooner because he felt sure Father Pagano would be acquitted. Clouser knew details about the crime that only the robber could have known—details never disclosed either in court or in the news media. Clouser was fourteen years younger than Pagano and had a full head of hair, but he nevertheless bore a striking resemblance to the priest.

August 23, 1982. Lenell Geter was arrested in Greenville, Texas, and charged with the robbery of a Kentucky Fried Chicken restaurant. Geter was twenty-five years old, college educated, and employed as a mechanical engineer at a design engineering firm in Greenville. Five eyewitnesses positively identified him, but nine of Geter's coworkers argued that he could not have been the robber because he was at work all day; the robbery occurred at 3:20 P.M., fifty miles away in a Dallas suburb. The director of the engineering firm explained that Geter, the only black man in his work group, "stood out like a raisin in a bowl of rice"; if he had skipped out for several hours in the middle of the day, they would have known about it.

The case came to trial in October 1982. The five eyewitnesses pointed to Geter in court and positively identified him as the robber. Geter's court-appointed lawyer argued that the eyewitness identifications should be thrown out of court because the restaurant workers, who were all white, originally described the robber as five feet six inches tall—and Lenell Geter stands a full six feet tall. The judge denied the motion.

An all-white jury found Geter guilty, and he was sentenced to life imprisonment. He spent sixteen months in prison, while his coworkers joined with lawyers from the National Association for the Advancement of Colored People (NAACP) in an effort to get his case reviewed. Then in March 1984 another suspect was arrested, and four of the five eyewitnesses who positively identified Geter now changed their minds—this new suspect was the man who had robbed the restaurant. After serving sixteen months in prison for a crime he did not commit, Lenell Geter was a free man.

I met Father Pagano and Lenell Geter in 1985 when we appeared together on a Boston television show about mistaken identifications. Father Pagano was bitter still, because he never received the apologies that he felt he deserved as a victim of mistaken identification. He was also deeply in debt, after spending more than $70,000 on his defense.

Lenell Geter, whose case of mistaken identification was made famous in a *Sixty Minutes* television segment, told me that he felt "shellshocked" by his experience. "Five people misidentified me," he said. "How could that happen? How could five people be so wrong?"

Eyewitness testimony, which relies on the accuracy of human memory, has an enormous impact on the outcome of a trial. Aside from a smoking pistol, nothing carries as much weight with a jury as the testimony of an actual witness. The memory of witnesses is crucial not only in criminal cases but in civil cases as well—in automobile accident cases, for example, eyewitness testimony carries great weight in determining who is at fault.

Implicit in the acceptance of this testimony as solid evidence is the assumption that the human mind is a precise recorder and storer of events. Human beings hold fiercely to the belief that our memories are preserved intact, our thoughts are essentially imperishable, and our impressions are never really forgotten. Sigmund Freud believed that long-term memories lie deep in the unconscious mind, too deep to be disturbed by ongoing events and experiences; most people today continue to accept Freud's view of memory.

In a published survey that I conducted with Geoffrey Loftus, my husband and fellow psychology professor, 169 individuals from various parts of the United States were asked to give their views about how memory works. Of these, 75 had formal graduate training in psychology, while the remaining 94 did not. The nonpsychologists had varied occupations. Lawyers, secretaries, taxicab drivers, physicians, philosophers, fire investigators, and even an eleven-year-old child participated. They were given this question:

Which of these statements best reflects your view on how human memory works?

1. Everything we learn is permanently stored in the mind, although sometimes particular details are not accessible. With hypnosis, or other special techniques, these inaccessible details could eventually be recovered.
2. Some details that we learn may be permanently lost from memory. Such details would never be able to be recovered by hypnosis, or any other special technique, because these details are simply no longer there.

Eighty-four percent of the psychologists and 69 percent of the nonpsychologists chose the first response, indicating a belief that all information in long-term memory is there, even though much of it cannot be retrieved. The most common reason for choosing that response was based on personal experience and involved the recovery of an idea that the person had not thought about for quite some time; a second reason, commonly given by psychologists, was knowledge of the work of Wilder Penfield, whose studies of brain stimulation in epileptic patients have been used as evidence to support the theory that memories are stable and permanent. Some respondents mentioned hypnosis, psychoanalysis, Pentothal, or even reincarnation to support their belief in the permanence of memory.

But, in fact, human memory is far from perfect or permanent, and forgetfulness is a fact of life. One of the most obvious reasons for forgetting is that the information was never stored in memory in the first place; even the most common, everyday items frequently fail to find a niche in our memory. Take a U.S. penny, for example. Most people would insist that they know what a penny looks like and would have no trouble recognizing one when they saw it. But in a study conducted in 1979, fewer than half of the subjects were able to pick the exact copy of a real penny from fifteen possible designs.[1] See the illustrations on the next page—can you?

Another common object that we look at every day is a telephone. Can you remember the letters that accompany the numbers of your telephone?

Even if we are careful observers and take in a reasonably accurate picture of some object or experience, it does not stay intact in memory. Other forces begin to corrode the original memory. With the passage of time, with proper motivation, or with the introduction of interfering or contradictory facts, the memory traces change or become transformed, often without our conscious awareness. We can actually come to believe in memories of events that never happened.

Child psychologist Jean Piaget, in his *Plays, Dreams, and Imitation in Childhood,* related a personal story about the malleability of memory:

. . . one of my first memories would date, if it were true, from my second year. I can still see, most clearly, the following scene, in which I believed until I was about fifteen. I was sitting in my pram, which my nurse was pushing in the Champs Elysees, when a man tried to kidnap me. I was held in by the strap fastened around me

1. R. S. Nickerson and M. J. Adams, "Long-Term Memory for a Common Object," *Cognitive Psychology,* 1979, 11, pp. 287-307.

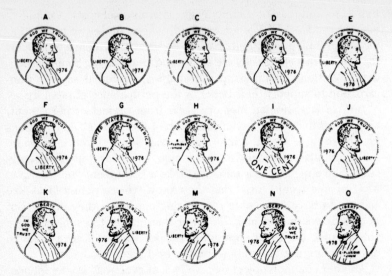

Which is the "honest" penny? (Reprinted from R. S. Nickerson and M. J. Adams, "Long-Term Memory for a Common Object," *Cognitive Psychology*, vol. 11, 1979, pp. 287–307.)

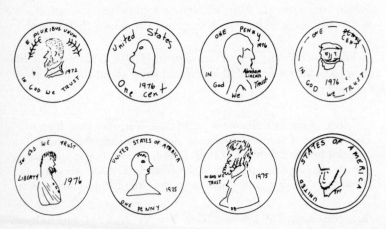

Pennies drawn from memory.

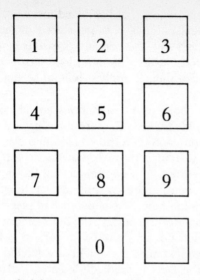

Can you remember which letters accompany the numbers on your telephone?

while my nurse bravely tried to stand between me and the thief. She received various scratches, and I can still see vaguely those on her face. Then a crowd gathered, a policeman with a short cloak and a white baton came up, and the man took to his heels. I can still see the whole scene, and can even place it near the tube station. When I was about fifteen, my parents received a letter from my former nurse saying that she had been converted to the Salvation Army. She wanted to confess her past faults, and in particular to return the watch she had been given as a reward on this occasion. She had made up the whole story, faking the scratches. I, therefore, must have heard, as a child, the account of this story, which my parents believed, and projected into the past in the form of a visual memory.

A visual memory, indeed—many years later Piaget could picture in his mind not only the scratches on his nurse's face but also the nonexistent crowd, the policeman with his cloak and baton, and the thief taking "to his heels"!

How *does* memory work, and why does it fail? Scientists generally agree that memories are formed when neurons link together to form new connections, or circuits, actually changing the contact between the cells; in the process, memories are stored. Long-term memories, which include experiences that happened just a few minutes ago to information several decades old, are stored in mental "drawers" somewhere in our brains. No one knows exactly where, although it has been estimated that in a lifetime, long-term memory can hold as many as 1 quadrillion (1 million billion) separate bits of information.

The "drawers" holding our memories are obviously extremely crowded and densely packed. They are also constantly being emptied out, scattered about, and then stuffed back into place. Like curious, playful children searching through drawers for a blouse or pair of pants, our brains seem to enjoy ransacking the memory drawers, tossing the facts about, and then stuffing everything back in, oblivious to order or importance. As new bits and pieces of information are added into long-term memory, the old memories are removed, replaced, crumpled up, or shoved into corners. Little details are added, confusing or extraneous elements are deleted, and a coherent construction of the facts is gradually created that may bear little resemblance to the original event.

Memories don't just fade, as the old saying would have us believe; they also grow. What fades is the initial perception, the actual experience of the events. But every time we recall an event, we must reconstruct the memory, and with each recollection the memory may be changed—colored by succeeding events, other people's recollections or suggestions, increased understanding, or a new context.

Truth and reality, when seen through the filter of our memories, are not objective facts but subjective, interpretative realities. We interpret the past, correcting ourselves, adding bits and pieces, deleting uncomplementary or disturbing recollections, sweeping, dusting, tidying things up. Thus our representation of the past takes on a living, shifting reality; it is not fixed and immutable, not a place way back there that is preserved in stone, but a living thing that changes shape, expands, shrinks, and expands again, an amoebalike creature with powers to make us laugh, and cry, and clench our fists. Enormous powers—powers even to make us believe in something that never happened.

Are we aware of our mind's distortions of our past experiences? In most cases, the answer is no. As time goes by and the memories gradually change, we become convinced that we saw or said or did what we remember. We perceive the blending of fact and fiction that constitutes a memory as completely and utterly truthful. We are innocent victims of our mind's manipulations.

A pointing finger of blame has a powerful hold on even the most informed and intelligent of juries. Several years ago I conducted an experiment in which subjects acted as jurors in a criminal case. First they heard a description of a robbery-murder, then a prosecution argument, then an argument for the defense. In one version of the experiment, the prosecutor presented only circumstantial evidence; faced with this evidence, only 18 percent of the "jurors" found the "defendant" guilty. In a second version, the prosecutor pled the exact case with one difference: There was testimony from a single eyewitness—a clerk who identified the defendant as the robber. Now 72 percent of the jurors found the defendant guilty.

The danger of eyewitness testimony is clear: Anyone in the world can be convicted of a crime he or she did not commit, or deprived of an award that is due, based solely on the evidence of a witness who convinces a jury that his memory about what he saw is correct. Why is eyewitness testimony so powerful and convincing? Because people in general and jurors in particular believe that our memories stamp the facts of our experiences on a permanent, nonerasable tape, like a computer disk or videotape that is write-protected. For the most part, of course, our memories serve us reasonably well. But how often is precise memory demanded of us? When a friend describes a vacation, we don't ask, "Are you sure your hotel room had two chairs, not three?" After we watch a movie, our companion wouldn't normally grill us with questions like "Was Gene Hackman's hair wavy, or was it curly?" or "Did the woman in the bar wear red or pink lipstick?" If we make a mistake, it usually goes unnoticed and uncorrected—does it really matter if there were two chairs or three, or if the actor's hair was wavy or curly? Belief in an accurate memory is confirmed by default.

But precise memory suddenly becomes crucial in the event of a crime or an accident. Small details assume enormous importance. Did the assailant have a mustache, or was he clean-shaven? Was he five eight or five eleven? Was the traffic light red, or was it green? How fast was the Cadillac going when it went through the red light— or was it yellow?—and smashed into the Volkswagen? Did the car cross the center line, or did it stay on its own side? Civil and criminal cases often rest on such subtle, seemingly trivial details, and these details are often hard to obtain.

In July 1977 *Flying* magazine reported the fatal crash of a small plane that killed all eight people aboard and one person who was on the ground. Sixty eyewitnesses were interviewed, and two eyewitnesses who had actually seen the airplane just before impact testified at a hearing to investigate the accident. The plane, one of the eyewitnesses explained, "was heading right toward the ground— straight down." This witness apparently did not know that several photographs clearly showed that the airplane hit flat and at a low-enough angle to skid for almost one thousand feet.

To be mistaken about details is not the result of a bad memory but of the normal functioning of human memory. When we want to remember something, we don't simply pluck a whole memory intact from a "memory store." The memory is actually constructed from stored and available bits of information; we unconsciously fill in any gaps in the information with inferences. When all the fragments are integrated into a whole that makes sense, they form what we call a memory.

Still other factors affect the accurate perception, and therefore recollection, of an event. Was there violence? How much? Was it light or dark? Did the eyewitness have any prior expectations or interests? A tragic real-life case illustrates the potential problems surrounding an initial perception of an event.

Two men in their mid-twenties were hunting for bears in a rural area of Montana. They had been out all day and were exhausted, hungry, and ready to go home. Walking along a dirt trail in the middle of the woods, with night falling fast, they were talking about bears and thinking about bears. They rounded a bend in the trail and approximately twenty-five yards ahead of them, just off the trail in the woods, was a large object that was moving and making noise. Both men thought it was a bear, and they lifted their rifles and fired. But the "bear" turned out to be a yellow tent, with a man and a woman making love inside. One of the bullets hit the woman and killed her. When the case was tried before a jury, the jurors had difficulty understanding the perceptual problems inherent in the event; they simply couldn't imagine how someone would look at a yellow tent and see a growling brown bear. The young man whose bullet killed the woman was convicted of negligent homicide. Two years later he committed suicide.

This dramatic case demonstrates what psychologists call "event factors"—those factors inherent within a specific event that can alter perception and distort memory. It was a dark night, and in darkness different colors can't be distinguished and details can't be resolved. The two hunters had strong expectations and motivations—they anticipated that they might see a bear, they wanted to see a bear, they were nervous, excited, and exhausted from a long day in the woods. When they saw something large, moving, and making noise, they automatically assumed that it was a bear, raised their rifles, and shot to kill.

Event factors have to do with the acquisition stage of memory, when we perceive an event and our brains make the instantaneous decision to either discard the information or insert it into memory. If the memory is stored, however, it does not just lie passively in our brains, waiting to be pulled out and recalled. Many things can happen during the retention and acquisition stages of memory—time passes, the memory fades, and more crucially, we are exposed to new information that adds to or alters the original memory.

Suppose that a crime occurs, the police are notified, they arrive at the scene and begin to ask questions. "What happened?" the witness is asked. "What did the assailant look like?" After the witness tells the police what he can remember, he may be asked to come to the police station to look through a set of photographs. The witness is now performing a recognition test, in which either a single item (a photograph) or a set of items (a group of people in a lineup) is shown, and the witness is asked to indicate whether he has seen any of them before.

Keep in mind that most witnesses are obliging—they want to help, and in the case of a violent crime or assault, they have an added incentive to help the police capture a violent criminal. In addition, research tells us that witnesses believe the police would not conduct a lineup unless they had a good suspect. Although witnesses try hard to identify the true criminal, when they are un-certain—or when no one person in the lineup exactly matches their memory—they will often identify the person who best matches their recollection of the criminal. And often their choice is wrong.

Obviously, the composition of the lineup—how many people are

Example of a biased lineup. (Reprinted from E. F. Loftus, *Eyewitness Testimony*, Cambridge, MA: Harvard University Press, 1979.)

included, what they look like, what they are wearing—is crucial. A lineup must be as free as possible from suggestive influences, or it could taint the witness's identification and lose its value.

As our rather fanciful illustration of a biased lineup shows, if the suspect is a large, bearded man, the lineup should not include children, women in wheelchairs, or blind men with canes. Unless people resembling the suspect are included in the lineup, the suspect may be picked out by default, not by true recognition.

But many lineups used in actual criminal cases are grossly suggestive, and the identifications they produce should be considered worthless. In a lineup conducted in Minnesota, a black suspect stood next to five white men; in another case, a six-foot-three-inch suspect was placed in a lineup with nonsuspects who were all under five feet ten inches tall; in a case where the offender was known to be in his teens, an eighteen-year-old suspect was placed in a lineup with five nonsuspects, all over the age of forty. In a case I worked on from 1986 to 1988, a man was accused of murdering eight people on a fishing boat in Alaska. Eyewitnesses had provided police with a general physical description of the man they saw at the murder scene, including one very specific detail—the man they saw wore a baseball cap. In the photo lineup, the suspect was the only person wearing a baseball cap.

But suppose a witness is presented with a fair lineup, in which everyone is at least approximately the same height and weight and fits a general physical description. The witness is looking at the lineup, concentrating hard, and the police officer suddenly says, "Take another look at number four." Perhaps the police officer stares conspicuously at number four while the witness is trying to identify the culprit. Or perhaps the witness hesitates while looking at number four and the interviewer leans forward and says, "What do you think about that one?"

The witness takes in these little bits of information and may use them—unconsciously—to "fill in" a vague and fuzzy memory with the image of the person in the photograph. The image shifts, the lines waver, and suddenly the face in number four fuses with the fading memory of the criminal. "Number four looks familiar," the witness might say. And later: "Yes, I'm sure it's number four."

A one-person lineup or viewing in which just one person is pointed out to the witness is particularly dangerous. In the fall of 1970, twenty-one-year-old Bobby Joe Leaster was chatting amiably with friends on a Boston street corner when two policemen jumped out of their patrol car, guns drawn, and accused him of murdering a store owner. They handcuffed Bobby Joe and drove him to Boston City Hospital where the murdered man's wife was brought to the patrol car and asked to peer in the window at the suspect. "What do you think?" the officer asked her. The woman began to shake and cry. "Yes," she said, sobbing, "this looks like the man who shot and killed my husband." That was the only evidence against him, but Leaster was charged with murder, and on June 22, 1971, he was convicted and sentenced to life without parole.

Six years later a father-son lawyer team, Robert and Christopher Muse, were appointed by the U.S. District Court in Boston to represent Bobby Joe Leaster in his appeal. After one interview with Bobby Joe, the Muses had a hunch that this convicted criminal might be different from the rest who claim that they are innocent—this one actually might *be* innocent. For more than nine years the Muses worked on Leaster's behalf, refusing to charge him a penny for their services. A friend once asked Robert Muse how much of his estate he would be willing to bet on Leaster's innocence. "All of it," he immediately answered.

In November 1986 the bullet taken from the murder victim was matched up with a gun linked to two men who had been arrested in October 1970, two weeks after the murder, for a liquor store holdup. In December 1986 Bobby Joe Leaster was given his freedom. He had spent almost sixteen years of his life behind bars.

Mistaken identifications do happen in real life, and they are sometimes brought about by common police procedures. When the police have a suspect, they often show the witness a photo array and produce the actual lineup only if an identification is made. Almost invariably, only the person identified from the photo lineup also appears in the in-person lineup, and almost invariably the witness identifies the person he saw in the photos. This is called a "photo-biased lineup," and the chances of a mistaken identification rise dramatically in such a situation.

A 1977 study conducted at the University of Nebraska shows the effect of photo bias on the memory of witnesses. Student "witnesses" watched some "criminals" committing a crime. An hour later they looked through mug shots that included some of the criminals they had seen. A week later lineups were staged, and the subject witnesses were asked to indicate those who had taken part in the original crime. Eight percent of the people in the lineups were identified as criminals, yet they had neither taken part in the "crime" nor were their pictures included in the mug shots. Twenty percent of the innocent people whose photographs were included among the mug shots were also falsely identified. None of these people had committed a crime, nor had they ever before been seen in person—and yet they were recognized from photographs and identified as criminals.

How often are mistaken identifications made? How many Father Paganos and Lenell Geters have been falsely arrested, wrongly convicted, and spent time in prison for crimes they never committed? In a classic text on the subject, *Convicting the Innocent*, legal scholar Edwin M. Borchard presents sixty-five cases of "erroneous criminal convictions of innocent people." In twenty-nine of these cases, or approximately 45 percent, mistaken eyewitness identification was responsible for the conviction. Borchard concludes: "These cases illustrate the fact that the emotional balance of the victim or eyewitness is so disturbed by his extraordinary experience that his powers of perception become distorted and his identification is frequently most untrustworthy" (p. 367).

Misidentifications are often blamed on the fact that the real criminal bears a close resemblance to the wrongly identified person. But in the twenty-nine cases in which mistaken eyewitness identification was responsible for the wrongful conviction, Borchard reports these facts: ". . . in eight of these cases the wrongfully accused person and the really guilty criminal bore not the slightest resemblance to each other, whereas in twelve other cases, the resemblance, while fair, was still not at all close. In only two cases can the resemblance be called striking" (p. 367).

In 1983 Arye Rattner, a graduate student at Ohio State University, completed his doctoral dissertation titled *Convicting the Innocent: Where Justice Goes Wrong.* Rattner estimated that 0.5 percent (one-half of 1 percent) of people arrested and charged for what the FBI calls "indexed crimes"—murder, robbery, forcible rape, forgery, larceny, assault, and arson—are wrongfully convicted. Although statistically this number seems small, it is one of the largest estimates I've seen, and it translates into an estimated 8,500 wrongful convictions in the United States in one single year.

Let's assume that Rattner's statistics are abnormally high—perhaps the percentage is twice what it should be, which would translate to 4,250 wrongful convictions in this country every year. Perhaps it's only half of that, in which case we would have 2,125 wrongful convictions. We could keep whittling the numbers down, but at some point the statistics have to hit us in the gut—these are real people, people like you and me, who are picked off the street, tried, convicted, and imprisoned—and yet they are *innocent.* If it were just ten people in one year, it would be too many.

How many people in Rattner's study were convicted on the basis of mistaken eyewitness identification? Rattner carefully examined over two hundred cases and found that 52.3 percent resulted from eyewitness misidentification. "Our data," Rattner concludes, "indicate that eyewitness misidentification is the factor most often associated with wrongful conviction" (p. 292).

What are the solutions to this grievous problem? Despite the obvious risks inherent in eyewitness identification, it would be a tragic mistake to exclude all eyewitness testimony, because very often, as in cases of rape, it is the only evidence available. And often the eyewitness's testimony is correct. But what about that small percentage of times when it is incorrect—how can we safeguard the rights of the innocent person who might be falsely accused? What can we do to give jurors a better understanding of the uses and pitfalls of such testimony?

Defense attorneys often ask judges to read a list of instructions to the jury on the dangers of eyewitness identification. But the instructions tend to be convoluted and hard for many people to follow. Moreover, numerous psychological studies have shown that jurors have difficulty understanding the instructions. Another possible solution in eyewitness cases is expert testimony—a psychologist can explain to the jury how human memory works and apply the experimental findings to the case in question.

That is what I do. I testify in court about the nature of human memory and the psychological factors that affect eyewitness testimony. I testify in cases where eyewitness identification is the sole or primary evidence against the defendant, including death penalty cases, where the consequences of a mistaken identification are potentially irreversible.

When I began my research on human memory twenty years ago, it had nothing to do with courts of law or expert testimony. When lawyers asked me if I would testify in cases where eyewitness identification played a major role, I was willing to speak out in hopes that the relevant psychological research might help to make our criminal justice system work more fairly.

When I testify in a criminal trial, my testimony does not guarantee that innocent people will go free—but it undoubtedly increases their chances. We cannot, we dare not, assume that our criminal justice system works perfectly and that all innocent men and women are sufficiently protected. "Trials are human affairs and therefore necessarily imperfect," wrote Judge Jerome Frank in his book *Not Guilty*. Mistakes will be made, innocent lives will continue to be pulled into the vast, complicated machinery of our justice system, and some will never make it back out again.

More than seven thousand people have been executed in the twentieth century in this country; a recent study indicates that at least twenty-five of these were innocent. *Twenty-five lives taken by mistake.* Nearly sixteen hundred people are now on death row—how many of them are innocent?

Hidden within the statistics and complicated discussions about guilt and innocence is an unanswerable question, an unsolvable dilemma. In some cases—in Father Pagano's and Lenell Geter's case—the innocent person is *proven* innocent. But in many cases, innocence cannot be proven beyond a shadow of a doubt. Of the cases I describe in detail in this book, only two have outcomes that are neatly and cleanly tied up, with the real criminal put safely behind bars and the innocent man completely and publicly exonerated. Hollywood can offer us pat, happy endings, but real life often does not give us the facts lined up in neat little rows, carefully sorted and assembled, every snag and tangle smoothed out. But in the absence of such absolute proof, is the person less innocent?

Consider the case of Jimmy Landano. Landano is a former heroin addict and ex-con who did time in Attica. He's now doing life plus fifteen years in Rahway State Prison in New Jersey for killing a policeman in 1976. He was also convicted of robbery, gun possession, breaking in, car theft, and conspiracy.

Four eyewitnesses and an accomplice who admitted his own role in the murder testified in court that Landano was the man who fired the fatal shot. Hairs found in the killer's hat were similar to Landano's; his name was in the address book of another accomplice to the murder; and he had no airtight alibi.

The case against the ex-con and ex-junkie was overwhelmingly persuasive. And when he threatened to "come after" the prosecutor when he got out of prison, the judge and jury were even more convinced that they had convicted a dangerous criminal who should spend his life behind bars.

But Landano claims that he was set up by members of a motorcycle gang known as The Breed in order to protect the real killer. They planted a hat similar to his own on the seat of the getaway car, Landano says. His history as a heroin addict and his incarceration in Attica for grand larceny made him a perfect "throwaway."

Four eyewitnesses pointed to a photograph of Landano as the cop killer; but not all of their facts fit. One eyewitness claimed the killer had a thick mustache while another described the man as having no mustache at all; Landano has a bushy mustache. One forensics expert testified that hairs found in the killer's hat might be Landano's; another expert said they probably weren't. The killer's ski jacket looked comical on Landano, the sleeves reaching only two-thirds of the way down his long arms, exposing two tattoos. Tight at the shoulders and around the chest, it restricted his movements; he couldn't even make the zippers meet. His mother and girlfriend testified that he had been with them during the morning of the killing; but even if the jury believed them, there was theoretically enough time for Landano to commit the crime.

Jim Landano spends his free time in prison reading court transcripts and police reports, pleading his case to anyone who will listen, writing letters to lawyers and reporters, and helping other inmates with similar cases. He is forty-four years old, and it will be twenty more long years before he is eligible for parole. The waiting makes him edgy; he is terrified of growing old in prison and missing out on the chance to straighten out his troubled life. Prisons breed hatred and desperation, he says. "When you treat people like animals," he repeats, over and over again, "they become animals."

The frequency of that angry refrain is matched only by another cliché-ridden assertion. "I've been framed," Landano says with fierce conviction. "I'm innocent."

It's one man's passionate declaration of innocence against the sworn word of four eyewitnesses, three accomplices, and a jury of twelve people who carefully weighed the evidence and found Jimmy Landano guilty.

Who is right and who is wrong?[2]

2. Jimmy Landano's conviction was overturned on July 27, 1989, by U.S. District Judge H. Lee Sarokin, who ruled that prosecutors and investigators withheld eyewitness identification evidence indicating that Landano was innocent and another man was guilty. Landano was released on bond. The State of New Jersey is seeking a review of the case.

PART
TWO

THE CASES

These real-life cases tell the story of how my life has intersected, through my work with memory and my fascination with the law, with the lives of people accused of violent crimes. It is also the story of their families, and of the victims and their families, and of the lawyers, judges, and jurors who play their crucial parts in the drama.

Ultimately, it is a story about memory—that fascinating, impossibly complicated human faculty that allows us to revisit and, in many cases, reinterpret our past. "Memory is the receptacle and sheath of all knowledge," the Roman orator Cicero said in the second century B.C. Two hundred years earlier, Saint Basil waxed eloquent about memory: ". . . the cabinet of imagination, the treasury of reason, the registry of conscience, and the council chamber of thought."

I love the literary flourish of those descriptions, the bright and haunting image of human beings standing awestruck before the magnificence of their own minds. But I have to admit I'm partial to Mark Twain's rumination on memory: "It isn't so astonishing, the number of things that I can remember, as the number of things I can remember that aren't so."

THREE

DARK JUSTICE: STEVE TITUS

"There they lie, never to hope, never to pray, never to love, never to heal, never to laugh, never to cry."
—President Ronald Reagan, May 5, 1985,
at the Bergen-Belsen concentration camp

I'll never forget Steve Titus. I can picture him clearly in my mind—boyish, with a round face and a wide, white-toothed smile and wrinkles that spread around his eyes when he laughed. I remember, too, the way he lowered his eyes, jaw clamped shut, mouth twisted in frustration and rage.

The irony, of course, is that I never met him. These images, so finely focused in my memory, came from black-and-white newspaper photos printed in the Seattle *Times* during the four years that Steve Titus fought for his life and his honor. Which is appropriate, for if there was any justice at all for Titus, it came through the news media and a tough-talking, chain-smoking reporter named Paul Henderson.

This is a story about Steve Titus's encounter with the dark side of justice. It is a story about the friendship that grew between Titus and Henderson, a strange partnership that would change both their lives. And it is a story about what happens afterward, after all the rest of us have forgotten the newspaper headlines and the grainy black-and-white images have faded from our memory.

The rest of us will never know what it is like to be falsely accused. Sitting on the outside looking in, we can only guess at the heat and the horror, the suffering and the outrage. The Steve Titus story brings us as close as we are likely to get to the agony of the falsely accused. It is the saddest story I have ever had to tell.

Seventeen-year-old *Nancy Van Roper* was standing on the narrow asphalt shoulder of Pacific Highway South, ten miles south of Seattle, with her thumb out, waiting for somebody to offer her a ride. It was about 6:45 P.M. on October 12, 1980. Night was falling fast, and the tall highway lights gave the rain-slicked road an eerie, other-worldly glow. Nancy shivered in the cold and began to worry about the inevitable confrontation with her mother when she got home. "Where were you?" her mother would ask, her voice shrill. "I was worried sick!"

A light-blue compact car pulled over to the side, and the sound of tires scrunching the pebbly surface of the roadway made Nancy jump back. A bearded man leaned across the passenger seat, opening the door. "Hi," she said. "Where you headed?" "Tacoma," he answered. "Great," she said, getting in and closing the door. "That's where I'm going."

The driver was young, maybe twenty-nine or thirty, dressed in a three-piece suit. He looked over his shoulder and eased his way back into the traffic. They drove in silence for a few minutes. Nancy always felt a little awkward sitting in a stranger's car, hitching a ride. She reached into her purse and put on some lipstick, smoothing her lips together, enjoying the feel of the slick gloss.

At South 208th Street, the man suddenly exited the highway and drove down the hill. Nancy looked at him, confused. "I have to stop and see my sister, Liz," he said. He turned again on 22nd Avenue South and then drove down a narrow dirt lane that ended at the broken-down foundation of a demolished house. *Is this where his sister lives?* Fear began to gnaw at the edges of Nancy's mind. She looked around for lights, people, cars, anything moving, alive, but there was nothing, just a bunch of dilapidated houses and huge mounds of dirt, stones, and rotten wood.

The man suddenly jerked the car to a stop, turned toward her, and pushed something sharp against her throat. Nancy's mind, blank with fear, registered one thought: *It's not a knife, too dull, feels like a screwdriver.*

"Do as I say, or I'll hurt you," he said. He told her to take off her blouse and jeans. Hands trembling, she unbuttoned her blouse. "Please," she begged him. "Take off your jeans," he said, pushing the weapon against her neck. When she was undressed, he forced her to perform fellatio; then he raped her. When he was finished, he told her to get dressed, step outside the car, and wait for him to leave. He backed out of the lane and drove off, the tires tossing dirt and mud into the air. She ran for help then, stumbling, sobbing, terrified of the night and the dark, silent hills of dirt and wood. At the end of the road, 650 feet from the rape scene, was a house with the porch lights on.

The call to the Port of Seattle police from the house at the end of 22nd Avenue South was logged at 7:22 P.M.; four officers responded immediately. They interviewed the victim, who was crying softly but appeared unharmed. Her clothing was clean and untorn and there were no cuts or bruises to indicate a violent assault. She described the rapist as twenty-five to thirty years old, six feet tall, medium build, with a full beard and shoulder-length, light-brown hair. He wore a three-piece, cream-colored suit. The car was royal blue, one of the compact models, new, possibly a 1980. The bucket seats were covered with velveteen upholstery. Temporary license plates were displayed in the rear window. The victim recalled seeing a necklace or maybe it was a pair of garters hanging from the rearview mirror. On the backseat was a brown vinyl folder or binder.

She accompanied the officers to the crime scene, pointing out the exact location where the rapist had parked the car. There were fresh tire tracks, perfectly preserved in the mud, which backed out to the right and then took off down the dirt lane. The officers took numerous photographs.

Detective Ronald Parker was placed in charge of the investigation. Theorizing that the rapist might be familiar enough with the area to live nearby, Parker instructed the officers to cruise through the night spots and parking lots along Pacific Highway South, looking for a blue compact with temporary license plates displayed in the rear window.

At 1:20 A.M. Detective Parker and Officer Robert Jensen spotted a light-blue Chevette with temporary plates parked outside the Raintree Restaurant and Lounge on Pacific Highway South near the Seattle-Tacoma airport. They parked the patrol car out of sight and waited.

Inside the restaurant, Steve Titus and his fiancée, *Gretchen Abraham*, were finishing their drinks. Thirty-one-year-old Titus was the district manager for a Seattle restaurant chain; Gretchen worked as a waitress at a Denny's restaurant south of Tacoma. It was after 1:30 A.M. when they left the lounge and walked across the parking lot. Titus opened the door of the company car, a brand-new, light-blue Chevette, and waited while Gretchen fastened her seat belt and pulled her raincoat away from the door.

They started driving south on Pacific Highway toward Titus's apartment in Kent. The four-lane highway, jammed most hours of the day with commuters and airport traffic, was eerily empty, the yellow highway lights flooding the dense, foggy air with a sickly glow. A jumbo jet rumbled overhead, its smooth metal belly suspended just several hundred feet above the ground.

Titus hadn't driven very far when he noticed the red lights flashing in his rearview mirror. He pulled over to the side of the road, swearing softly. Parker and Jensen walked up to the Chevette and politely asked Titus to step outside the car.

"What's the matter, Officers?" Titus asked, keeping his voice calm, a smile on his face.

Parker asked to look at Titus's license and registration. He asked Titus where he had been that afternoon and evening, pressing him for facts, details. Titus explained that he'd been at his parents' house near the airport celebrating his father's birthday all afternoon. "What time did you leave?" Parker asked, his pen poised above his notebook. "After six," Titus answered. "It was six-ten, I remember looking at the clock when I left."

"What did you do then?" Parker asked, writing rapidly.

Titus explained that he drove back to his apartment in Kent, a fifteen to twenty-minute drive. He arrived there at 6:30 P.M., made a few phone calls, watched TV with his best friend. He left the apartment around 9:20 P.M. to pick up Gretchen for their date.

Parker thanked Titus and told him to get back in the car. He questioned Gretchen separately. Then he asked Titus's permission to search the car and take photographs of the inside and outside. "Sure," Titus said, "help yourself."

They're probably looking for a stolen car, he thought as he watched the two policemen searching around, shining flashlights into the backseat, writing down the temporary license plate numbers. Why else would they want pictures of the inside and outside of the car? The Chevette was leased by his employer, the Yegen Seafood Corporation, franchised owners of Ivar's Seafood Bars, a popular chain of Seattle restaurants. As district manager for the company, Titus supervised approximately one hundred employees at seven different seafood outlets; the company car was his to use whenever he needed it. He explained these facts to the officers, who wrote the information in a notebook.

When Officer Jensen asked if he could take his photograph, Titus smiled. Sure, why not? The front and profile photographs show him smiling, looking untroubled, the left eyebrow slightly raised. He joked with the police, asking if they would mind taking his picture with his fiancée. Now it was Parker's turn to shrug his shoulders. "Sure," he said, "no problem."

After Parker told him he was free to go, Titus continued driving south toward his apartment in Kent. He kept checking his rearview mirror, spooked now. "Don't worry," Gretchen reassured him. "It was just one of those strange things. It's all over now." But Titus kept thinking about the photograph—why did they want a picture of him? And why did they search his car and take down his license plate number?

Detective Parker returned to the Port of Seattle police department offices at Sea-Tac airport. It was now after 2:00 A.M., but Parker was fired up. He had a rape, he had a description, he had a suspect who fit in almost every detail. You couldn't ask for much more than that in just seven hours of work.

Referring constantly to the Polaroid pictures he'd just taken of Steve Titus and keeping in mind the victim's description of the rapist—a white male, twenty-five to thirty years old, six feet tall, medium build with a full beard and shoulder-length brown hair—Parker began to sift through the police department's mug-shot file. Titus was only five eight but that little inconsistency didn't bother Parker. Rape victims often made mistakes, errors, miscalculations. How the hell are you going to remember all the details with a knife at your throat?

Parker selected six men, two photographs of each, one side view and one face-on view. He pasted the two photos of Steve Titus at the right top corner of the montage. All the men in the photo lineup had brown hair and full beards. They were all average-looking, between twenty-five and thirty years old, with no distinguishing marks or blemishes on their faces. There weren't any giants, freaks, or sadists in this group, Parker thought, just an all-American bunch of guys. He looked from one photo to the next, comparing his prime suspect with the rest of the mug shots, and felt satisfied. It was a good lineup, no question about it.

On Monday, October 13, Parker and Officer Scott Pierson knocked on the door of the victim's home in Tacoma. "We have some photographs here," Parker said to Nancy Van Roper. His tone was gentle, fatherly. "We want you to look at these photographs and see if you can pick out the man who raped you."

Nancy studied the photographs for several minutes, her teeth biting her lip so hard that all the blood was drained out. She shook her head several times, confused, near tears. Parker urged her to concentrate, to think hard. "You can do it," he said. With a shaking hand she finally pointed to the pictures at the righthand corner of the page.

"This one is the closest," she said, her finger trembling slightly, poised just an inch above the Polaroid picture of Steve Titus. "It has to be this one."

On October 14, a squad car from the Port of Seattle police department arrived at the Yegen Seafood Corporation offices at Southcenter, a sprawling office and shopping complex ten miles south of Seattle. Officers walked into the company offices and asked for Steve Titus. When he appeared, they read him his rights, walked him out to the waiting patrol car, handcuffed him, and pushed him into the backseat. A few hours later a tow truck arrived and hauled away Titus's company car, the light-blue Chevette with the temporary plates pasted on the back window.

That afternoon in a police interview room at the airport offices of the Port of Seattle police department, Titus gave a voluntary statement to Detective Ronald Parker and Officer Robert Jensen, describing his whereabouts on the afternoon and evening of October 12. Titus did not have an attorney present, the officers did not take notes, and the conversation was not recorded.

Over the next several weeks the special assault unit of the prosecutor's office reviewed the evidence against Steve Titus and decided to offer him a deal: If he passed a polygraph, they would drop the charges against him. If he failed, he would be prosecuted for the rape, although the results of the polygraph, by law, could not be used against him.

Titus had hired Tom Hillier, reputedly one of the finest criminal defense attorneys in the state of Washington. Hillier, who had never lost a rape case, discussed the prosecutor's deal with Titus, explaining that it was basically a no-lose situation, which indicated the prosecutor's confusion regarding the evidence. In the absence of overwhelming evidence of guilt, a truthful polygraph result reported by a reputable examiner is often adequate to cast a reasonable doubt, leading to a dismissal of charges.

"If you pass, the prosecutor's office has a convincing reason to drop the case," Hillier told his client. "If you fail, he has a moral justification to go forward. Coincidence argues that you could be the rapist—the car, the temporary plates, the victim's description, the fact that you were in the area that night. But you've got a solid alibi, character and alibi witnesses, a steady job, and no criminal record. Go ahead and take the polygraph—it's our best shot at having this case dismissed."

Titus took the polygraph and failed miserably. All four black needles measuring his blood pressure, heart rate, respiration, and galvanic skin response scratched out a trail that could be read as "deception." The polygraph is based on the theory that when a person lies, emotionally triggered physiological responses occur that can then be measured and compared with "control" responses to emotionally neutral questions. But people can figure out which are the "relevant" questions and experience a stress/fear reaction to those questions that the machine would then pick up. Fear and stress are all that the polygraph measures.

"Did you rape Nancy Van Roper on the twelfth of October?" Steve Titus was asked. Knowing that his answer to this one question would determine his future, Titus apparently panicked, and the scratching black needles indicated that panic.

After looking at Titus's appalling performance on the polygraph, the prosecutor's office made the decision to go ahead with the case. Steve Titus would stand trial for rape.

The trial was scheduled to begin at the end of February, and Tom Hillier knuckled down to the hard work of defending a client whose rage and bitterness could only work against him. Titus was outraged, filled with spite and hostility directed at Detective Parker and the entire Port of Seattle police department. He would pace around Hillier's office, his hands curled into fists, his entire body rigid with tension. He reminded Hillier of a caged animal driven wild by imprisonment, a creature who could not be tamed or calmed. Hillier knew he was in trouble if he couldn't get Titus to settle down before the trial. Jurors would take one look at this hostile, suspicious, bitter man and reach a disastrous conclusion—*guilty*.

Hillier sat down with Titus and his parents and plotted out exactly where Steve was and what he was doing from noon until midnight on October 12, 1980. They all agreed that he'd left his parents' house, two miles north of Sea-Tac airport, at 6:10 P.M., arriving at his apartment in Kent at 6:30 P.M. When he entered the apartment, his phone was ringing, but when he picked it up, the line was dead. He had plans to meet his best friend, Kurt Schaefer, and was running late; he immediately called Schaefer, who lived in the same apartment complex.

Within ten to fifteen minutes, Schaefer showed up at Titus's door. "It was no later than 6:50 P.M.," Titus told Hillier, because the two men sat together in the apartment and talked for at least ten minutes before Titus made the 7:00 P.M. long-distance phone call to Gretchen in Tacoma. After the phone call, Titus and Schaefer watched *Superman* on cable TV. At 9:20 P.M., Titus left to pick up Gretchen for their date.

The alibi was rock solid except for the fifty minutes from 6:10 P.M. when Titus left his parents' house to the 7:00 P.M. phone call, which was verified by long-distance phone records. Titus and Schaefer both insisted that Titus had called Schaefer around 6:30 and that Schaefer arrived at Steve's apartment between 6:45 and 6:50 P.M. But there was no solid proof, and a jury could easily conclude that Schaefer was lying to cover up for his best friend. Still—the rape victim told police that she was picked up by the rapist at 6:45 P.M., and the call to the Port of Seattle police was logged in at 7:22 P.M. It would have been virtually impossible for Titus to leave his parents' house, pick up the girl, drive her to the abandoned house, rape her, and make it home in time to make the long-distance phone call at 7:00 P.M. No matter how much you might like to stretch the facts, you can't fit a rape and a twenty-minute drive into a fifteen-minute time slot.

Another factor in Titus's favor was the victim's description of the rapist's clothing. Nancy Van Roper told police that the rapist was wearing a cream-colored, three-piece suit. When Titus left his parents' home, he was wearing dark slacks, a dark sweater, and a green shirt. Pictures were taken during the birthday party that proved it. Why would Titus have changed his clothes before the rape? Even if someone in the prosecutor's office could come up with a good reason for a rapist to wear a three-piece suit (and Titus claimed he didn't even own one), they couldn't slow down the clock enough to allow time for Titus to change his clothes, commit the rape, change his clothes again, and get back to his apartment, twenty minutes away, by 7:00 P.M. It just wasn't possible.

The alibi, confirmed by long-distance telephone records, was the strongest part of Titus's defense, but there was other good news. The prosecutor had absolutely no physical evidence tying Steve Titus to the rape. The state crime lab had gone over Titus's company car and the victim's clothing with a fine-tooth comb, and they came up with nothing, zero, zip—no matching hair samples, no matching clothing fiber samples, no fingerprints, no nothing. Port of Seattle police lifted eighteen fingerprints from Titus's Chevette but not one matched the victim. Police cut sections from the Chevette's blue vinyl seats—vinyl, not velveteen, as the rape victim had reported—and tested them for semen stains; they all proved negative. Head hairs recovered from the victim's sweater did not match Titus's head hair.

And there was more good news; fabulous news, in fact. The Western Washington State Crime Laboratory determined that the Michelin tire tracks photographed at the rape scene, a crucial piece of evidence for the prosecution, could not have been made by Titus's car. The steel-belted radial tires were standard equipment on many imported cars similar in appearance to the company-owned Chevette.

The strongest evidence against Titus was the eyewitness identification. Nancy Van Roper had identified Steve Titus as her rapist, and Hillier had no reason to believe that she would change her mind at the last minute. She would undoubtedly point to Titus in court and utter those deadly words: "He's the one; he did it." Hillier knew that any case resting on eyewitness identification is problematic, but in a rape case, when the victim is eyeball to eyeball with her attacker, the ID is given even more weight. The emotional trauma of rape can also play a big part in the jury's decision. A seventeen-year-old girl's life had been ripped apart by a random act of violence, and the jury was not going to be looking at the accused with anything remotely resembling sympathy.

The eyewitness identification was unshakable, but Hillier knew just by looking at Parker's photo montage that it was grossly suggestive. The Polaroid pictures of Titus were smaller, approximately half the size of the five other pairs of pictures. Titus also stood out on the sheet because, unlike the other subjects, there was no dark-line border between his front and profile shot. And he was smiling. Hillier argued in a pretrial hearing that the montage was suggestive and should not be shown to the jury, but the judge denied the motion, ruling that the jury would have to decide whether or not the montage was suggestive.

Hillier's problems didn't end with the eyewitness identification; he would also have to contend with the remarkable similarity between the license plate numbers given by the rape victim and the plates on Titus's car. According to Detective Parker's report, the victim claimed that the beginning numbers displayed on the temporary license plate in the rapists's rearview window were either 667 or 776. Titus's company-owned Chevette had temporary license plates with the six-digit number 661-677.

And it was, truly, an incredible coincidence that two cars, similar makes, similar color, with virtually identical temporary license plate numbers, driven by two men fitting the same general description, were in almost the same place at almost the same time. The prosecutor would be sure to hammer that point into the jury, insisting that such a coincidence was statistically impossible.

Hillier called the State Department of Licensing and discovered that newly purchased cars could, indeed, have similar license plate numbers. In the months of September and October of 1980, for example, all temporary plates issued from Olympia, Washington, began with the numbers 66. It *was* conceivable that another car, purchased around the same time as Titus's Chevette, would have nearly identical license plate numbers.

As the February trial date approached, Tom Hillier found himself believing with unusual intensity in his client's innocence. There was no doubt in his mind that Steve Titus was a victim of mistaken identification. Still, he couldn't rid himself of a feeling of nervousness, a sense that this case was slippery, uncontrollable, unpredictable. Nancy Van Roper would walk in that courtroom, point her finger at Titus, and insist, under oath, that he had raped her. That was his biggest problem by far.

But right up there, working against him, was his own client. Steve Titus was scared to death and his fear had taken on a frantic, hysterical edge. Hillier tried time and time again to calm Titus down. He coached him to think before speaking, to loosen up, to try to control his anger. But whatever was eating at Titus had eaten all the way through. As the trial date approached, Tom Hillier began to wonder if his client wasn't his own worst enemy.

The trial began on February 25, 1981, in a small courtroom located on the third floor of the King County Courthouse. The witness box was only a few feet from the jury box; when the victim testified, the jurors were close enough to see the tears welling up in her eyes. Chris Washington, the prosecutor in the case, questioned her closely about the events of the evening of October 12. Exactly what time was it when she was picked up by the man in the compact blue car, he asked.

"Six-thirty P.M.," she answered immediately and confidently.

Titus and Hillier looked at each other, Hillier's face registering disgust, Titus's expression panic-stricken. The victim had just rolled back her time by fifteen minutes, from 6:45 P.M. to 6:30 P.M. With that extra fifteen minutes, it was conceivable that Titus would have had time—barely enough time—to commit the rape and return to his apartment by 7:00 P.M. Hillier would point out the inconsistency in his cross-examination and argue that this was a move of desperation on the part of the prosecution. But if Nancy Van Roper now remembered that she was picked up by the rapist at 6:30 P.M., she had every right to say that in court.

The prosecutor showed the victim the photo montage and asked if she recognized the pictures. "Yes," she replied, pointing to Titus's photograph. "Do you see this person in the courtroom?" "Yes," she answered again, pointing at Titus. The prosecutor asked her to step down, walk toward the defense table, and get as close to Titus as she was on the night of the rape.

Nancy Van Roper stepped out of the witness box, took a few steps toward the defense table, and then broke down, sobbing uncontrollably. Hillier, stunned at the prosecutor's outrageous tactic, was on his feet, screaming out objections. The judge hurriedly excused the jury, but Hillier continued to yell at the top of his lungs, hoping the jury would hear his outrage. The judge tried to calm him down, sustaining his objections and reprimanding the prosecutor. But the damage was already done. The jury filed back in, faces closed, eyes downcast, refusing to look at Hillier or Titus.

The parade of prosecution witnesses marched, one by one, through the small, claustrophobic courtroom. Ironically, most of the experts called to the stand offered evidence that vindicated Titus. Specialists from the state crime laboratory told the jury they found no evidence that the rape victim had been in Titus's car. Another specialist testified that none of the fingerprints lifted from Titus's Chevette were from the rape victim. Sections of blue vinyl upholstery cut out from the seats of Titus's Chevette proved negative for seminal fluid. Hair fibers from inside the car were analyzed microscopically, and not one hair matched the victim's. Clothing fibers recovered from the car did not match the clothes the victim had worn the night of the rape. Numerous head hairs taken from a blue sweater worn by the victim did not match hairs from Steve Titus's head.

No screwdriver or knife was found in the Chevette, although the prosecutor argued that a black-felt pen found in the well between the front passenger's seat and the door could have been the weapon the rapist held to the victim's throat.

It was Detective Ronald Parker's turn to take the stand. Overweight, open-faced, hands folded in his lap, Parker looked the part of the good, decent cop. Calmly, in a clear, steady voice, Parker testified that the tire tracks he photographed the night of the rape were not, in fact, the tire tracks from the rapist's car. He had recently returned with the victim to the crime scene, he explained, and she recalled that the rapist drove straight in and backed straight out. The tracks that were photographed—the tracks that did not match Titus's Chevette—turned to the right.

Hillier listened in amazement. The police were simply changing their story, throwing out the old evidence because it didn't implicate Titus and introducing new evidence that might have no basis in fact, that could not be proven, and yet would almost certainly prejudice the jury against Titus.

Minutes later Parker delivered his second blow. He testified that he'd seen a brown vinyl binder in the rear seat of Titus's Chevette, just like the binder described by the rape victim. Hillier and Titus looked at each other, flabbergasted—no binder was ever mentioned in the report filed by the officer who searched Titus's car the night of the rape.

But Parker wasn't finished. He offered into evidence a typed statement that he claimed was the one voluntarily given by Titus after his arrest on October 14, in which he explained his whereabouts the night of the rape. Parker had waited until a week before the trial began to type up his recollections of that conversation— memories that Titus, when he saw the written report the night before Parker's testimony, insisted were a pack of lies. In the report, Parker stated that Titus told him he had arrived home the night of the rape at 6:55 P.M.—not 6:30 P.M., as Titus had insisted from the moment he was first questioned by Parker early in the morning of October 13.

"He's a liar," Titus snarled under his breath. Hillier put a hand on Steve's arm. "Steve, be careful," he whispered. "You can't go out there and call him a liar, or you'll turn the jury against you. Calm down. We'll have our chance to give our side."

In his cross-examination, Hillier repeatedly brought up the inconsistencies in the prosecution's case, arguing that the last-minute changes and manipulations were a desperate move to make a weak case look stronger. But he was hesitant to make a direct attack on either the victim or the Port of Seattle police for fear of looking desperate himself. In his cross-examination of the rape victim, Hillier was gentle and considerate, always careful not to alienate the jury by attacking her or coming on too strong. He phrased his last question to her carefully.

"If I could prove to you that Steve Titus was somewhere else when the rape occurred, would you still say he's the one who did it?"

"Yes," Nancy Van Roper answered without a moment's hesitation.

Hillier looked at the jury, hoping the point had sunk in. *This victim,* Hillier was hoping to communicate, *is fixed on Steve Titus to the point that she will dismiss even iron-clad, airtight information showing that he couldn't possibly have done it.* Hillier hoped that her answer to his final question would prove to the jury that her identification of Steve Titus had become an irresponsible and unreasonable obsession.

In his closing statements to the jury, Hillier continued with his nice guy, straight-line approach. *This is all a tragic mistake,* he tried to convey to the jury. *Nobody meant to harm Steve Titus. The police are just trying to do their job, but this man is innocent; he didn't commit these crimes. Look at all these inconsistencies. There's absolutely no physical evidence linking him to the crime. Look at the facts. Be calm, be reasonable.*

But as he took his seat next to his client and looked up at the skeptical, narrow-eyed members of the jury, Hillier felt fear rising within him. Maybe I should have played rough, he thought. The prosecution played dirty. They lied and fabricated and twisted the evidence, and here we are, caught with a smile on our faces and our hands outstretched. Damn.

Hillier suddenly felt the case slipping away from him. It just happened so fast; there was no time for it all to sink in, but the prosecution had nailed them to the wall. He could see it in the jurors' eyes, in the way they sat, heads turned slightly to the side, as if they were afraid to look at him straight on. He'd lost some of them, he felt sure of it. Sitting at the defense table, he offered a quick mental prayer. Don't let me lose them all. Just let one hold out—just one, and Steve will get another chance.

The jurors deliberated for twelve hours. On the first two ballots they voted eight to four for acquittal. On the third ballot they split seven to five, with the majority still arguing for acquittal. Two hours later, on the fourth and final ballot, the jury agreed on a verdict. Steve Titus was found guilty of first-degree rape.

The reaction in the courthouse was hysterical. Members of Titus's family began to scream at the jury; his fiancée collapsed on the floor sobbing. The judge hurriedly ordered guards to escort the jury from the courtroom. Steve Titus sat at the defense table, isolated from the tumult, a condemned man.

*   *   *

Early in April 1981 Seattle *Times* news reporter Paul Henderson got a phone call from a man who identified himself as Steve Titus. Titus talked fast, as if he feared that Henderson would hang up on him in mid-sentence. He had been convicted of rape, he said, but he was innocent, a victim of mistaken identification. The sentencing date was just a few weeks away. Would Henderson investigate the story?

Henderson lit a cigarette, perhaps his fortieth that day, and listened to Titus's story. Titus told him about the events of October 12 and 13: the birthday party, the drive to his apartment, the 7:00 P.M. phone call to his girlfriend. He told him about the trial, how the victim broke down in tears in the courtroom, how her memory about the time when she was picked up by the man in the three-piece suit changed from 6:45 to 6:30 P.M., how Detective Parker lied about the tire tracks and the vinyl folder.

Henderson lit another cigarette. There might be a story here; this just might be a Big Story. It was the voice that got to him. Titus was *driven*.

That same afternoon Henderson drove south on Interstate I-5 to Kent, approximately fifteen miles south of Seattle. He stopped to buy a six-pack of beer, figuring that would loosen up the conversation. He found the apartment complex, knocked on the door of Titus's apartment, and a nice-looking kid, with light-brown, wavy hair, a beard, maybe thirty years old, opened the door. Henderson put out his hand, shook hard. He took off his jacket, sat down on the sofa, lit a cigarette, and opened a beer.

For the next four hours, Paul Henderson sat in the living room of Steve Titus's apartment, listening to a desperate man. After an hour or so, Henderson found himself thinking, Hey, this guy just might be innocent. If Titus were guilty, he'd be talking slower, moving slower, and he'd be more calculated in his statements. He'd have the whole thing planned out, step by step. But this "thing" had Titus by the throat—it was pushing him right off the deep end. You could see it in the way he kept jumping up and down, moving papers from one pile to another and talking a mile a minute.

Titus explained that the only way they could overturn the conviction and win a new trial was to uncover "new evidence of a material nature." He waved at his kitchen table, stacked high with police reports, legal documents, and trial transcripts. Every night he stayed up until one or two in the morning, comparing the reports, reading them over and over again, trying to find the holes, the contradictions and inconsistencies. He had a list of seventy discrepancies. *Seventy.*

But that wasn't enough for the prosecutor's office; no, they would only be satisfied with "new evidence of a material nature." So for three weeks Titus sat on the shoulder of Pacific Highway South, watching for cars that matched the description the victim gave, cars that looked like the Chevette he was driving that night. One day he spotted a light-blue Chevy Citation heading south. The driver had a beard and wore a tan suit and vest. Titus followed the car to Tacoma, parked out of sight, wrote down the address and the license plate number, and drove home. But when he checked with the Department of Motor Vehicles, he discovered that the car had been purchased after the rape.

Titus told Henderson that he spent a lot of time at the DMV, looking through the yearly sales files for a car purchased within the two-week period prior to October 12, 1980. Searching through the files of just one dealer took him between six and eight hours; and there were twenty-five local dealers. He paid an office worker to keep looking, but she didn't have any luck either.

"I'm broke," Titus said. "I have nothing left." The trial lawyer cost him $5,000. The appeal attorney was charging $10,000. Bail bond set him back $2,500 cash. A private detective handed him a bill for $1,200. Titus's employer told him that he believed in Titus's innocence, but he couldn't keep a convicted rapist on the payroll; Titus would be terminated in May, the official reason being that he couldn't "cope with the job."

Titus emptied his beer, put the can on the kitchen floor, and squashed it with the heel of his boot. "You know, I used to be a carefree guy, sort of reckless in my ways," he said. "Those were the good old days."

It took Paul Henderson six weeks to research the Steve Titus story, double-check all the facts, and write it up for publication. On Friday, May 15, the Seattle *Times* published Henderson's story titled "One Man's Battle to Clear His Name." After reading the article, which covered approximately eighty-five inches of newsprint, the judge in the case decided to delay sentencing for several weeks.

On Friday, May 29, the Seattle *Times* published a second story about the Steve Titus case, and once again the judge postponed sentencing for a week. But for everyone who believed in Titus's innocence, that felt something like putting an extra set of brake pads on a logging truck loaded with several tons of trees going seventy miles per hour down a thirty-degree incline. They could feel the new sentencing date bearing down on them, brakes squealing, horn blowing, the smell of burning rubber thick in the air.

With just a few days remaining before Titus's sentencing date, Henderson was playing croquet and drinking beer with some buddies in the middle of a Seattle summer rainstorm. That's when the revelation hit, coming out of nowhere, taking his breath away. What a perfect place to commit a rape, he thought, croquet mallet in hand, rain dripping off the rim of his baseball cap. A rapist's paradise, with all those condemned houses, overgrown driveways, the piles of dirt and wood scraps, the dead-end roads leading nowhere. Maybe the guy didn't stop at one rape. Maybe he went back there more than once. Maybe the victim reported it, and maybe the police had it on file.

That was a powerful bunch of maybes. Henderson knew that *maybe* 10 percent of rape victims report the assault. Maybe, he thought, they'd get lucky, maybe not. He went home and got a few hours' sleep. Early the next morning he was on the phone, calling police departments in Kent and Normandy Park to check the files— was there, by any chance, another rape reported on 22nd Avenue South, sometime between September and November 1980?

Two days later the call came back. A detective at the Sex Crimes Unit of the King County Department of Public Safety told Henderson that yes, there was a rape at the same place; he'd found it in the back of the "low-priority" file. The victim was a fifteen-year-old runaway who reported the rape by phone; she never showed up for the scheduled interview.

The case was listed as number N. 80-187676. At 2:40 P.M. on October 6, 1980, the victim was hitchhiking on Pacific Highway South. A well-dressed man in a light-blue sports car stopped and offered her a ride to Tacoma. He turned off the highway, telling the victim he was going to see his brother. He took her to a secluded dirt lane on 22nd Avenue South, held a pocketknife to her throat and said, "Do what I ask, and I won't hurt you." The victim described the rapist as bearded, with brown hair, twenty-nine to thirty years old, dressed in a tan sports coat, a brown tie, and blue dress slacks.

Pay dirt! Everything fit—the date, the car, the beard, the excuse the guy gave for turning off the highway, the dirt lane, the weapon at the throat, even the threat. Everything. But best of all, October 6 was a Monday—Titus would have been at work.

Henderson called the Yegen Seafood Corporation personnel office and asked Titus's former supervisor, Bob Dennis, to check through the personnel files. Was there a record showing where Steve Titus was, what he was doing, on Monday, October 6, 1980? Dennis found an expense account form that showed on Monday, October 6, Titus was reimbursed for driving ninety-one miles, from his apartment in Kent to downtown Seattle, back to Ivar's Seafood Bar in Kent, and then to the company's store in Federal Way.

What car was he driving? Henderson asked. A company-owned 1979 Pontiac LeMans station wagon, the answer came back.

Titus was driving a station wagon on October 6; whoever raped the fifteen-year-old runaway was driving a sports car.

Henderson took his information to the police, who located the October 6 rape victim at a Tacoma foster home. Sergeant Harlan Bollinger prepared a photo sheet of eight bearded subjects, including Steve Titus, and showed it to the fifteen-year-old victim. If she pointed at Titus's picture, he would be back in the soup, even with the alibi provided by the personnel report. But the rape victim didn't give Titus's photo a second glance.

On Monday, June 8, 1981, armed with Paul Henderson's investigative report, Steve Titus's attorney argued in Superior Court that the obscure rape case represented "new evidence of a material nature" which entitled Titus to a new trial. The prosecutor's office vigorously opposed the motion for a new trial. Judge Charles V. Johnson reviewed the evidence, threw out Titus's conviction for the October 12 rape, and granted the new trial motion.

Three weeks later, on June 30, 1981, the prosecutor's office dismissed charges against Steve Titus and announced that they had a new suspect in the October 12 rape—*Danny Stone*, an unemployed salesman from Kent, Washington. Stone and Titus were considered "look-alikes"—they both had beards and were approximately the same age, height, and weight. Danny Stone was charged with the October 6 and October 12 rapes, another rape that occurred in January 1981, and a rape committed just two weeks before his arrest in June; he was considered a suspect in three additional rape cases.

Nancy Van Roper was brought into police headquarters for an in-person lineup. She looked through the one-way mirror at Danny Stone and began to cry. "Oh, my God," she said, sobbing. "What have I done to Mr. Titus?"

Danny Stone confessed to the rapes and was committed to the sexual psychopath program at Western State Hospital in Steilacoom, Washington.

This is where the Steve Titus story should have ended. The prosecutor's office and the Port of Seattle police should have publicly apologized to Titus. Steve should have picked up the scattered pieces of his life, going back to work at Yegen Seafood, marrying Gretchen, and raising a family. He should have remembered those nine months of his life as a terrible nightmare, but one that was finally over.

Justice had been momentarily derailed, but it had gotten back on track. Steve Titus was vindicated, and there was no doubt left in anyone's mind that he was an innocent man. All's well that ends well.

But Steve Titus didn't think things had ended well. Steve Titus thought he'd gotten one lousy deal. Yegen Seafood Corporation never offered to give him back his job. The prosecutor's office never made a public apology. Gretchen decided that she couldn't live with this angry, obsessed man who had forgotten how to smile. She broke off their engagement.

Steve Titus couldn't just forgive and forget. The system that he believed in, the system that he thought would give him justice, had turned around and declared him a guilty man. It had wiped out his job, his fiancée, his savings account, his reputation. It had destroyed his life, and he wanted to make someone pay for what had been done to him.

In mid-August 1981, on a hot, sunny day, I drove to Pioneer Square for a meeting with Richard Hansen and David Allen, two criminal defense attorneys I had worked with on other cases of possible mistaken identification. Pioneer Square is the old, historic part of Seattle, with cobblestones, century-old brick buildings, four-star restaurants, and quaint bars. It is also the congregating place for the city's down and out: the winos, panhandlers, and bag ladies who inhabit the sidewalks and sprawl over the newly painted park benches. I parked my car on the street a few blocks from the law offices, walked along the sidewalks with their strange mixture of panhandlers with arms outstretched and beautifully dressed professionals hurrying to their next appointment, and stepped into the Pioneer Building, the oldest office building in Seattle, listed in the National Register of Historic Buildings.

We met in the library of David and Richard's third-floor offices, a room of dark wood and heavy law books, the kind with the red leather spines and thick gold lettering. Richard introduced me to Paul Henderson, a slightly built man, perhaps forty years old, with thinning hair, a shy smile, and a pushed-in nose. He looked like a welterweight who had taken a few too many punches in his day.

"Nice to meet you," he said in a low, gravelly voice that showed the effects of many years of heavy cigarette smoking. I shook his hand and told him how excited I was to finally meet him. "I feel as if we're kindred spirits," I said.

"Fighting for truth, justice, and the American way?" he asked.

"Something like that," I said, and we both laughed. We sat down in the comfortable chairs grouped around the conference table and listened as Richard Hansen explained why he brought us all together.

"Steve Titus is going to sue the Port of Seattle police," Richard began. "He believes that Detective Parker lied on the witness stand and fabricated evidence, and he wants to confront him in court and expose the truth about what happened to him. He's hired us"— Richard nodded toward David—"to represent him in the civil case, and we'd like both of you to testify as expert witnesses."

Richard leaned forward in his chair, hands clasped, blue eyes intense. "Paul, you broke the case through your excellent skills and instincts as a reporter and investigator. We want to bring up the point that the police should have done what you did, before they ever accused Steve Titus of this rape. They should have been able to figure out, like you did, that there had been an identical rape in the identical place, within a few days of the Van Roper rape. Everyone who works in criminal justice knows that rape is often a repeated crime, and it's standard procedure to look for similar crimes. Paul figured this out on his own, and I think citizens of this state have the right to expect their police officers to be able to take certain fundamental steps. If they had done their job, Steve never would have been charged. In summary, we'd like you to help us show that the police screwed up and to tell the story of how you proved Steve's innocence. We have Stone's confession, but we want the jury to know, to believe with every cell of their body, that Steve is innocent."

Richard shifted his gaze to me. "Beth, we hope you will agree to enlighten the jury about how easily eyewitnesses can be manipulated in subtle ways, how quickly they can be led into believing that they have picked the right person. We all know what interviewers can do to manipulate their witnesses in ways that the witness doesn't even understand. Based on interviews with the victim, we believe that Parker prepped her by telling her that they had caught the guy who did this terrible thing to her. Parker sat her down on the couch, said some comforting words to her, and then indicated that he had some photographs, and he wanted her to identify the man who raped her."

"If that's indeed what he said," I said, "then you could argue that these were suggestive statements, which planted the idea in the victim's mind that the police had the rapist in custody and all she had to do was identify him. Biased instructions—statements that lead the witness to believe that the culprit is there, in the photo or in-person lineup—put pressure on witnesses to identify someone, anyone."

I briefly described a study conducted by Roy Malpass at the State University in Plattsburgh, New York, in which students witnessed a "crime" and were then given either biased instructions ("We have the culprit and he's in the lineup") or unbiased instructions ("The culprit may not be in the lineup; if you don't see him, say 'not there.'") Two different lineups were then conducted. In the first, the culprit was indeed in the lineup. One hundred percent of the witnesses given the biased instructions picked someone; 25 percent picked the wrong man. Eighty-three percent of the witnesses given the unbiased instructions chose the real culprit, while 17 percent erroneously said that the culprit wasn't there.

But even more interesting were the results of the second lineup, when the culprit was not included—thus, everyone in that lineup was "innocent." When subjects were given an unbiased instruction, 33 percent chose a member of the lineup; but when subjects were given a biased instruction, an astonishing 78 percent made the decision to pick one of the innocent men as the criminal.

Richard nodded his head. "Even without biased instructions, there's a problem, because people have a strong expectation when they're shown a lineup that the guy will be there and all they have to do is pick him out. The pressure is intense to pick someone— even if you're uncertain. These subtle suggestions, as you've said, have a big impact, an unconscious influence on the minds of the victims. Particularly when the person making the suggestions is an authority figure. In this case we've got an impressionable, uneducated seventeen-year-old girl; and we have a fatherly type policeman, unimposing, soft-spoken, concerned. It's a situation ready-made for disaster."

"I've always wondered about something," I said. "Why didn't Titus's lawyers hire an expert witness to testify about memory and the problems with eyewitness testimony? After all, the entire case against Titus hinged on the word of one eyewitness."

"First there's the problem of getting the expert testimony admitted, which is extremely difficult in this state," Richard said. "I'm sure that played a part in Hillier's decision. Then there's the fact that there was absolutely no physical evidence linking Titus to the rape, and the fact that Titus had this seemingly ironclad alibi, confirmed by long-distance phone records. You know, I happened to run into Tom Hillier at Merchant's Café the afternoon after closing arguments, when he was waiting for the jury's decision. I've known Tom a long time, and he's a great trial attorney, one of the best. I could see he was depressed, anxious about something, so I sat down next to him and asked what was bothering him. He told me about the case—the license numbers, the description of the car and the rapist, the eyewitness identification—and then gestured at Titus, who was sitting at the bar drinking a beer. 'I think they're going to convict him, and he's innocent.' Hillier said. 'Why do you think he's innocent?' I asked him. All that evidence seemed damned convincing to me. 'Titus didn't rape her,' Hillier said. 'He's not a rapist. The victim rolled back her times; Parker lied on the witness stand. Titus has been framed.' "

Richard shuddered slightly. "You know, this case is a defense lawyer's worst nightmare. Hillier believed in his head and his heart—he knew in his *gut*—that Titus was innocent. They had the alibi, the phone records, the timing was impossible. There was absolutely no physical evidence tying Titus to this crime. How could the jury find him guilty? But then, out of the blue, the stories start changing: the victim changes her mind about the time she was picked up; the cops monkey around with Titus's statement; Parker changes his mind about the tire tracks; and the jury, caught up in the emotions of the case, fed up like we all are with rapes and murders, comes back with a conviction."

Richard tapped his pen against the conference table, absorbed in his thoughts. "So what could Hillier do then?" he said after a moment. "He couldn't get a retrial on his gut feeling that Titus was innocent; he had to come up with new evidence, material evidence, something that would prove Titus's innocence. He had other clients to represent and Steve didn't have the money to finance a full-scale investigation. It looked like Steve was going to jail."

Richard waved his hand at Paul Henderson. "Enter the Seattle *Times* in the person of Paul Henderson. Paul investigates the case, becomes a believer, and eventually uncovers evidence that another person committed this rape. His articles helped to correct a horrendous injustice and at the same time expose the fallibility of eyewitness identification and the abysmal failure of polygraph examinations to get at the truth."

David Allen, Richard's law partner, spoke up for the first time. "All the rest of us are satisfied with this conclusion. Justice swerved off course, but through the masterful art of investigative reporting and the glories of a free press, it is brought back into line. The guilty are brought to justice and the innocent are freed. What a nice, neat conclusion to a messy six months. All the rest of us can live with this conclusion, but for Steve Titus nothing will ever again be nice and neat. His life is in ruins. He can't sleep, he can't eat, he lost his job, his savings account is depleted, his fiancée left him, and he feels that his reputation is destroyed. Many people haven't heard that Titus was completely cleared, that another man confessed to the rape. They remember the name—Titus—and they look at him and think 'convicted rapist.' Steve Titus's life has been shattered into so many little pieces, and he wants justice. Justice, and perhaps a little bit of revenge."

Watching Richard and David, it struck me, as it always does when I work with them, what a perfect pair of opposites they are. Richard is tall, trim, with tight blond curly hair and delicate features. David is half a foot shorter, with dark hair, a salt-and-pepper beard, and wire-rim glasses. Richard is extroverted, a quick-thinking, articulate man who is always in the center of the fray. David is introverted, watchful, with gentle brown eyes that take in every word, every gesture.

"Justice and revenge," I repeated. "In the civil case, then, does Steve hope to be reimbursed for the expenses incurred in the criminal trial? Or is he hoping for even more?"

"Even more." Richard and David looked at each other; Richard nodded slightly, giving the floor to David. "We believe that Detective Parker lied on the witness stand," David said. "We believe he persuaded the rape victim that she was wrong about her times, that he made up the story about the tire tracks and the brown vinyl folder. And we believe he manufactured evidence against Steve Titus, namely the license plate numbers. We believe that either the victim never gave Parker a license plate number or that she gave him a completely different number. After Parker had arrested Titus and written down his temporary license plate numbers, he changed the police report and added in Titus's plates."

Paul Henderson jumped in. He said he smelled something rotten from the first time he met Steve, when he drove down to his apartment in Kent and drank a six-pack of beer with him. It had to be police misconduct, Henderson figured; how else could they nail Titus when his alibi was so tight? Henderson kept talking, jabbing at the air with his lighted cigarette. The license plate numbers were always Titus's biggest problem, he said, because the numbers the rape victim gave Parker were almost identical to Titus's temporary plate numbers. But when Danny Stone, the real rapist, was caught and confessed, his license plate numbers were completely different from the numbers listed in the police report. When he heard that piece of information, Henderson figured that Parker had lifted the numbers right off Titus's plates and stuck them in his report.

"We think that's exactly what he did," Richard said. "We hired Jan Beck, a documents examiner who worked for years with the FBI and CIA. Beck went over the police reports and determined that they'd been altered. Titus's license plate numbers were inserted later, after the original police report was typed and signed by the victim. The page with the license plate numbers was out of sequence, and the typed plate numbers were out of alignment with the rest of the typing on the page."

"Why would Parker do something so outrageous?" I asked. "Why would he fabricate evidence and lie on the witness stand just to put away Steve Titus?"

"Why not?" Richard smiled at me benignly. "Consider this scenario: Parker's got a rape, he's got a victim, he's even got a suspect who fits the description in almost all respects. He interviews the victim, but she can't remember the license plate numbers; or maybe she's given him a number that doesn't match the numbers on Titus's car. Later, after he arrests Titus, he realizes he has only this minor discrepancy, only the license plate numbers don't fit. But Titus looks so good, everything fits except for maybe a few small things: his height, the beard, a license number here or there. So, he thinks to himself: She's got the license plate number wrong. She couldn't remember the numbers, because she was scared and confused. Titus is the guy, there's no doubt about it, but he'll walk unless we get some concrete evidence. He'll walk and then he'll rape again. I can't let that happen. So in the interest of law and justice and getting criminals off the street and behind bars, Parker took Titus's license plate numbers and inserted them into the original report. It's just a little extra padding to his case; that's how he probably justified it. Just a little extra insurance."

"We went backward and forward over these reports," David said. "Once Beck told us about these suspicious pages, all we had to do was get a ruler and magnifying glass to see that somebody took the finished report, put it back in the typewriter, and added Titus's license plate numbers. It was as simple and insidious as that."

It would have worked too," Richard said, "if Titus weren't such a fighter, and if Paul Henderson hadn't come on the scene. They almost had Steve locked away. He was just a few days away from sentencing when Henderson discovered this other rape case. Parker almost got away with it."

"What's happening to Parker now?" I asked.

"The department is standing behind him," Richard said, "and they're ready to fight us with everything they've got. Their reputation is on the line, and they're filing motions left and right, trying to knock the case out of court."

Richard and David looked at each other, a glance that spoke of partnership, friendship, and long, hard nights ahead. Richard sighed. "Any direct attack on the police, any attempt to sue a police department for negligence or incompetence is going to be hotly contested. We've got one long, nasty fight ahead of us."

Through the remaining four months of 1981, through the years 1982, 1983, and 1984, Steve Titus and his attorneys fought their way through the labyrinth of paperwork and pretrial contests that marked the course of this incredibly complex civil suit. The Port of Seattle police fought back every inch of the way, and the case ground along, slowly, painfully progressing on its way to the courts.

Every few months I'd get a call from Richard or David, telling me about new developments, a positive ruling by the court, a new review requested by the police, a scheduling delay. I would always ask how Titus was holding up, and there would inevitably be a slight hesitation.

"He's frustrated," Richard said during one of these conversations. "He's become very distrustful."

"Of you?" I asked.

"Of everyone. This is so much worse than any of us could imagine. Time, it is clear, does not heal all wounds, at least not Steve Titus's wounds. He spends every waking moment and every sleeping moment consumed by this case. It rips him apart, still, that nobody apologized to him. If just one person at the police department or the prosecutor's office had said, 'Hey, we're sorry, we screwed up,' I think he might be able to let go of some of his bitterness and anger. But instead he's made to feel like the whiner, the complainer, the pain in the neck, while they're out covering their butts, hiding behind the excuse that he *looked* guilty, and so they had no choice but to prosecute. 'We did nothing wrong,' they said. 'Considering the evidence, we had no choice but to proceed.' Imagine how those words sound to Steve Titus's ears. These people grudgingly give him their regrets, but they refuse to apologize. They ruined his life, and they won't even say, 'I'm sorry.'"

"Ruined his life," I repeated. "Temporarily or permanently?"

"I don't know," Richard said. "I honestly don't. I saw Steve smile the other day, and I realized it was the only time I'd ever seen him smile. We were in the Court of Appeals and there was an intensely spirited argument over the police department's motion to dismiss our claim of negligent investigation. Two major law firms were fighting us tooth and nail, an all-out, no-holds-barred defense. At the end of a series of intense arguments, the commissioner gave us a great ruling—he looked down at us and said, 'You can have your day in court, I'm not going to interfere.' I looked at Steve and he was grinning from ear to ear. It lasted about three seconds, and then it was gone. I wonder if I'll ever see him smile again."

"Will he eventually be able to put all this behind him?"

"I don't think so," Richard said. "That's the question all the rest of us are asking—we all watch this man's ceaseless struggle and we think: Why can't he get on with his life? But we haven't experienced his horror and so we can't know what he's going through. We just can't know."

The Titus case was finally about to come to trial. All the motions filed by the Seattle Police department had been defeated in court, all obstacles had been removed, and a trial date was scheduled for February 19, 1985. It had taken four and a half years for Steve Titus to have his day in court, the day when he would be the accuser, pointing his finger at the defense table.

As the months before the trial turned into weeks and the weeks to days, I found myself thinking about Steve counting down the days. On January 30, nineteen days before the trial, Steve Titus woke up in the morning, doubled over in pain. He collapsed to the floor, reached out to the woman he was living with, and whispered, "Don't leave me."

When the paramedics arrived, Steve was in a coma. His heart had stopped. He was rushed to the Coronary Care Unit at Valley Medical Center in Renton, where he lay comatose, hooked up to a respirator and a heart monitor.

On February 8, 1985, eleven days before he would have faced his tormentors in court, Steve Titus died. He was thirty-five years old.

On December 17, 1985, Steve Titus's estate was awarded a $2.8 million settlement from the Port of Seattle.

On June 8, 1987, six years to the day after Titus's conviction was overturned, Detective Ronald Parker was found slumped next to his gym locker, dead of a heart attack. He was forty-three years old.

Steve Titus is buried in Washington Memorial Cemetary on Pacific Highway South, near Sea-Tac airport. I drove out to the cemetery one blustery spring day and found his grave under two small evergreens. A one-foot-by-one-foot plaque was set into the ground; the grass around the stone was well-trimmed. Behind me I could hear the sounds of steady traffic on Pacific Highway South, the highway where this tragedy began so many years ago.

I knelt down, moving the fresh flowers off the stone so that I could read the epitaph.

> *Steven G. Titus*
> *1949–1985*
> *He fought for his day in court,*
> *he was used, deceived, betrayed*
> *and denied justice even in death.*

THE ALL-AMERICAN BOY:
TED BUNDY

"He was the all-American boy murdering all-American girls."
—James Sewell, Assistant Chief of Campus Police,
Florida State University

Now that I think back on it, I don't remember John O'Connell ever telling me that his client, twenty-three-year-old law student Ted Bundy, was innocent. I have a letter from O'Connell in which he refers to the kidnapping charge against Bundy as "one of the more interesting cases involving eyewitness indentification." I remember a phone conversation in which he talked about the "extremely weak case" against his client. He often stressed the confusion and uncertainty of the kidnapping victim—the only eyewitness, it would turn out, who lived to tell about her few moments of terror with Ted Bundy.

But when I dredge up the strange and painful memories of my involvement with Ted Bundy, I have no recollection of John O'Connell insisting with his characteristic passion and intensity that his client was innocent. Maybe that particular silence should have given me a clue.

The name Ted Bundy meant nothing to me back in December 1975 when John O'Connell first contacted me about the kidnapping charge against his client. The name might as well have been anyone's. But one comment in O'Connell's letter did set off an alarm system in my memory. It was the second line of his five-page, single-spaced letter.

Dear Dr. Loftus,

I am representing Ted Bundy on a charge of aggravated kidnapping here in Salt Lake. Mr. Bundy is a law student from the Seattle area and has achieved a great deal of notoriety there because this case has made him a prime suspect in the "Ted cases." . . .

I knew all about the "Ted cases"; I'd be willing to bet that every woman living in the state of Washington knew about the "Ted cases." Beginning in January 1974, young women in their late teens and early twenties, all pretty, all with long brown hair parted down the middle, began to disappear. Every month another woman would vanish. The media, in a hideous display of insensitivity, began referring to the missing women as "Miss February," "Miss March," "Miss April," and "Miss May."

In June 1974 the pace speeded up as two more women disappeared, and in July two women vanished on the same day from the same park at Lake Sammamish, twelve miles east of Seattle. But now, finally, there were witnesses who told police that an attractive, polite young man calling himself "Ted" and wearing his left arm in a sling approached several women and asked for their help in lifting a sailboat onto his car. He couldn't do it himself, he explained with a shy grin, because of his sprained arm.

The disappearances seemed to stop then, but the grisly discoveries began. In September the remains of three women were discovered by a grouse hunter near an abandoned logging road twenty miles east of Seattle. The next spring another "dumping site"—a favorite media expression—was discovered by two forestry students hiking on the lower slopes of Taylor Mountain near the town of North Bend. Four skulls and assorted bones would eventually be unearthed there, each cranium fractured by a heavy blunt instrument wielded with tremendous force and fury.

I turned to page 2 of O'Connell's letter, where he described the kidnapping incident, and continued on to page 3 where he discussed

Bundy's arrest on a traffic charge almost ten months after the kidnapping.

> There is no other evidence whatsoever connecting the defendant to this crime except that he has type O blood and some type O blood was found sometime later on the victim's clothing. All this, despite the fact that Ted Bundy has been subjected to the most thorough police investigation that I have ever seen. Due to the great time lapse, we are unable to establish an alibi for the time concerned.

O'Connell included with his letter a twenty-page police report and typed transcript of a taped statement the victim made the night of the incident. Throughout both the police report and the transcript, O'Connell used a thick black pen to underline certain words and phrases and scrawl notes in the margins. I began reading.

OFFENSE: Abduction
DATE OF OCCURRENCE: 11–8–74
SUSPECT: Male, white, American, 25–30 years, brown hair, medium length, approximately six feet tall, thin to medium build, moustache neatly trimmed. Wearing green pants and sports jacket, color unknown. Patent leather, shiny <u>black</u> shoes.

An arrow led from the underlined word to the left-hand margin where O'Connell had scrawled, "See taped statement—reddish brown shoes."

I leafed through the remaining pages of the police report, noting the other underlined parts.

Victim believed that she scratched suspect, probably on either the hands or arms, that she did note some blood on her hands that must have come from the suspect, that she was not injured herself. <u>However, does not remember actually hurting the suspect.</u>

In talking to victim, she states she believes she could identify suspect if she saw him again, that she spent approximately <u>20–30 minutes</u> with him in the mall and walking through the parking lot and in the vehicle. Victim <u>taped a report</u> which will be included as a supplement of this report.

The supplementary report contained the transcript of a conversation between the victim, Carol DaRonch, and Detective Riet. I leafed through the pages, noting O'Connell's underlines and comments. On page 4, Detective Riet asked the victim how old she estimated her assailant to be.

"Between twenty-five and thirty," she answered.

"How old do you think I am?" Riet asked.

"I can't tell age," DaRonch answered.

O'Connell had underlined the words "I can't tell age." On the next page was this exchange:

RIET: Did he have a beard or any mustache or any sideburns?
DARONCH: He had a mustache.
RIET: Was it a long, bushy mustache? Short? Medium?
DARONCH: Just a medium.

Bundy had no mustache! These words, carefully printed, were enclosed in parentheses in the margin.

This seemed odd to me. Why would the victim remember a mustache, even partially describing it as a "medium" mustache, when there wasn't any mustache? On the other hand, maybe Bundy had a stick-on mustache that he used for a quick disguise.

A few lines down on the same page, Detective Riet asked about the assailant's shoes.

RIET: Shoes? Did you notice any shoes?
DARONCH: Yes, they were patent leather.
RIET: Color?
DARONCH: Kind of a reddish brown.

Kind of a reddish brown. There it was, reddish brown, not black as reported on the first page of the police report. It was a small discrepancy, but when combined with the victim's other hesitancies and contradictions, it could be argued that, just a few hours after it occurred, she was having difficulty reconstructing her attempted kidnapping.

On page 6 of the transcript there was a discussion about the car:

RIET: Do you remember his car?
DARONCH: Well. Yes. Kind of.
RIET: What kind was it?

DARONCH: Volkswagen.

RIET: They all pretty well look alike, don't they? Typical bug type?

DARONCH: Yes.

RIET: Did you notice what color it was?

DARONCH: It was a light color, a <u>light blue or white</u>.

RIET: Are there any cracks in any of the windows? Do you remember?

DARONCH: No, <u>I can't remember</u>.

RIET: Was there any stickers in any of the windows?

DARONCH: <u>I can't remember</u>.

RIET: Can you remember what color the upholstery was?

DARONCH: <u>No</u>.

RIET: Was it dark or light?

DARONCH: <u>I don't remember</u>.

O'Connell's thick, black marking pen didn't miss one of those
memory lapses. "No," "I can't remember," "I don't remember," all
underlined. I wondered if Detective Riet was getting frustrated. I
could picture him leaning back in his creaky chair, stabbing at his
gums with a toothpick. Suddenly, in my imaginary scenario, he
tossed the toothpick into his dirty metal wastebasket, leaned forward
with his hands clasped tightly together, and asked DaRonch to be
specific, please, about what had happened when she was approached
in the mall.

RIET: What was his story when he approached you? What did he
say?

DARONCH: He asked me if I had a car parked in Sears parking lot
and I told him I did . . . then he told me someone was trying
to break in with a piece of wire and someone saw him trying
and went into Sears and reported it to him. And then we walked
out the doors between Auerbachs and Ropers and walked over
toward my car in Sears parking lot and then I got my keys out
and opened the door on my side, the driver's side, and nothing
was gone.

RIET: Then what did he do?

DARONCH: And then we went around to the other side of the door
and he wanted me to open it and I told him—I asked him what
for. I said, "I know what's in my car and nothing's gone."

RIET: Were you suspicious of him then?
DARONCH: Yes.

Stress, Fear, I wrote on a piece of note paper. DaRonch described, then, how she accompanied "Officer Roseland" back into the mall where he offered to drive her to police headquarters so that she could sign a complaint. At that point, she asked to see his ID.

DARONCH: . . . he opened his wallet and showed me a badge that was all gold and I couldn't see any writing on it or nothing. He put it back inside of his jacket. Then we walked to the car . . . and he opened—he was really nice, opened all the doors for me.

Opened all the doors for me. Something clicked in my memory, like a door opening, a shaft of light penetrating the darkness. I remembered what one of the Lake Sammamish victims told the police about "Ted." He was "very sincere," she said. "Easy to talk to. Real friendly. He had a nice smile." And I remembered another fact—the Lake Sammamish Ted drove a beige VW. And all of his victims were pretty young women with long brown hair parted in the middle.

Did Carol DaRonch have long brown hair? Was the Volkswagen blue, as DaRonch first testified, or was it beige, as she later claimed? When did Ted Bundy move from Seattle to Utah? Could the Utah Ted be the Lake Sammamish Ted?

Stop it, Beth. Stick to the facts. I took a deep breath, then another, and focused my attention again on the faded, Xeroxed copy of the police report.

DARONCH: [He] helped open the car door for me and I got in and [he] went around and got in and told me to "put your seat belt on" and I said . . . no, I don't want to put it on. And then he turned around and then I started wondering why he didn't go on State, but he turned around and went east and then he turned back at the stop sign . . . and then he stopped the car and kind of went up on the curb a little bit and came back down and I told him "What are you doing" and then I opened the car door and stuck my foot out and then he grabbed my right arm and he stuck the handcuffs on it and I started screaming and I pulled away and he pulled out a gun and he said he'd shoot me.

Detective Riet questioned her about the gun, but DaRonch could only describe it as black and small. "I didn't get that good a look at it," she said.

Weapon focus, I wrote in my notes. With a gun being waved in her face, it was no wonder she had trouble remembering details.

DARONCH: And then I started screaming again and I started pulling on the car and he said he would shoot me but I just started pulling out of the car and I got outside of the car with him and had a hold of his . . . left hand. He had a crowbar in it and so I grabbed the crowbar so he couldn't hit me with it and he kept trying to push it down and me and I don't remember if I fell or not and finally I don't know how I did it but I tore away and then I ran out into the street. I thought he was following me so I saw a car and stood in the middle of the street and started waving and running towards it and they stopped.

There were no commas in the transcription. No commas, I imagined, in Carol DaRonch's voice either as she spewed out the details of those few, horrifying moments when she fought, tooth and nail, for her life.

Carol DaRonch had been terrified, no doubt about that, and when people are afraid, their memories slip and slide, neglecting details, rearranging facts. When we remember, we pull pieces of the past out of some mysterious region in the brain—jagged, jigsaw pieces that we sort and shift, arrange and rearrange until they fit into a pattern that makes sense. The finished product, the memory that seems so clear and focused in our minds, is actually part fact, part fiction, a warped and twisted reconstruction of reality.

The warping occurs even when there is no stress, fear, anxiety, or terror. It is the nature of our imperfect ability to store and retrieve data. But when there is extraordinary stress, as there undoubtedly was in this situation, the warping can also be extraordinary.

When Carol DaRonch told Detective Riet that she couldn't remember certain details of the kidnapping, she was telling the truth.

Just an hour after her ordeal, she couldn't remember the most obvious details about her assailant, his car, or the weapon he waved in her face. Her memory was eaten through by the acid of fear.

Just one page remained of the supplementary report. Riet asked DaRonch about "Officer Roseland's" badge.

RIET: Could you read any writing on it at all? Did it have an eagle on it or anything like this, this is a police badge here. Did it have an eagle or anything like this?
DARONCH: It wasn't as big as that but it was the same shape.
RIET: Was it the same color?
DARONCH: <u>No, it was all gold.</u>

A final, thick black underline—<u>No, it was all gold</u>—and in the margin this penciled statement in O'Connell's now-familiar scrawl: "At hearing she testified that it was blue and white and gold which is same color as Murray badge shown to her by police officer."

I picked up the phone and dialed John O'Connell's number in Salt Lake City.

"This is Elizabeth Loftus," I said when O'Connell came on the line. "I received your letter and the police transcripts in the Bundy case and from what I've read so far, it appears that there are some psychological issues I could discuss regarding the eyewitness identification in this case."

"Great!" O'Connell's voice boomed across the line. I moved the receiver off center in an attempt to protect my eardrums. "As I wrote in my letter, the kidnapping case is one that I would ordinarily regard as a very weak case, but in view of the massive pretrial publicity, this trial presents an extremely dangerous situation for my client." O'Connell stopped talking for a moment, and in the background I heard the sound of a match lighting and then an exhale. Pipe or cigarette? I wondered. "I should tell you that three weeks before this kidnapping incident occurred in Murray, the daughter of the Midvale chief of police disappeared. Midvale is about five miles from Murray. Her body was found ten days later; she'd been raped and murdered. Although there is no evidence whatsoever linking these two incidents, the Murray police seem to regard both incidents as an attack on their department by the same person. They are more than a little uptight about the situation."

Overzealous police? I wrote in my notes. "How large a town is Murray?" I asked.

"About twenty-six thousand people," O'Connell answered.

I added half a dozen question marks after *overzealous police*. A murder and an attempted kidnapping within two weeks seemed like an unusual amount of violence for a small town. If I lived in Murray, I'd be a little uptight too.

"What about the connection to the Washington murders and disappearances?" I asked.

"It's all circumstantial," O'Connell said, his tone soothing. "The Seattle cops have been meeting with the Utah and Colorado cops, and they haven't been able to come up with any solid evidence linking Bundy to these other crimes. But the pressure is on to find a suspect, and Bundy seems to be the only one they've got. They're convinced that they're on the trail of a multistate mass murderer. The publicity has been outrageous. Just last month I saw a Seattle newspaper story with the headline 'Is Utah Ted the Seattle Ted?' "

I ignored the churning sensation in my belly and flipped to page 2 of his letter. "You mention that Mr. Bundy was arrested on a traffic charge nine months after the attempted abduction."

"Right. A highway patrolman stopped him last August, around 2 A.M. for running some stop signs."

"How did a traffic violation get him into this fix?"

"They found a ski mask, handcuffs, ice pick, crowbar, and some other tools in his car. They arrested him for possession of burglary tools."

Handcuffs, ice pick, burglary tools? I wrote in my notes. That little stash certainly didn't look good for Mr. Bundy. Why was he driving around residential streets at two in the morning with handcuffs and an ice pick in his car?

"What happened then?" I asked.

"Shortly after his original arrest on the traffic charge, Mr. Bundy was interrogated regarding the missing girl cases, which he, of course, denied knowing anything about," O'Connell explained. "Then the kidnapping victim was shown Mr. Bundy's photograph in a rather large group of photographs—she had looked at literally hundreds of photographs since the incident, attempting to identify the individual involved—and she picked it out as one that looked more like her abductor than other photographs she had seen. 'I guess it looks something like him' were, I believe, her exact words.

"But here's the really interesting part," O'Connell continued in a low, confidential tone. I could imagine him sitting at a wide oak desk, loosening his tie and staring out at the Mormon Tabernacle from the window of his high-rise, glass-faced office building. "A few days after the victim's first ID of Bundy, a police officer showed her another photo of Bundy, a driver's license photo this time. Suddenly her memory is dramatically improved, and she's convinced that Bundy is the man. The cops might as well have planted the picture in her brain."

O'Connell had a point. By showing her two different photos of the same man, the police could actually have created a memory in DaRonch's mind. When she viewed the second photograph, she would have "remembered" the face in the first photograph. With that memory fixed firmly in mind, it would be easy to put Bundy's face—which she had now seen in two separate photographs—into her original memory of "Officer Roseland."

"When was the lineup?" I asked.

"October second, nineteen seventy-five."

"Almost eleven months after the attempted kidnapping," I calculated out loud. "Was the lineup fair in your opinion?"

"Hell, no," O'Connell exclaimed. "She'd seen two photos of Bundy and had never seen any of the other guys in the lineup. They were all policemen, by the way. Who do you think she'd pick?"

Photo-biased lineup. I capitalized the letters and underlined the words twice. This would be a critical point for the defense. Once a witness has seen a person's photograph, that person will look familiar when he or she appears in a lineup. The witness may incorporate this familiar face into her memory of the crime and the criminal—and make a mistaken identification.

I put my pen down. "Mr. O'Connell—" I began.

"John," he interrupted. "Please call me John."

"Okay. John, it's clear to me that there are several factors that could have led to a mistaken identification in this case. But what are the chances of getting my testimony introduced?"

The Supreme Court had traditionally ruled that an expert witness may not testify to anything a layman can reasonably be expected to know. The prosecutor in the Bundy case would almost certainly challenge my testimony on the basis of this standard ruling, just as other prosecutors had challenged expert psychological testimony in previous cases. In the two years since I first appeared in a courtroom as an expert witness on memory and perception, I had been asked to testify in seven cases; in only three of those cases was the testimony permitted in court.

"We believe there's a good probability that we'll be able to put you on the stand," O'Connell said. "The rules of evidence in Utah are more liberal than they are in Washington or California, and we succeeded in getting such testimony admitted on the one other occasion that we tried it. However, this case will be tried in front of a different judge, and the state will no doubt be trying a lot harder to keep you off the stand. It could be a battle."

"I'm used to that," I said. I asked O'Connell to send me the preliminary hearing transcripts, mug shots, lineup photos, newspaper articles, and anything else he had on Bundy. Then I hung up the phone and looked over my notes.

STRESS
FEAR
OVERZEALOUS POLICE??????
HANDCUFFS, CROWBAR
PHOTO-BIASED LINEUP

AUGUST 16—	ARREST BUNDY
	FOUND HANDCUFFS
	QUESTIONED
SEPTEMBER 1—	SHOW PICTURES TO DARONCH
	TENTATIVE ID
SEPTEMBER 4—	NEW PICTURE, STRONG ID
OCTOBER 2—	LINEUP. POSITIVE ID

On August 15 Ted Bundy was a law student about to begin his second year. On August 16 he was a burglary suspect; two weeks later he'd become a suspected kidnapper. Over the next few months, circumstantial evidence would make him a serial murder suspect.

Life, it would be safe to say, had not proceeded according to plan for Ted Bundy.

I thought for a while about the mass murder suspicions. Was this law student a diabolical mass murderer, as the police seemed to think, or was he innocent, caught in the wrong place at the wrong time? I knew what could happen when a suspect *looked* right. An arrest is made, preliminary hearings held, defense attorneys hired, depositions taken, newspaper articles published. The pressure gradually intensifies, facts are accumulated, conclusions are constructed, and the heavy, cumbersome machinery of the criminal justice system is cranked up. And caught up in the gears and the cogs, an essential part now of the equipment itself, is the person called "defendant."

Most of the time, perhaps 99 percent of the time, the defendant *is* guilty; his screams are the final protest of a human being about to lose his most precious possession, his freedom. But every once in a while an innocent person is pulled into the system.

I had a file folder full of such cases, dozens of them. Lawrence Berson, a seventeen-year-old college freshman, was arrested in 1973 and held for a week in a New York City jail on multiple rape charges after five women identified him as their attacker. Berson was freed when a New York City taxi driver, whom he resembled strikingly, was arrested, identified, and charged with the rapes.

William Schrager, thirty, an assistant district attorney of Queens County, New York, was identified by four women as the man who had sexually molested them. John Priolo, forty-five, a Sanitation Department chauffeur, was identified by several victims of similar sexual attacks as the perpetrator. Both Priolo and Schrager were exonerated when a twenty-nine-year-old postman confessed to some of the crimes for which Schrager and Priolo had been charged. Schrager had this to say about the victims who mistakenly identified him: "They were so intelligent and so convincing that they almost made me believe I did it."

Frank Doto, forty-three years old, was identified by *seventeen* witnesses as the man who robbed three supermarkets and shot a policeman in the head. Doto was cleared when police checked his airtight alibi and discovered that he was nowhere near the scene of the crimes.

Each of these cases provides dramatic proof that memory is fallible, that eyewitnesses make mistakes, and that innocent people are convicted and imprisoned. "But what about the victims of these crimes?" people ask me. "Don't you care about them?" Yes, I care; of course I care. But as an expert witness I try to make sure that two victims do not emerge from this crime, that an innocent person is not put behind bars while a guilty person is allowed to go free.

In the Bundy case, I couldn't let myself think about Carol DaRonch's shattered perception of the world as a sane and peaceful place. I couldn't allow myself the luxury of sharing her fear or participating in her pain, because I had to concern myself with the possibility that she might be pointing her finger at an innocent man. I had to focus on the factors that might have reduced the accuracy of her memory, and thus the accuracy of her identification of Ted Bundy.

"But how could you get up on the stand and call the eyewitness a liar?" I've been asked, and I answer that it is not my place to call anyone a liar. I would be called to testify about the general nature of human memory and the factors that reduce its accuracy. My testimony is detached and disassociated, in the same sense that a pathologist, testing a piece of tissue for malignancy, is disconnected from the pain and fear of the human being waiting to hear the diagnosis.

"But how do you justify testifying for people accused of such horrible crimes?" the same people ask me. I'm not defending them, I answer; I'm simply presenting the research on memory. The defense attorney has the duty of defending the client, and the jury has the duty of deciding guilt or innocence. I just present the facts as I know them to be true.

"But aren't you concerned that the jury might acquit a guilty person because you've planted a doubt in their mind?" And I answer: In order to convict, a jury must believe that the defendant is guilty beyond a reasonable doubt. If my testimony causes members of the jury to doubt the defendant's guilt, then according to the most basic, indispensable principles of our justice system, the defendant *should* be acquitted.

When a person is charged with a crime and brought to trial, our system theoretically assumes innocence until guilt is proven, and the burden is placed on the prosecutor to prove the defendant's guilt beyond a reasonable doubt. But when we move from the world of theory to the world of reality, the situation can be quite different. In the process of arresting, charging, and trying a defendant, a subtle transformation often occurs. We begin to presume guilt, and the burden is actually shifted onto the defense to prove innocence. Having to prove someone's innocence implies, of course, that guilt is already presumed. The worse the crime, the bloodier the act, the harder the defense attorney must work to overcome this presumption of guilt.

The emotions associated with bringing a criminal to justice can undermine reason by invoking savage passions. The most primitive part of our mind cries out for revenge. Not justice, but revenge: an eye for an eye, a tooth for a tooth, a life for a life.

This is mob mentality, and someone needs to block the way. I am a specialist in memory and perception, a scientist who conducts research experiments in controlled environments. It is my job to be rational and clearheaded, to prevent emotions from swelling up and distorting reason, bending reality, twisting facts.

I seek justice, because I fear revenge. I ask only that we think about the plight of those innocent people accused of crimes they did not commit. Imagine their bitterness, fear, and despair. Envision, if you can, the horror of being put on trial, the anguish of losing the respect and love of your friends and family, the mind-numbing hell of prison life. Translate the statistics into the flesh and blood of thousands of men and women who sit in their prison cells knowing too well the dark side of justice.

I believe the rights of these innocent people are worth fighting for. If we do not fight for them, we will lose the best part of ourselves.

Early in the evening of February 24, 1976, John O'Connell showed me through his home, apologizing for the fact that I would spend the night in his son Will's room. "I'm afraid you'll have to share the room with Luther," O'Connell said, pointing to the chest-high dresser where a large snapping turtle stared at me from the bottom of a grimy fishbowl.

"Luther lives in the nightmares of many of our guests," O'Connell confided. "I hope you're not terrified of reptiles."

"Just snakes," I said, laughing, feeling relieved to be staying in this comfortable, safe home. The thought had occurred to me as I was flying to Salt Lake City earlier that day that Ted Bundy might offer to let me stay in his apartment. I'd been reviewing my notes and studying the mug shots taken the night of Bundy's arrest in August 1974. Sitting in my aisle seat on the DC-10, I brought the mug shot close and stared into Bundy's face. With his lips pressed tightly together, his nostrils slightly flared, one eyebrow raised, he appeared arrogant, defiant, angry. His eyes were cold, lifeless, vacant; it was as if I could see right through them.

O'Connell handed me a glass of white wine and ushered me into his study. "Let's review the basics of your testimony tomorrow," he said, settling his long, lanky body into a brown leather chair. A cowboy hat, big as a briefcase and probably weighing as much, rested on the polished desktop. "First things first, however. We waived the right to a jury."

"What?" I said, my voice registering my shock. I carefully set down my wineglass and waited for O'Connell to explain. Waiving a jury was an extremely unusual legal maneuver, rarely used in such high-stakes cases as this one. In a jury trial, Bundy's fate would be decided by twelve men and women, and all twelve would have to agree that he was guilty beyond a reasonable doubt. By waiving the jury, O'Connell had decided that Bundy's guilt or innocence would be determined, instead, by one individual—a judge.

O'Connell smiled at the look on my face. "We need your testimony, it's as simple as that," he said. "The prosecution's case rests primarily on Carol DaRonch's ID of Bundy as the man who abducted her. You're our star witness. You can raise questions about her ID by testifying about the fallibility of memory and the problematical nature of eyewitness identification. As you know, we'd have one hell of a time getting this information before a jury—the prosecutor would try every trick he knows to prevent you from testifying. But the judge will hear it; I feel confident about that."

O'Connell stood up and began pacing the room. "There's another reason," he said. "The typical, average guy on the street thinks circumstantial evidence is flimsy, but it's a whole hell of a lot more trustworthy than an eyewitness. Eyewitness testimony is lousy testimony, you and I know that, but juries are more likely to convict on the basis of eyewitness testimony than almost anything else."

O'Connell held his hands out, palms up, pleading his case. "Our theory is simple. Why not go with one juror, the judge, who we know is intelligent rather than testing our chances on twelve unknowns?"

I took a deep breath. O'Connell had rearranged his entire case so that I could testify. It was a risky move. The judge would have to hear my testimony, even if the prosecutor protested, because O'Connell would insist on "putting it in the record." But judges are notoriously tougher on defendants than jurors. They deal with hard-core criminals every day, and every day they hear the familiar litany: "I'm innocent, I didn't commit this crime, it's all a mistake."

Such repetition, such day-in, day-out exposure to the details of these horrific crimes hardens the heart. Judges are toughened to defendants much as butchers are inured to the sight of blood. Now there's a fascinating legal sidelight. It's a little-known fact that butchers rarely get to sit on criminal juries—prosecutors reject them immediately, because they know that it takes a house full of horrors to shock someone who spends eight hours a day cutting dead animals into little pieces.

I figured O'Connell's gamble must have something to do with the personality or track record of the judge in this particular case. "Tell me about the judge," I said.

"His name is Stewart M. Hanson, Jr. I went to law school with him." O'Connell picked up a pipe, struck a match, and puffed a few times. "He's honest, he's fair, he respects the principle of the law, and he's not afraid of controversy. Just last month he dismissed a civil suit brought by the city against a theater featuring the movie *Deep Throat*. Hanson didn't even give it to a jury; he just threw it out. We think he can stand up to public pressure."

I hoped Hanson would play by O'Connell's script. I wanted to testify in this case, not just because of the potential for a mistaken identification but because I believed that the research on memory needed to get out of the laboratory and into a real-life forum where it might make a difference. For the concept of innocent until proven guilty, I believed my testimony deserved to be heard in court.

"Let's review the major eyewitness issues in this case," I said.

O'Connell searched through some papers on his desk and handed me a lined, legal-size piece of paper with "Loftus—Main Points" handwritten at the top of the page. "I took notes from our telephone conversations," he explained, grinning at me.

I read the first point.

Perception and memory do not function like T.V. camera and videotape. Only that which was perceived can be remembered—i.e., memory cannot be "replayed" to get details which were not noted in original perception. Analogy to watching football play. If observer did not notice great block because concentrating on runner, cannot replay and recall from memory the block as one could do with the videotape of the same play.

"Nice analogy," I said.

"I'm a great football fan," O'Connell said, puffing on his pipe. "Why don't you explain this videotape concept to me again."

I'd given this particular lecture dozens of times to college students; I was on automatic pilot. "Most theoretical analyses of memory divide the process into three separate stages," I began. "First, the acquisition stage, in which the perception of the original event is put into the memory system; second, the retention stage, the period of time that passes between the event and the recollection of a particular piece of information; and third, the retrieval stage, in which a person recalls stored information.

"Contrary to popular belief," I continued, "facts don't come into our memory and passively reside there untouched and unscathed by future events. Instead, we pick up fragments and features from our environment and these go into memory where they interact with our prior knowledge and expectations—information that is already stored in our memory. Thus experimental psychologists think of memory as being an integrative process—a constructive and creative process—rather than a passive recording process such as a videotape."

I switched from the general to the specific. "All the 'I don't knows' and 'I don't remembers' in Carol DaRonch's testimony could mean that the information was never stored in the first place—there was a failure, in other words, in the acquisition stage. Or it could mean that the information was stored but then forgotten—a failure in either the retention stage or the retrieval stage. There's really no way of telling exactly what happened."

I looked at O'Connell's list and read number 2: Memory deteriorates at an exponential rate.

"The accumulation of research shows that memory decays or deteriorates as times goes by," I explained. "After a week, memory is less accurate than after a day. After a month, memory is less accurate than after a week. And after a year, memory will be less accurate than after a month."

"Eleven months is presumably one hell of a long time for Carol DaRonch to hold a memory of Ted Bundy's face in her mind," O'Connell observed.

"That's right," I agreed, "although many people are under the mistaken impression that memory for faces lasts a lifetime. The distinction—and it's an important one—must be made between memory for faces of people we've known for years and memory for the face of a stranger whom we see once, for a short period of time. Many people do remember the faces of friends whom they haven't seen for years or even decades. We graduate from high school, go off on our own, and twenty years later come back to a reunion where we immediately recognize the faces of our former friends.

"But this is not the same thing as remembering the face of a stranger. When it comes to strangers—people seen only briefly and only once—the overwhelming trend is that memory deteriorates as time passes. Most of the studies have used periods of time much shorter than eleven months and have shown great deterioration of memory for faces."

O'Connell nodded his head and looked at the paper, reading over my shoulder. "Some stimulation improves perception and memory, but great stress interferes. Fear to the point of hysteria has a negative effect on memory."

"This third point refers to the relationship between stress and memory," I said, "which is explained by the Yerkes-Dodson law, named after the two men who first noted the relationship back in 1908. At very low levels of arousal—for example, when a person is just waking up in the morning—the nervous system may not be fully functioning and sensory messages may not get through. Memory is not functioning very well. At moderate levels—say if you were slightly nervous about an upcoming trial or anxious about a confrontation with your teenage son—memory performance will be optimal. But with high levels of arousal, the ability to remember begins to decline and deteriorate."

"Tell me, Elizabeth," O'Connell said. "If you were in a car with a man who had identified himself as a police officer but who was driving the wrong way to the police station in a rundown Volkswagen, who then ran the car up onto the curb, snapped handcuffs on your wrist, brandished a gun, and raised a crowbar in an effort to hit you over the head—would you rate that as a high level of stress?"

"Yes, I would," I said. "But I should warn you about a potential problem."

O'Connell raised his eyebrows at me.

"Carol DaRonch wasn't under great emotional stress for the first five or ten minutes that she was with 'Officer Roseland,'" I said. "Part of that time she walked around with him in a well-lighted mall. It could be argued that she was under a moderate level of emotional arousal, which tends to produce alertness and fairly good recall."

"The prosecutor will be sure to pick up on that," O'Connell said. "Still, if you put all the facts together, we've got a good case for reduced accuracy of memory." He pointed to number 4 on the list. "Difficult to maintain separate visual images without transference and merging."

"This point refers to a process known as unconscious transference," I said, "a phenomenon in which a person seen in one situation is confused with or recalled as a person seen in a second situation. Again, with reference to this particular case, when the police showed Carol DaRonch two different photos of Ted Bundy—a mug shot and then, within a few days, a driver's license photo—they could have created a memory for her. 'Planted it in her brain,' as you once said."

O'Connell nodded his head. He understood that point well enough.

"Point 5," I said, reading the last paragraph on the list. "Effect of interviewer bias—particularly unintentional cueing and reinforcing. Support proposition that increasing excitement and activity of peace officers from September 1 (original photo selection) to October 2 (lineup) had effect of changing weak identification to positive identification."

"Do you always refer to the police as peace officers?" I asked.

"Yup," he said. "That's what I call them, because that's what they're supposed to be." But in this case O'Connell believed that the "peace officers" had gone too far and biased their witness, transmitting through words, gestures, or other "cues" their belief that Ted Bundy was, in fact, the kidnapper. After DaRonch tentatively identified Bundy's photo on September 1, 1975, and then more firmly identified him a few days later from a different photograph, the police may have communicated to her, intentionally or unintentionally, the feeling that they had "a live one." In her desire to help

79

the police and finally put an end to her ordeal, DaRonch might have picked up on the signals and decided in her own mind that Bundy was, in fact, her abductor. Questions suggested answers that encouraged more sharply detailed questions until the whole thing picked up speed, steamrolling neatly ahead, with Bundy—guilty or innocent?—trapped beneath the wheels.

"You've looked at the transcript, Elizabeth," O'Connell said. "You can see for yourself how DaRonch changed her statement from the night of the crime to the preliminary hearing. Why would she change it in so many details? Why would she change her original statement, 'It looks something like him' to 'He's the one'? Because the police pressured her. Because they intentionally or unintentionally communicated to her that Ted Bundy was their man. She's been subtly brainwashed, there's just no doubt about it."

O'Connell picked up the transcript of the preliminary hearing and quickly turned the pages. "On page thirty-seven, Yocom—he's the prosecutor—asks DaRonch about the crowbar. DaRonch answers that the kidnapper held it in his right hand. 'Are you sure it was the right hand he had it in, Carol?' Yocom asks. 'Yes,' she answers."

O'Connell chuckled. "Yocom didn't like that answer at all. Bundy is left-handed."

He turned more pages. "Page fifty-seven," he said. "Yocom asks her about the color of the car. 'Was it light beige or white?' he asks. 'Yes,' she answers. He pumps her. 'Could it have been light blue, green?' 'No.' Yet right here in the police report, just an hour or two after the event, she claims it was light blue or white. What do you suppose happened to change her mind?"

It was a rhetorical question. O'Connell believed that when the police found a suspect with a beige car, the witness's memory gradually conformed to the new information, and the color of the car began a subtle transformation from white or light blue to beige.

"Page sixty-seven," O'Connell continued reading from the transcript. "I'm cross-examining DaRonch, and I ask how many times she's looked at pictures in regard to this case. 'Quite a few,' she admits. 'Can you give me some idea? Ten times?' I ask. 'Yeah,' she answers." He turned the page. " 'How many times have you seen Mr. Bundy's picture?' 'A few times. About three or four times.' 'Have you looked at his picture in the newspapers?' 'Yes,' she answered."

O'Connell rolled his head around his shoulders, first to the left, then the right. He adjusted his glasses. "Okay, I'm going to read these next sections verbatim from the preliminary hearing transcript, pages seventy-nine to eighty. I'm asking the questions of Carol DaRonch, and we're talking about the set of mug shots she was shown eleven months after her attempted kidnapping. Eleven months filled with looking at literally hundreds of photographs. Here goes:

Q: How many photographs did they give you?
A: About eight or nine.
Q: And that was when you looked through and said—exactly what happened on that occasion? Was it that you gave them back and that you took Mr. Bundy's out from the pack and then you gave the pack back and said there wasn't anybody there of the person and they asked, "Well, why did you take that one out," and you said, "Well, that one looks more like him than any other picture"?
A: Yes.
Q: In fact, your first statement was that the man's picture—that the man who had done it wasn't in there but that Mr. Bundy's was closer than other people?
A: Yes.
Q: All right. Then how long was it until you were brought Mr. Bundy's picture again to look at?
A: I don't know. I don't remember. A week after or something.
Q: Okay. Now what kind of photos were these; mug shots or driver's license photos or what?
A: I don't remember what they were. They were both.
Q: Did you make a positive identification the second time?
A: No.
Q: All the picture identifications were tentative; is that right?
A: Yes.

O'Connell tossed the 150-page transcript on his desk, glanced at his watch, sighed. "It's after eleven. I'm sorry to go on like this, but let me briefly review what's happened in court the last two days. Yocom began his direct examination by taking his witness through the night of the abduction and her ID of Bundy eleven months later.

81

In cross, I highlighted the inconsistencies of her ID—for example, that she had originally described Ted as having a mustache, shortly after the incident decided he didn't, and then sometime later decided again that he did.

"Okay, day two, today. Jeez, it's been a long day." O'Connell ran his hand through his hair. "Detective Jerry Thompson testifies that when searching Bundy's apartment he found two or three pairs of shiny patent leather shoes. DaRonch claimed in her original statement that her assailant wore black or dark-red patent leather shoes. We had witnesses who testified that Bundy wouldn't be caught dead in patent leather shoes, but there they were in his apartment. Not good for us." O'Connell shrugged his shoulders.

"Let's go back to September 1975, when Detective Thompson showed DaRonch a packet of photos. She looked through them, took Bundy's photo out, and gave the rest back to Thompson, saying 'I don't see anyone in there who resembles him.' Thompson said, 'What about that one there?' and pointed to the photo in her hand. And she said, 'I don't know. I guess it looks something like him.' But now, when he's questioned in court by the prosecutor, Thompson reported that DaRonch said, 'Yes, I believe that looks a lot like the individual, but I'm not sure.'

"So in cross, I had to make two crucial points: first, that she didn't say 'a lot like him,' but in fact she said 'something like him'—that's what Thompson wrote in his original report. Now my next point, dealing with the second photo lineup when DaRonch was shown Ted's driver's license picture, is critical to your testimony.

" 'You knew it was improper, didn't you,' I asked Thompson, 'to show a witness two different pictures of the same individual, to show a witness another picture of an individual after she had made somewhat of an identification: "This looks something like him."?' Thompson replied, 'I figured it was improper to show the same photo, but an entirely different one that looked so much different, I didn't feel there was anything wrong with it.'

"But of course there is something improper and wrong about it," O'Connell concluded, "and that's where your testimony comes in."

"Unconscious transference," I said. "DaRonch sees one picture, the detective draws attention to it, and then she is shown another picture of the same man. Now it looks familiar. But it's possible that she's recognizing the picture of the man she saw in the first photograph. A memory may actually have been created for her by the police.

"Precisely." O'Connell grinned at me and looked at his watch one last time. "Enough practice, we have to be in court in nine hours. Are you ready to face Luther, the incredible snapping turtle?"

In court the next morning I sat at a table in the judge's chambers. On the other side of the table, close enough for me to reach across and touch him, sat Ted Bundy. He's adorable, I thought, surprised at my first impression, because I'd pictured him in my mind as brooding, dark, intense. But he was all Ivy League charm, clean-cut, freshly shaved and showered, bright and eager. I could imagine him tossing a Frisbee on a California beach, or dressed in immaculate tennis whites, sipping a gin and tonic on the country club lawn while earnestly discussing his backhand. His face was almost square, with a strong, prominent jaw and cheeks chiseled by handsome smile lines. His forehead seemed permanently wrinkled, the thick layers of skin pushed up by well-formed eyebrows, raised in apparent contempt and disdain.

We were seated around a table in the judge's chambers, O'Connell, Bundy, Judge Hanson, Yocom, and I. I averted my eyes from Ted Bundy and concentrated on the legal arguments that would determine whether or not I'd testify that day. Yocom, as expected, had objected to my testimony, citing the traditional Supreme Court rulings that an expert may not testify to anything a layman can reasonably be expected to know. Judge Hanson didn't need an "expert's" assistance in evaluating Carol DaRonch's testimony, Yocom argued; surely a judge, who must deal with eyewitness issues every day, knows the strengths and weaknesses of such testimony?

Hanson listened intently, nodding his head, acknowledging Yocom's carefully prepared, persuasive arguments. He waited patiently for Yocom to finish and then the judge spoke, citing the fact that both the Utah and the U.S. Supreme Courts had formally recognized that eyewitness testimony is the most problematical type of testimony that can be offered. The fact that he was somewhat of an expert himself could only help him evaluate the strengths and weaknesses of my testimony. Yocom's objection was overruled. I would testify.

As we were leaving the judge's chambers, I glanced at Bundy to gauge his reaction to Hanson's decision. He was grinning at Yocom, an ingratiating, insinuating sort of smile that showed his straight, white teeth. That smile seemed to say "Hey, look, I'm not this bad guy you think I am. Come on, give me a break." I was shocked. Why would Bundy smile at his prosecutor, his chief accuser? What the hell was he doing?

The memory of that smile burned in my brain. Everything else about Bundy seemed right—his conservative gray suit, his neatly trimmed hair, even the worried furrows in his brow. But that smile was wrong. It was dead wrong.

I had worked on behalf of innocent people before, and I'd never seen one of them, not one, smile at the prosecutor. These were angry, bitter people who had been falsely accused, who were horrified by the events that had brought them to the courtroom to fight for their reputations and sometimes for their lives, who lived in terror of this mighty system that could crush them. The prosecutor was the hangman, and these innocent defendants feared his power.

And yet here was Ted Bundy, confident, relaxed, and smiling at his prosecutor.

It was disconcerting. As I took the stand, raised my right hand and took the oath to tell the truth, the whole truth, and nothing but the truth, I looked over at the defense table. Judge Hanson had provided extra chairs for Bundy's family, and his mother was staring intently at me, her lips parted, her eyes swollen from crying, her head tilted back slightly. In her eyes I saw the terror I had come to expect.

O'Connell approached the witness stand. "Dr. Loftus," he began, taking his very first opportunity to emphasize my academic credentials. "What does 'unconscious transference' mean?"

"That's a term used to refer to the mistaken recollection or the confusion of a person seen in one situation as the person who has been seen in a different situation," I said, keeping my voice strong, calm, thoroughly professional. "The classic example is the case in which a clerk in a train station was held up, I believe at gunpoint. Later on the clerk identified a sailor in a lineup. The clerk said that the sailor had committed armed robbery. It turned out that the sailor had an ironclad alibi but had purchased tickets from the clerk on three prior occasions. So when the clerk went to the lineup, the face did indeed look familiar, but the clerk confused that familiarity and recalled the face as being the face of the robber rather than properly recalling it as the person who purchased the tickets."

"Could you describe your own experiment for us?"

"I showed thirty subjects in my experiment six photographs, one at a time, while they heard the story of a crime being committed. All of the people involved in this incident were innocent except the fourth person, who committed an assault. My subjects learned, then, that this person was essentially a criminal. Three days later the subjects came back. They didn't even know that they were going to be asked any questions. They thought they were coming back for their checks. We presented them with four photographs of people they had never seen before and one innocent bystander from the previous story and asked them to select the criminal. Their correct answer would have been 'The criminal is not here.'

"What my subjects did is as follows: sixty percent chose the innocent bystander, sixteen percent chose another incorrect person— meaning that seventy-six percent were incorrect. Only twenty-four percent refused to make a choice. This experiment indicates that the phenomenon of unconscious transference can be demonstrated in the laboratory and is a very real phenomenon."

O'Connell led me into a discussion about the effects of postevent information. After witnessing an important event, people are sometimes exposed to new information that can not only enhance existing memory but actually *change* their memory, even causing nonexisting details to become incorporated into the previously acquired memory. In this particular case, Carol DaRonch initially remembered "Officer Roseland's" badge as "all gold." After being shown the Murray police badges, which are gold, silver, and blue, she changed her description and "Officer Roseland's" badge became "gold, silver, and blue." Her memory, I suggested to the courtroom, may have been altered by later exposure. The same type of memory alteration had occurred with the suspect's mustache, which DaRonch's memory put on, removed, and put on again—as if "Officer Roseland" was an imaginary paper doll that could be dressed and undressed at will.

Throughout my testimony that afternoon, O'Connell asked questions that allowed me to emphasize the effects of severe stress on memory. I tried to communicate the fact that fear and terror do not solidify memory, compressing it into a coherent, accurate mass, but instead create gaps in our recollections. Bundy's fate hinged on this one basic point—was Carol DaRonch's memory of that night correct, or was it mistaken?

After O'Connell was finished with his questions, Judge Hanson leaned toward me across his massive desk. "Dr. Loftus," he said in a surprisingly soft voice, "do you have any data to form a conclusion about how a victim in an actual situation might be affected?"

I knew the meaning of his question. He was asking me, in effect: Does all this laboratory research have anything to do with real life?

"When a person experiences extreme stress, arousal, or fear," I said, phrasing my answer carefully, "research studies suggest that the performance of memory will be less accurate and detailed. If you assume that a crime victim is experiencing extreme arousal, her memory will not be as accurate and detailed as if the arousal were more moderate."

"Let's assume you have a time continuum as represented by a straight line." Hanson continued with his line of questioning. "At one point in time there is no stress whatsoever. As that continuum proceeds, the stress begins to build. The victim begins to suspect that she might be a victim. At a point further down the line, the victim becomes assured of the fact that there is a real problem. In your judgment, how would stress affect eyewitness identification under those circumstances? That is, would the victim be more likely to be able to identify that perpetrator under those circumstances than in a situation where there was a sudden violent event, like a breaking in through a door or window?"

"The sudden event would produce a less accurate identification," I answered, "because the whole experience would be while the victim was in an extreme state of stress."

Hanson had this issue by the throat, and he wasn't letting go. He briefly outlined Carol DaRonch's fifteen-minute encounter with "Officer Roseland." How would such an encounter affect memory?

I didn't hesitate. "Performance when the person was moderately stressed prior to extreme stress? In that case, you might expect fairly optimal memory performance."

Judge Hanson would probably have kept these questions to himself if Ted Bundy was being tried by a jury. Judges in jury trials are careful to remain impartial observers in order to avoid biasing the jurors with questions or concerns of their own. But as the sole arbiter of this case, Hanson obviously felt an obligation to understand the subtle nuances of my testimony. I was impressed with his determined efforts to get at the truth. He clearly established that Carol DaRonch's fifteen-minute ordeal of moderate stress prior to extreme stress led to "fairly optimal memory performance," a crucial point for the prosecution. Carol DaRonch, in other words, presumably had enough time to fix "Officer Roseland's" face into her memory at a time when she was not severely stressed.

The strong points for the defense, however, were the eleven-month gap between the attempted kidnapping and DaRonch's first, tentative identification of Ted Bundy, and the possibility that by showing their witness two pictures of the same man prior to the lineup, the police had molded the face in her memory to conform to the face of the suspect they had in custody.

I heard later that Judge Hanson spent an agonized weekend sifting through the evidence, reviewing the trial notes, and formulating his decision. In the end, his decision was based on the fact that he didn't believe Ted Bundy. It wasn't that he didn't have doubts—no one can know anything for certain, he told the press—but there were no longer any reasonable doubts in his mind that it was Ted Bundy who tried to kidnap Carol DaRonch.

On Monday, March 2, 1976, at 1:30 P.M., Judge Hanson announced his verdict. "I find the defendant, Theodore Robert Bundy, guilty of aggravated kidnapping, a first-degree felony, as charged." Hanson gave Bundy a relatively light sentence of one to fifteen years in the Utah State Prison; in less than three years he would be considered for parole.

On January 27, 1977, ten days after Gary Gilmore was executed by firing squad in the same Utah prison where Bundy was incarcerated, Bundy was transferred to the Pitkin County Jail in the basement of the Aspen, Colorado, Courthouse; three months later he changed addresses again, moving to a tiny cell in a one-story brick building in Glenwood Springs, Colorado.

Colorado authorities had charged Bundy with the murder of Caryn Campbell, a twenty-three-year-old nurse who had disappeared from a ski resort in Snowmass, Colorado, on January 12, 1975; her nude body was found twenty-six days later, the skull bashed in from a vicious blow. Several witnesses had tentatively identified Bundy, gas credit card receipts placed him in Colorado on January 12, and an FBI lab specialist pronounced a hair sample vacuumed from Bundy's car to be "microscopically indistinguishable" from hairs taken from Caryn Campbell.

On June 7, 1977, during a recess of the pretrial hearing in the Aspen Courthouse, Bundy strolled into the law library. The deputy assigned to watch him walked out into the hallway for a smoke, and Bundy jumped from the open second-story window.

He was arrested less than a week later, early in the morning on June 13, and again incarcerated in the Garfield County Jail in Glenwood Springs, Colorado. On December 30, 1977, Bundy escaped through an old light fixture in the ceiling of his jail cell.

Then there was silence. Six weeks of ominous, portentous silence. In those weeks there were moments when I would find myself staring into space, urging the police on, hoping that Bundy would get caught. He had to be tried for the Caryn Campbell murder in Colorado and for the murders in Washington and Utah—how else would the police know if he had committed these crimes? How else would the families of these young women find an end to their torment? And, if Ted Bundy had committed these crimes, if he was, in fact, this appalling creature who murdered women so randomly and casually, what was he doing now, on the loose? How many more women would be killed?

On February 17, 1978, around 8:00 A.M., I walked into the psychology department office to check my phone messages. "Did you hear about Ted Bundy?" one of the secretaries asked, handing me the front section of that morning's Seattle *Post-Intelligencer*.

SHOTS FLY IN FLORIDA
BUNDY RECAPTURED

ESCAPED CONVICT THEODORE R. BUNDY OF TACOMA WAS CAPTURED DURING A HIGH-SPEED CHASE PUNCTUATED BY GUNFIRE IN PENSACOLA, FLA. YESTERDAY.

BUNDY, WANTED BY THE FBI FOR QUESTIONING IN 36 SEX KILLINGS IN WESTERN STATES, ESCAPED DEC. 31 FROM A GLENWOOD SPRINGS, COLO., JAIL WHERE HE WAS AWAITING TRIAL FOR FIRST-DEGREE MURDER.

EVEN BEFORE POSITIVE IDENTIFICATION OF BUNDY HAD BEEN MADE BY FLORIDA AUTHORITIES, POLICE SAID THEY WERE QUESTIONING HIM IN THE JAN. 15 CLUBBING DEATHS OF TWO COEDS AT FLORIDA STATE UNIVERSITY IN TALLAHASSEE.

The sounds of life, of ongoing, routine-filled life, pounded in my ears: the hot air blowing through the vents, the intermittent clacking of the typewriter, the rain softly tapping at the windows, a door closing in the hallway. Footsteps, people breathing, soft laughter.

I turned and ran down the hallway, my high-heel boots clicking on the linoleum. I looked at my watch; Geoff had a class in ten minutes. I felt a sudden and immense gratitude that my husband and I were both professors of psychology at the same university with offices in the same building. In nine years of marriage, Geoff had always been there when I needed him.

Geoff was staring at a complicated series of numbers on his computer printout when I burst into his office and handed him the newspaper article. "What if my testimony had helped to acquit Bundy in Utah?" I said, talking fast. "What if he really did murder those women?"

Geoff read the article, stood up, and put his arms around me. "Sometimes you will testify for people who are guilty," he said. "That happens, there's no way around it. You can't possibly know whether the defendant is innocent or guilty before you decide to take a case. You are not judge and juror; you are simply an expert witness, a social scientist in a court of law."

"I should know," I said. "I deal with facts, statistics, figures. I should be able to determine which facts add up to innocence and which add up to guilt."

"You are a scientist," Geoff said. "You are not a mind-reader, and it is not your job to pronounce guilt or innocence on another human being. It is your job to testify about what you know to be true."

The world seemed suddenly black and white, all the confusing paradoxes, alternative hypotheses and statistical norms vanished, and in my mind I saw Ted Bundy's handsome face with the cold eyes and the sly grin, and I thought: This is the face of evil. I remembered my first impression of Ted Bundy. He's adorable, I thought, as I sat just three feet away from him. In the beginning had I been fooled, as so many others were fooled, by the all-American boy with the polite manner and the deep smile lines? Unaccustomed to evil, could I not recognize it when it stared me in the face?

Once or twice a year I have a particularly disturbing nightmare. I'm in an elevator, going up fast, hundreds of feet above the ground. The buttons don't work, I can't get the elevator to stop. Terrified of heights, I lean against the windows, my palms pressed against the cold glass, my knees buckling underneath me. With a sudden lurch, the doors open, and I spin downward, eventually hitting the ground with bone-crushing force.

"That's impossible," a friend of mine says. A clinical psychologist, she assures me that in falling dreams, you don't hit the ground. *But I do*, I tell her. *I do.*

I hit the ground hard that day, standing in my husband's office, clutching the newspaper, agonizing about my role in this grisly drama. Eleven years later, early on a foggy Seattle morning, I hit the ground again. I remember waking up that morning, Tuesday, January 24, 1989, looking at my alarm clock and immediately pressing the remote-control button to turn on the TV. My hands were shaking. "That's funny," I remember thinking. "I'm nervous."

"Ted Bundy was executed this morning, three minutes after schedule," a voice announced. The TV screen panned the crowd of several hundred spectators outside the Starke, Florida, prison, and then zoomed in on their placards: "Roast in peace," "Too bad so sad you're dead Ted," and "This Buzz Is for You." One man wore a T-shirt with a recipe for "Fried Bundy" printed on the front. Vendors sold electric chair pins to the celebrants, and a group of older spectators sang these words to the tune of "On Top of Old Smokey":

> *He bludgeoned the poor girls*
> *all over the head*
> *Now we're all ecstatic*
> *Ted Bundy is dead.*

The scene switched to an interview with Ted Bundy the night before his electrocution. Prison had removed the arrogance from his smile, sharpening his features. The eyes seemed deeper set, the nose longer and straighter, the creases in his forehead permanently etched.

The image flashed off, and the announcer described the last conversation between Ted Bundy and his mother. Louise Bundy's voice had trembled with emotion when she said the last words she would ever say to Ted Bundy: "You'll always be my precious son."

I turned off the television and watched the fog drifting and swirling in the streetlights outside my window. I felt lightheaded, slightly sick to my stomach. The TV images flashed in and out of my mind, mixing with the older pictures of Bundy at his trial, talking with O'Connell, smiling at the prosecutor, sitting at the defense table and watching me, eyes unwavering, as I testified about the fallibility of memory.

In the last years of his life, Ted Bundy had confessed to "two or three dozen murders." Some investigators believe he may have murdered fifty, perhaps as many as a hundred women. Bundy didn't understand why he was driven to rape and kill with such viciousness and unimaginable cruelty, although he rambled on once about hunters who stalked and killed deer and were never plagued by a guilty conscience. Why are we so moralistic, Bundy wanted to know, when it comes to human life? Why is a human life worth more than a deer's life?

It was an interesting question. Society had just extracted its most severe penalty, taking a life in exchange for lives taken, and spectators were in a party mood. One of the arguments used against capital punishment is that it desensitizes the public and trivializes life. My concern is less philosophical and more concrete—I am concerned that mistakes cannot be corrected. If a person is innocent and executed, it is not in our power to turn around and give that life back.

Sitting in my room that winter morning, the TV screen vacant and silent, the images and faces already fading from my memory, I kept hearing Louise Bundy's words: "You will always be my precious son." Bundy was guilty; there was no longer any doubt about the fact. But he was also a human being, and now he was dead. Where, I wondered, is the triumph, the glory in that?

A KNOCK ON THE DOOR: TIMOTHY HENNIS

"I wish to tell you that I am an innocent man. I never committed any crime but sometimes some sin. I wish to forgive some people for what they are now doing to me."

Bartolomeo Vanzetti, as he was being strapped into the electric chair,
August 23, 1927

They think it began with a knock on the door, sometime around 10:00 P.M. on May 9, 1985. The knocking must have alarmed Kathryn Eastburn, who was in the living room of her one-story home in Fayetteville, North Carolina, folding the laundry. Perhaps she stood there, holding a pair of socks or a child's T shirt in her hands, her heart racing. Who could that be? Her husband was out of town and her three small children were fast asleep. Who could be knocking at the side door at that hour?

She walked through the kitchen into the utility room and opened the door. There was no sign of a forced entry. The intruder forced Mrs. Eastburn back into the living room, used rope to tie her hands behind her back, and pushed her to the floor. He pulled at her blouse, popping two buttons, and used a knife to cut her bra up the front, sliding it back over her arms. Holding the knife to her neck, he pulled off her shoes and jeans. One sock came off with her jeans. He sliced with the knife at one side of her underwear and yanked them so violently that he bruised the skin on her hip. Then he raped her.

The police pieced together this scenario from the evidence found at the scene of the crime, but unanswerable questions remained. Did Kathryn Eastburn answer the door, letting the intruder in, or did he somehow break in without leaving any sign of forced entry? Did she look out the window and recognize the man? Was he someone she knew? Or was she so trusting and fearless that she would open the door to anyone at 10:00 in the evening when her husband was away?

There are few unknowns, however, in the pathologist's report. Kathryn Eastburn's body was found on the floor of the master bedroom to the right of the bed, a pillow covering her face. She had fifteen stab wounds to the chest and an extensive cut across the neck that severed her trachea, esophagus, both major arteries, and both major veins. Because of the relative lack of bleeding from the chest wounds, the pathologist concluded that the neck wound, which would have produced unconsciousness within ten seconds and death within one or two minutes, occurred first. The stab wounds were produced by a weapon with a sharp blade at least several inches long and less than an inch wide; the pathologist was unable to determine if more than one weapon was used.

Three-year-old Erin Eastburn's body was found on the floor of the master bedroom to the left of the bed, a pillow partially covering her face and chest. She had been stabbed ten times in the chest and upper abdomen, and there was an extensive cut across the neck that severed her trachea, esophagus, and right carotid artery and partially severed the left carotid artery. The neck wound would have produced unconsciousness within ten to sixty seconds and death within one to two minutes. One of the stab wounds severed the major artery from the heart, which would have caused death almost immediately, within seconds to a few minutes.

Down the hallway in the middle bedroom, covered just above the waist with a bedspread, was the body of five-year-old Kara Eastburn. She was stabbed ten times in the front and back of the chest and had an extensive cut across her neck from the left side of the midline around to the back. According to the pathologist, the neck wound would have produced death within one or two minutes.

At some point before or after his killing spree, the murderer stole cash and a bank card from Kathryn Eastburn's purse. A metal strong-box containing the code for the bank card and other important documents was taken from the house.

On the way out of the house, the killer had to pass twenty-one-month-old Jana's room. He may have hesitated there, thinking, *Another bedroom, another potential witness.* Perhaps he opened the door and listened for a moment to the baby's light, rhythmic breathing. His eyes, well adjusted by now to the darkness, would have been able to distinguish the crib, the baby quilts, the changing table, and stuffed animals. Did he have a fondness for infants, or had he simply had enough killing? The baby's room faced the street; perhaps he heard a car door slam, or a shrill siren in the distance jolted him out of his reverie.

He shut Jana's bedroom door and continued walking down the hallway, through the kitchen, into the utility room, leaving the house by the side door, and disappearing into the foggy, drizzly night.

On Saturday morning, May 11, Captain Gary Eastburn waited for the weekly phone call from his wife. He was temporarily stationed in Alabama, attending officers' squadron school; in just a few months, he would be moving his family to England, where he was being transferred. As the minutes ticked by and Kathryn didn't call, he began to get worried; at 8:30 A.M., he tried to call her, and he tried again at 11:00 A.M. and at 2:00 P.M.

By 5:00 P.M., Captain Eastburn knew that something was wrong. He called a friend in Fayetteville and asked him to drive to the house and check things out. His friend knocked loudly on the front door, rang the doorbell several times, and walked around to the back of the house to look in the bedroom window where five-year-old Kara's body was lying out of sight on one of the twin beds, the quilt pulled up to her chest, a pillow over her face. He didn't see anything out of the ordinary and after returning home, he called Gary Eastburn to reassure him. But Eastburn knew something was wrong. *Call the sheriff,* he told his friend.

Around midnight that night, a sheriff's deputy went to the Eastburn home, knocked several times, and left a note tacked to the front door, informing Kathryn Eastburn that her husband was trying to reach her.

By the next morning, Sunday, May 12, the Eastburns' neighbors, Robert and Norma Seefeldt, were getting worried. Why weren't the children outside, playing on the gym set? Why were the newspapers piling up in the front yard? At 11:30 A.M. Robert Seefeldt knocked on the side door, then walked around to the front door, knocking loudly and ringing the bell. He put his ear to the door, listened for a few minutes, and thought he could hear the faint sound of a baby crying. "Norma, get over here quick!" he shouted. Mrs. Seefeldt listened at the front door and then leaned across the porch railing to listen at the front bedroom. She looked at her husband, then, her expression frightened and bewildered. "I hear the baby crying," she said. "We better call the police."

Just before 1:00 P.M., a sheriff's deputy walked onto the Eastburn porch, leaned over the porch railing, and looked through the front bedroom window. The shade was pulled down, but through a small space at the side he could see a baby standing in her crib, crying and holding out her arms. *What the hell was going on in there?* He cut the screen, opened the window and climbed in. Twenty-one-month-old Jana Eastburn, exhausted from hunger and dehydration, held out her hands to the stranger. The deputy picked up the baby, hugged her for a moment, and handed her out the window to Mr. Seefeldt. Then he took a deep breath, trying to ease his nervousness. *Something is wrong here*, he thought; *something is very, very wrong*.

"I'm going to take a look around," he said to the Seefeldts through the window. Less than a minute later, the deputy stuck his head out the baby's window and used his hand-held radio to call in the news to the sheriff's department. Then he waited for the detectives and the technicians who would try to make sense of this senseless carnage.

It was Sunday, May 12, 1985. Mother's Day.

On Tuesday morning, May 14, a grief-stricken Gary Eastburn remembered the dog. His wife had placed an ad in the Fort Bragg newspaper, seeking a new home for Daisy, their four-year-old, liver-spotted English Setter. In her last letter to her husband, Kathryn Eastburn wrote that a "nice" man had picked up Daisy on Tuesday night and was taking her home on a trial basis to see if she got along with his other dog, a black Labrador retriever; Kathryn planned to call the man that Thursday to see how the dogs were getting along.

On Wednesday morning, May 15, the Cumberland County sheriff's department issued a news release that was broadcast on television and radio stations, requesting that the man who had picked up the Eastburn's dog immediately contact the sheriff's office. The news release included the name and description of the Eastburn's dog and the available data about her new owner: he drove a white Chevrolet Chevette and he owned a black Labrador retriever.

Just after noon that day, Army Staff Sergeant Timothy Hennis arrived home from Fort Bragg to have lunch with his wife, Angela, and their two-month-old daughter, Kristina. While they ate lunch, they watched the news on television. When the news bulletin about the Eastburn's dog flashed on the screen, Hennis turned to his wife. "My God," he said, "that's me they're looking for!" He immediately called his company commander, explained why he wouldn't be back at work that afternoon, and taking his wife and baby with him, drove down to the police station.

For six and a half hours, Timothy Hennis was interrogated. The detectives repeatedly assured him that he was not under arrest, nor was he a suspect in the case; it never even occurred to Hennis to ask for a lawyer. In a voluntary statement, Hennis gave detectives a detailed description of his activities from Tuesday, May 7 through the following Monday, May 13. On Thursday night, May 9, the night before the murders, Hennis had arrived home about 8:30 P.M. At around 8:45 P.M., Mrs. Eastburn called to ask how the dogs were getting along. "Great," he said, "everything is working out just great." About 9:00 P.M., he called his wife's parents' house. About 9:30 P.M. he went to the grocery store for some Pepsi. He returned home before 10:00, did some chores, and went to sleep. He was up by 4:00 A.M. on Friday, May 10, and off to work by 5:00 A.M.

While Hennis was being questioned, detectives hastily assembled a photo lineup. Hennis's photo was pasted in position number 2. All photographs used in the photo lineup were cropped so that only the head and part of the upper body was visible, making it impossible to tell the relative size or weight of the people in the photos. Hennis's picture was the only one in the photo array of a blond male with short hair wearing a dark Members Only jacket.

A detective took the photo lineup outside to a police car. Inside the car was *Chuck Barrett*, a black maintenance worker, who had flagged down a sheriff's deputy on Sunday, May 12 with the information that he had seen a white male walking down the Eastburn driveway about 3:30 A.M. on Friday, May 10. The man, Barrett said, was wearing a black Members Only jacket and a black knit hat pulled down below his hairline, and he was carrying a dark-colored garbage bag over his shoulders. At the end of the driveway, when the man was approximately four feet away from Barrett, he said, "Leaving kind of early this morning." He continued walking down the street, got into a white Chevette parked on the side of the road, and drove away.

Sitting in the back of the police car, with a detective on either side, Barrett studied the pictures. "Do you see him?" one of the detectives asked.

"Well, you know, I'm still thinking, still looking," Barrett said. He looked, rubbed his eyes, looked some more. Four of the six men didn't look anything like the person he had seen on Summer Hill Road, so he concentrated on the two individuals that did—it was the haircut and the nose that he recognized, he explained to the detective. Number 5 had a straight narrow nose like the man he saw, but number 2 looked more like him, even though his nose was wide and flared.

"Have you got him yet?" the detective kept asking.

"Well, you know," Barrett said, pointing to photograph number 2, "that's him, you know, right there."

"Are you sure?" the detective asked.

"Naw," Barrett said. "I can't answer that."

The detective handed Barrett the lineup photos, asked him to initial the one he had selected, photo number 2, and then they accompanied him back into the Law Enforcement Building. As they were walking through the parking lot, one of the detectives pointed out Timothy Hennis's white Chevette. "Do you recognize that car?" he asked Barrett.

"Yeah, that looks like the car I saw on Summer Hill Road," Barrett said. The detective turned to his partner and Barrett thought he heard him say, "We've got a hit."

Timothy Hennis had no idea that he was now considered the prime suspect in the Eastburn murders. He volunteered to be fingerprinted and photographed, and he permitted the police laboratory technicians to take samples of his blood, head hair, and pubic hair. At 7:30 P.M., after nearly seven hours of interrogation, detectives told Hennis he was free to go home.

Less than six hours later, at 1:00 A.M. on Thursday morning, May 16, Timothy Hennis was awakened by loud and persistent knocking on his front door. He hurriedly dressed in jeans and a T shirt, turned on the porch light, and opened the door. The porch was swarming with policemen. "Sergeant Hennis?" one of the officers said in an official tone of voice. Hennis nodded. "We have an arrest warrant and a search warrant. You have the right to remain silent . . ."

Hennis's mind went blank. He stared at the street lights, blinking the sleep from his eyes, trying to wake up. Somebody put handcuffs on him, somebody else grabbed his arm, and they started pushing him down the steps, toward the police car parked in the driveway. Hennis looked back at his wife standing in the doorway in her bathrobe, holding their baby. He couldn't think what to say. *Goodbye? Give me a call? I love you?* The words floated into his mind and out again, and he was aware only of putting one foot in front of the other and choking back the fear that kept rising into his throat, fear so thick that he felt as if he were drowning in it. Someone placed a hand on his head, gave a push, easing the six-foot four-inch, 200-pound man into the back seat. Climbing in next to him, the officer said, "You're in big trouble, buddy. Big, big trouble."

Timothy Hennis was charged with the triple murder of Kathryn, Kara, and Erin Eastburn. For the next six months he was locked up in the Cumberland County jail without bond. He hired Gerald Beaver and William Richardson, two young defense attorneys who had just won a highly publicized police brutality case in Fayetteville, to represent him. Henry Z. Spell had been arrested and was being questioned in the booking room when a police officer kneed him in the groin, bursting his testicle, and permanently sterilizing him; the plaintiff was eventually awarded a $900,000 verdict plus $235,000 in attorney's fees.

Less than a month after the verdict in this lengthy, hotly contested trial, thirty-seven-year-old Beaver and twenty-nine-year-old Richardson agreed to take Timothy Hennis's case. After reviewing the evidence against their client, the two lawyers agreed that it was one of the flimsiest cases they had ever encountered. The only evidence linking Timothy Hennis to the crime was the eyewitness testimony of Chuck Barrett. Not one piece of physical evidence linked Timothy

Hennis to the crime scene. Beaver and Richardson were encouraged by what they perceived to be serious weaknesses in the government's case.

But it didn't pay to be overconfident; a crime as gruesome and bloody as the Eastburn murders worked on people's passions and emotions. And, of course, there were the striking parallels to the infamous Jeffrey MacDonald murder trial. Early in the morning of February 17, 1970, in Fayetteville, the pregnant, twenty-six-year-old Colette MacDonald and her two young daughters, five-year-old Kimberly and two-year-old Kristen, were brutally murdered. Colette's skull was smashed by blows from a heavy club, and she had been stabbed more than twenty-eight times. Kimberly was stabbed between eight and ten times, and her skull was shattered by blows from a club. Kristen was stabbed thirty-three separate times in the back, the chest and the neck. Captain Jeffrey MacDonald was discovered lying on the floor next to his wife, with one stab wound in the abdomen. MacDonald later told investigators that hippies carrying candles and chanting "groovy" and "kill the pigs" broke into his house and slaughtered his family. But investigators saw things differently, and MacDonald was charged with the gruesome crimes.

It would be safe to say that just about everybody who lived in Fayetteville knew about the MacDonald murders; fifteen years later, heated arguments about MacDonald's guilt were still taking place. Hennis's lawyers feared that the memories of the MacDonald murders would spill over into the Eastburn murders and, by association, implicate their client. MacDonald, after all, insisted that he was innocent, but a jury pronounced him guilty; Hennis was claiming he was innocent—*But*, people might think, *he's probably guilty, too*.

Jeffrey MacDonald was sentenced to three life terms in prison to be served consecutively; it was the harshest sentence he could receive at that time, since the death penalty was not applicable at that time under federal law. But the death penalty was reinstated in North Carolina in 1977. If convicted of the Eastburn murders, Timothy Hennis could be sentenced to death.

In November, the lab results started coming in, all negative: negative for fingerprints, clothing fibers, and blood type. Not one shred of evidence placed Timothy Hennis in the Eastburn house. Hennis began pleading with his lawyers to get him out of jail. Beaver and Richardson cautioned restraint and patience. "The state's case is weak, ridiculously weak," they told Hennis. "But if we ask for reconsideration of bond based on lack of physical evidence, and if the judge agrees to let you out, we might as well send a telegram to the prosecutor's office: *You've got a weak case. Better find some new evidence.*"

"Believe me, Tim," Billy Richardson told his client, "the state won't take that information and file it away—they'll get out there and do everything they can to strengthen their case."

"I've got to get out," Hennis said. Sitting in that tiny jail cell with his large frame curled up and compressed, he reminded the lawyers of a huge jack-in-the-box ready to spring. "It's almost Christmas, I need to be home with my wife and baby."

"Just a few more months," Beaver tried to argue with him. "That way, we won't tip our hand, the case will come to trial, it will be immediately clear to the judge and jury how weak the evidence is, and you'll be a free man."

Hennis shook his head. He couldn't stand the thought of another day in jail. "Please," he begged, "you have to get me out."

On December 11, 1985, Beaver and Richardson argued in the Superior Court of Cumberland County that the state's evidence was so weak and insubstantial that Hennis should be released on bond. The judge agreed and released him on a $100,000 bond posted by his parents and in-laws. Hennis was home in time for Christmas.

On January 22, 1986, Billy Richardson tracked down Chuck Barrett, the state's star witness, at his sister's house in Gibsonville, North Carolina. "Are you positive it was Sergeant Hennis you saw that night?" Richardson asked Barrett. Barrett's memory kept slipping and sliding; he wasn't sure of this, he wasn't sure of that. He had doubts, he admitted to Richardson.

"Would you mind if we tape recorded this conversation?" Richardson asked.

Barrett said he wouldn't mind.

In the tape-recorded conversation, Barrett freely admitted that he had doubts about his identification of Hennis, that he could have been mistaken, that he might have been wrong.

"You're saying you're just not sure he's the man that you saw?" Richardson asked.

"Yep," Barrett answered.

With a transcription of the tape recording in hand, Richardson and Beaver tried to decide what their next step should be. Beaver wanted to file a motion to suppress Barrett's identification as inherently unreliable. Richardson argued that they should keep the tape recording as a surprise, presenting it during the trial. Beaver countered that if Barrett held to his story and refused to identify Hennis, the state would have to dismiss the case and Hennis would be spared the agony of a jury trial.

Eventually the two lawyers agreed to file a motion to suppress Chuck Barrett's eyewitness identification, and they asked Barrett to sign an affidavit. They met in the office of an independent lawyer, James F. Walker, who interviewed Barrett alone in his office. Walker showed Barrett the affidavit prepared by Richardson and Beaver, asked him to read it and confirm that the facts in the affidavit were true. Barrett swore on the Bible that no one had forced or coerced him in any way, and he willingly signed the affidavit admitting his doubts about his identification of Timothy Hennis.

> I thought that I was positive that the person that I picked out in the lineup was the person I had seen. However, after thinking about the matter, I have doubts as to whether or not I picked out the right person. I cannot say that the person I picked out in the lineup is the person I saw on Summerhill Drive.

At a pretrial suppression hearing held on February 13, 1986, Richardson and Beaver presented the judge with Barrett's tape recording and signed affidavit. The prosecutors hurriedly called a recess and disappeared with their witness for nearly two hours. When they returned to the courtroom, Chuck Barrett completely recanted the affidavit and tape recording, claiming that the defense lawyers had pressured him and forced him to say things he didn't intend to say. He claimed he didn't understand that he was signing an affidavit. The judge ruled against the suppression of Barrett's testimony, clearing the way for him to appear as a prosecution witness at Hennis's trial.

The trial began on May 26, 1986. The prosecutor placed photographs of the smiling Eastburn family on the banister in front of the jury box. "Before Hennis," he intoned. He removed the photographs and brought out a new set of photographs, which he held as if they were literally covered with blood. He placed the police department photographs of the Eastburns' mutilated bodies on the banister. "After Hennis," he said.

The judge had authorized the construction of a special screen in the courtroom, large enough to permit the side-by-side projection of two slides simultaneously. From where the jury was seated, the screen was located just above Timothy Hennis's head, on the courtroom wall. In every color slide that was projected onto the wall, Timothy Hennis could be seen at the left-hand corner, staring up at the carnage.

A slide projector clicked on and a color slide, five feet by eight feet, blasted three-year-old Erin Eastburn's body onto the screen. Click, another color photograph; click, another. Thirty-five times the projector clicked, blasting the bloody, macabre photographs of the victims directly over the head of the defendant. Soft moans could be heard throughout the crowded courtroom.

Nine slides depicting the crime scene and the placement of the bodies were shown over strenuous defense objections; during the testimony of two pathologists, the prosecution was permitted to display twenty-six slide projections of autopsy photographs of the victims. At the conclusion of the state's evidence, the prosecutor was allowed to pass to the jury members the glossy color photographs that duplicated the slides projected in the courtroom. The photographs were passed one at a time, a process that took a full hour.

Chuck Barrett took the stand and testified that he was sure, now, that Timothy Hennis was the man he had seen walking down the Eastburns's driveway at 3:30 A.M. the morning of the murders. "That's him—Mr. Hennis," he said, pointing to the defendant. "I had doubts. I don't have doubts now. I'm positive."

The defense tried to establish that Barrett had seen someone else, a man who roamed the neighborhood in the early morning hours, a man dubbed "the walker" by neighborhood residents. Richardson and a private investigator had staked out the neighborhood at 3:00 A.M. every morning for a month, but "the walker" never showed up. He'd simply disappeared. The best the defense could do was to present witnesses who claimed that they had seen a man walking the neighborhood early in the morning hours.

After Barrett left the witness stand, Richardson and Beaver thought the prosecution had called its best witness, and they felt confident they would win an acquittal. Barrett was the only eyewitness to link Timothy Hennis to the crime, and that "link" was so thin and tenuous, it couldn't possibly be strong enough to convict a man of murder.

But then something happened that would turn the whole case around. Billy Richardson would later tell his friends and associates that it was the most devastating event that had ever happened to him in a courtroom. The prosecutor announced a surprise witness— *Sandra Barnes*. Richardson and Beaver looked at each other, aghast, and in that moment they felt the beginning of a growing fear that they might lose this case. They knew about Barnes; they had interviewed her within two months of the crime. The murderer had stolen Kathryn Eastburn's wallet, containing an automatic teller bank card, and a metal strongbox which included, among other valuables, the code for the bank card. At 10:54 P.M. on Friday, May 10, 1985, the murderer had used the bank machine to withdraw $150. The card was used again at 8:56 A.M. on Saturday, May 11 to obtain another $150.

On Saturday morning, May 11, at 8:59 A.M., three minutes and thirty-five seconds after the murderer had withdrawn the cash from the Eastburn's account, Sandra Barnes made a withdrawal from the same machine. When she was contacted by law enforcement officers a few weeks later, she told them firmly and emphatically that she had not seen anyone at the bank that day. Richardson and Beaver contacted Barnes again in September, and again, she insisted that she had not seen anyone at the bank that morning.

But Sandra Barnes was now in court, testifying that she had suddenly found her memory. Sometime in February or March 1986, she claimed she remembered that she did see someone at the bank. When she drove up to the automatic teller machine, she saw an "unusually tall" man with blond hair, wearing a white T shirt and military pants, walking away from the machine. She watched him for perhaps a minute as he left the bank machine and walked toward his car. Several strands of the man's hair were falling down over his face as he leaned over the steering wheel of his small, light-colored, two-door car.

The prosecutor asked her to look at the defendant. "Is that the person that you saw?"

"He looks like the person I saw, yes, sir," she replied.

Billy Richardson glanced over at the jury and knew that they were in serious trouble. Up to that point in the trial, the jury had been with them, Richardson could almost feel a bond being created between them. But then this surprise witness took the stand, and she was very believable, very confident as she pointed at Tim Hennis and said, "He looks like the man I saw." Sandra Barnes had found her memory, and it occurred to Billy Richardson that one seemingly insignificant memory can make all the difference in the world. One memory can change innocence into guilt.

The defense attorneys did their best to call that memory into doubt. What happened, Beaver asked Barnes in his cross-examination, to make you find your memory? Mrs. Barnes answered that the memory just came to her, out of the blue. Did you tell anyone about your sudden change in memory? Beaver asked her. No, she said, she didn't tell anyone for several months. Not even your husband? No, not even her husband.

"Are you absolutely certain the defendant is the same person you saw at the bank?"

"If it's not, it looks just like him, you know, that's all I can say," Sandra Barnes replied.

"It's either Mr. Hennis or someone who looks a great deal like him."

"Yes, sir."

Witnesses called by the defense testified that Sergeant Hennis was at work at 10:54 P.M. Friday night May 10, the first time the Eastburn's bank card was used, and that he left work only a few minutes before the card was used the second time at 8:56 A.M. Saturday morning. He clocked out that morning at 8:45 A.M.—how could he have driven the eleven miles to the bank machine through stop lights and stop signs in just eleven minutes?

The defense emphasized the complete lack of physical evidence linking Timothy Hennis to the crime. Dozens of fingerprints and palm prints were lifted, over two hundred hairs were collected and analyzed, and not one print, not one hair, matched those of Mr.

Hennis. Vaginal swabs were taken from Mrs. Eastburn and an FBI expert testified that although Hennis could not be ruled out as the rapist, neither could 88 percent of the male population.

The defense called Paul Stombaugh, a former FBI chemist, who agreed to testify because of the parallels to the Jeffrey MacDonald crime. Stombaugh appeared as a key prosecution witness in the MacDonald case, arguing that the physical evidence could be considered strong enough to link Jeffrey MacDonald to the murders of his wife and children. In the Hennis case, however, Stombaugh's conclusions were different. He told the jury that he hadn't found one iota of evidence to tie Timothy Hennis to the crime scene.

One piece of evidence actually seemed to exonerate Hennis—a bloody left shoe print revealed by chemical tests conducted by a state investigator. The serologist from the State Bureau of Investigation tested the Eastburn house for invisible blood stains and found a pattern of footprints inside and outside the house, all of which appeared to be made by the left foot of a hard-soled shoe. Photographs were made of the prints with an inch ruler along the side to show their scale. An agent from the State Bureau of Investigation testified that in his opinion it wasn't possible to determine the shoe size from the photographed prints because the same size shoe had different size soles and heels.

But Dr. Louise Robbins, an anthropologist who had made a special study of the prints left by human feet with and without shoes, testified that a number of the prints were complete and showed sharply defined edges at the sole; all but one-eighth inch at the back of the heel did not appear in the print. The prints measured between 9.31 inches and 10.9 inches from the heel to the tip of the sole, and it was Dr. Robbins' opinion that all the prints were made by the same, hard-soled shoe, size 8½ to 9½.

Timothy Hennis's size-12 feet measured 12¼ inches from heel to toe with shoes, and 11½ inches without shoes. The defendant's foot could not possibly fit in the shoe that made the prints, Dr. Robbins testified.

No traces of blood were found on the defendant's clothing, none were found on his shoes, his jacket, or on the folding buck knife the defendant had in his pocket at the time of his arrest. The interior and the exterior of the defendant's car had been exhaustively searched, vacuumed, sprayed, and chemically tested, and no trace of blood was found. How could Sergeant Hennis have brutally murdered three people, the defense lawyers asked the jury, and emerged from the carnage without one trace of blood on his body, his clothing, his knife, his car? How could that possibly have happened?

The jury began its deliberations at 4:30 P.M. on Wednesday, July 2, 1986. They deliberated for almost an hour and then were excused for the evening. They returned on Thursday, July 3, 1986, and deliberated all day, taking an hour off for lunch. They returned again on Friday, July 4, staying in the jury room from 9:30 A.M. until late afternoon. At 4:19 P.M., on Friday, July 4, the jury returned with a verdict: Sergeant Timothy Hennis was pronounced guilty of three counts of first degree murder and one count of first degree rape.

Hennis turned to Billy Richardson, twisted his wedding ring off his finger and said, "Give this to Angela. Tell her I love her."

Richardson took the ring and closed his fingers around it. He knew what it meant. Tim Hennis believed he would never get out of prison; he believed that his life was over.

On July 7, 1986, the penalty phase of the murder counts began. After listening to the defense requests for leniency, the jury sentenced Sergeant Timothy Hennis to death, offering him a choice between the gas chamber and lethal injection. Hennis chose death by lethal injection.

For 845 days, Sergeant Timothy Hennis lived on death row. Every one of those days he wore white socks, a white T shirt, and green trousers. His cell was unlocked at 7:30 A.M. He ate breakfast, wrote letters, read books, ate lunch, read books, wrote letters, talked with the other sixteen prisoners who shared the cell block's day room. At 4:00 P.M., he was permitted to watch TV. Dinner was served at 5:00 P.M. After dinner he cleaned his cell, took a shower, washed his clothes. Lockup was at 10:30 P.M.

One day a week he was allowed to watch a movie. Twice a week he was permitted outside exercise. Once a week his wife and child came to visit. Kristina would pound on the clear plastic wall separating them and cry, "Open it, Daddy! Open it!" After several months of weekly visits, Kristina began calling the prison "Daddy's house."

Early in March 1987, Hennis received a hand-written letter that had been forwarded from the sheriff's office.

Dear Mr. Hennis,

I did the crime, I murdered the Eastburns. Sorry you're doin the time. Thanks.
Mr. X

Hennis stared at the letter for a long time. Then he took a piece of paper, put the pencil in his left hand, and wrote his name. Looking at the awkward scrawl, comparing it to the childish, block-type handwriting in the letter, he felt sure "Mr. X" had used his left hand to write the letter.

Thanks. That one word drove him crazy. *Thanks.* As if he had willingly sacrificed his life; as if he and "Mr. X" were somehow in collusion, partners, collaborators, inside traders.

Hennis gave the letter to his attorneys, who told him that a murder case will draw out the kooks. They filed the letter away and focused on the appeal brief.

On September 14, 1988, twenty-six months after Hennis was pronounced guilty, Richardson and Beaver appeared before the North Carolina Supreme Court and argued that Timothy Hennis's convictions should be overturned because of trial errors. The evidence against Hennis was so insubstantial, they said, that it should never have been allowed to go to the jury. The prosecution, lacking the necessary evidence and physical proof, had aroused the jurors' emotions by showing them the color slides and photographs of the murder victims. The trial court had erred by failing to suppress the testimony of Chuck Barrett.

On October 6, 1988, in an unusually swift decision, the North Carolina State Supreme Court ordered a new trial for Sergeant Timothy Hennis, ruling that the "grotesque and macabre" photographs shown to the jury had prevented him from receiving a fair trial. The justices ordered a new trial.

Beaver and Richardson developed a new strategy for this trial. First, they hired a new private investigator, Les Burns, an ex–Green Beret with seventeen years' experience as a private investigator dealing primarily with cases involving mistaken eyewitness identification.

The second major change in defense strategy was the decision to have Tim Hennis take the stand. In the first trial Richardson and Beaver feared that Hennis's bitterness over his arrest and incarceration as well as his intense dislike for prosecutor William VanStory might be construed as outright hostility, which might lead the jurors to conclude that this was, indeed, a nasty, unpleasant, potentially violent man. Trial lawyers know that a witness's demeanor—his gestures, grimaces, intonations, hesitancies, and facial expressions—are picked up by jurors and weighed as "demeanor evidence" along with the other evidence presented in the trial. Juries pay close attention to the mannerisms and attitudes of witnesses when they testify, and they are often more strongly influenced by appearances than by actual words. If Hennis acted belligerent, quarrelsome, or unnecessarily aggressive on the stand, it might have aroused the jury's distrust or even dislike.

But as it turned out, Tim Hennis's stoic expression and composure during the first trial worked against him; observers commented that he was too cool, too calm, and wondered out loud if an innocent man would be so quiet and restrained. This time the lawyers decided they would try a different strategy, and put Hennis on the stand.

The third and final strategy change involved the decision to hire an expert witness to testify about the problematic nature of eyewitness testimony and the power of suggestion to change and even create memories. The person they decided to hire was me.

Gerald Beaver called me early in December, briefly recounted the facts of the case, and asked if I would be interested in looking over the materials pertaining to the eyewitness identifications.

"You bet," I said without a moment's hesitation. The case intrigued me for several reasons. First, it was a death penalty case. If Timothy Hennis were, in fact, innocent, and if he were sentenced to die, the consequences would be irreversible. In lesser crimes like burglary or rape, the penalties are less severe and temporary; if a person is mistakenly convicted, the government can later admit its mistake, offer its apologies and perhaps even make financial restitution. But in a death penalty case, the consequences are permanent.

No one knows how many innocent people have been put to death by the U.S. government, but a recent capital punishment study reports that in this century 343 people were wrongly convicted of crimes punishable by death and twenty-five were actually executed. Twenty-five innocent people put to death. Was it possible that Timothy Hennis might be the twenty-sixth?

My second reason for wanting to testify in Hennis's trial was less altruistic and more personal. In his first trial, Hennis was convicted and sentenced to die; in his second trial, Hennis would have an expert witness on his side. Would it make a difference? In most criminal cases, the defendant is allowed only one trial, and thus there is no way to know if the jury's decision might have been different if a certain feature had been changed. My testimony would not be the only variable that was altered in this trial, but the outcome promised to give me some valuable information about the power of expert testimony to affect jurors' decisions.

I had one additional reason for being interested in the case. After fifteen minutes on the phone, Gerry Beaver had convinced me that *he* believed 100 percent in his client's innocence. "This man is innocent," he said, simply and without equivocation. "He did not commit these crimes." I didn't get the feeling that Beaver was trying to persuade me or manipulate the facts so that I would take the case, which can sometimes happen when lawyers want to get me on their client's "side." Beaver was straightforward, earnest, and honest— he wanted me to read the file and make the decision for myself. From the very beginning, it was clear to me that he believed wholeheartedly in his client's innocence.

I received the file several days later and quickly separated the materials into two piles relating to the eyewitness identifications of Chuck Barrett and Sandra Barnes. I began with Barrett.

On May 14, 1985, two days after the murders were discovered, Barrett gave a voluntary statement to the police. At the top of the typed statement were the words "Not Under Arrest."

On Friday the 10th of May it was about 3:30 A.M. I had just left my girlfriend's and I was coming down Summer Hill Drive and I saw a white car to the left it was a white Chevette. I kept walking, and I was just about under the second street light, and I saw a white guy coming down from the carport or driveway with a garbage bag over his shoulders and I thought he was breaking in but I could not say nothing, so I just kept walking and as I was walking past, he spoke to me and he said, "Leaving kind of early this morning," so I walked up under the streetlight to see where he was going, so I bent down and turned around to look, and he was looking at me, so he got in the white Chevette and started to turn around, so I walked up in this lady's yard and he turned around and made a right turn on Yadkin Road, so I went home and told my dad what had happened. He told me not to worry about it and that was it.

A question-and-answer session with a sheriff's detective followed his statement.

"Which driveway did you see the white male with the garbage bag walk out of?" the detective asked.
"Where the people were murdered?"

Barrett's sentence ended in a question—was that significant?

"Are you sure, if so, why?"
"Positive, because I saw him."
"How was this white male dressed to the best of your recollection?"
"He had on a black knit cap, white like T shirt, thin dark-colored jacket, jeans and tennis shoes."
"What other description can you give of this white male you saw leaving the house where the people were murdered?"

The questioner, I noticed, now had the white male leaving the house, not just walking down the driveway.

"He had a mustache, short hair, like a G.I. haircut, light brown . . . he weighed about one sixty-seven, and was six foot tall . . ."

Beaver had attached a handwritten note to this voluntary statement. "We first heard this description at trial; see page forty-four of the appeal brief."
The last paragraph on page forty-four of the appeal brief contained this information:

. . . at trial the defense discovered, to its surprise, that the initial description given by Chuck Barrett to investigating detectives was that of a <u>brown-headed,</u> Caucasian male, <u>six feet</u> tall, who weighed

110

167 pounds and was thus smaller than the witness Barrett himself. The defendant was blond, six-foot four inches tall and weighed 202 pounds; a discrepancy of four inches and forty pounds. Therefore, the defense was denied access to this vital exculpatory and impeaching information at the time of the pre-trial hearing . . .

The defense was not given this original description at the time of the pre-trial hearing. Based on the obvious discrepancies between their client's physical appearance and this original description, Beaver and Richardson argued in the appeal that Barrett's identification testimony was untrustworthy and unreliable.

When he testified at the first trial, Chuck Barrett changed his original description. The man he saw walking down the Eastburns' driveway was not six feet tall, as he had first described, but six feet *four* inches tall; the man he saw didn't have brown hair, he had brownish-*blond* hair. Barrett had revised the physical description to fit Timothy Hennis.

I read through the transcript of the January 22, 1986 tape-recorded conversation between defense attorney Billy Richardson and Chuck Barrett. On page two there was this exchange:

"You indicated to me that you had thought long and hard about your identification of Hennis," Richardson said. "What did you tell me?"

"I said that I wasn't too sure," Barrett answered. "At first I was, but now I'm not."

"What do you mean by 'you're not too sure'?"

"Um, you know, I could have been mistaken about it, you know, that was the man."

"Do you feel that you have a reasonable doubt, or that you have a doubt as to the identity?" Richardson asked Barrett.

"Yeah, you know, for right now. But, you know, I'd like to think about it a little bit, you know, more, you know, but for right now, you know, that's how it stands, you know, I'm doubtful."

"Okay. And why do you have that doubt?"

"Cause, you know, I've read the papers and everything, you know, and it's not starting to add up like it was, you know at the beginning."

"It's nothing that I've said or anything like that that's made you have that doubt."

"No. Uh-huhmm," Barrett answered.

"And you don't have that doubt out of any fear?"

"No. I've had this doubt a long time ago, you know."

"You've had it a long time ago?" Richardson asked.

"Yeah, you know, I've been thinking about this a long time, you know."

"And you're saying you're just not sure he's the man that you saw?"

"Yep."

From this conversation it was clear that Barrett doubted his own eyewitness identification of Timothy Hennis. A week later, on January 29, 1986, Barrett agreed to sign an affidavit, under oath, admitting his doubts (". . . I have doubts as to whether or not I picked out the right person . . ."). At that point, Richardson and Beaver requested a pre-trial hearing in which they argued that Barrett's identification should be suppressed.

In the suppression hearing, prior to Barrett's testimony, the defense announced in court that Barrett had signed an affidavit. A lunch recess was announced, and a detective escorted Barrett back to the district attorney's office. When Barrett testified after the two-hour lunch recess, he recanted his statements of doubt and claimed he was pressured by the defense to sign the affidavit. Now he was sure, absolutely sure, that Hennis was the man he saw in the Eastburns' driveway the night of the murders.

What did the detective and the prosecutors say to Barrett to make him change his mind? We'll never know, but given his complete recantation of the tape-recorded conversation and the signed affidavit, the question arises: Was Barrett coerced or threatened in some way? I often hear intimations from defense attorneys that police or prosecutors have pressured their witnesses, using prior charges as blackmail, offering deals or immunity for testimony.

On the other hand, it's possible that there was an innocent type of persuasion in which the police may have said, "Look, everyone has doubts, a lot of our eyewitnesses go through this indecision and uncertainty. Trust your first instincts. You know what you saw." And Barrett, eager to please and hopelessly confused by the passage of time and intervening events, rejects his doubts and goes back to his original story.

What did the police have on Barrett? When Gerry Beaver first called to ask for my help in the case, he mentioned Barrett's prior arrests on a three-year-old charge of credit card fraud, in which

Barrett had allegedly tried to use a stolen credit card to withdraw money from an automatic teller machine. Barrett obviously was in trouble with the law; if the police wanted to use that charge as leverage, they wouldn't have much trouble making Barrett see their side of things.

Next, I turned to the material dealing with Sandra Barnes. Mrs. Barnes was the surprise witness who used the automatic teller machine at the Methodist College Branch of Branch Banking and Trust Company in Fayetteville at 8:59 A.M. on May 11, 1985—three minutes and thirty-five seconds after the murderer used the same machine. Sheriff deputies contacted Mrs. Barnes approximately one month after the Eastburns were murdered, in late June or early July, to determine if she had observed anyone in the vicinity of the machine when she used the card. She told investigating detectives that she was "in a big hurry" that morning and that "she didn't see anything." In September 1985, Mrs. Barnes was interviewed by an investigator employed by the defense team; again, she told him that "she didn't recall seeing anything out there."

In April 1986, spurred on by Hennis's release on bond and the vacillating testimony of the star prosecution witness, investigating detectives conducted follow-up interviews with everyone who had used the automatic teller machine the morning of May 11. At that time, Mrs. Barnes informed detectives that she *did* remember seeing someone, and her memory was astonishingly detailed. She described a tall, well-built, white male with wispy blond hair, wearing military trousers and a white T shirt, leaving the automatic teller machine and getting into a small beige or light-colored two-door car.

On April 16, 1986, sheriff's detectives showed Mrs. Barnes a photographic lineup consisting of several blond males, one of whom was Timothy Hennis. Mrs. Barnes pointed to Hennis's photograph but admitted that she wasn't sure whether she was identifying him from the newspapers or from seeing him at the bank that morning. She was shown a photograph of the defendant's car but said she could not identify it as being the same type of car she had seen near the teller machine.

The defense had no warning whatsoever that Sandra Barnes would appear in court with her "new" memory. In most states, the prosecution would have been forced by the laws of "discovery" to inform the defense that they intended to call a new witness to the stand.

But in North Carolina, apparently, the defense doesn't always find out in advance what the prosecution has in store.

In the appeal brief, Beaver and Richardson stated that they made

". . . repeated requests and motions to discover the facts and circumstances surrounding any identification of the defendant so as to allow a reasonable opportunity to prepare for hearings and motions to suppress their admissibility. All such motions were denied. . . . The identification by Mrs. Barnes and the facts surrounding her observation were concealed from the defense up until the moment of her taking the stand."

When defense counsel requested an interview with Mrs. Barnes, the request was denied.

In open court, Mrs. Barnes was directed by the assistant district attorney to look at Timothy Hennis. "Is that the person that you saw?"

"He looks like the person I saw, yes, sir," she answered.

In their appeal brief, Beaver and Richardson argued that this in-court identification was ". . . an unconstitutionally permissive and overly suggestive show-up." The defendant was sitting in court, at the defense table; he was the only person in the "lineup"; the prosecutor pointed to him and challenged Mrs. Barnes to make an identification—"Is that the person that you saw?" And she answered, "He looks like the person, yes."

In such circumstances—in open court, with just one person to choose from, with a prosecutor pointing his finger at that person—identification is almost inevitable. In numerous cases, judges have ruled that such a one-on-one "show-up" leads to a constitutionally impermissible eyewitness identification. In numerous cases, such identifications have been summarily thrown out.

I put the legal documents and handwritten notes back into the file folder and pushed it off to the side of my desk. There was no doubt in my mind: these were two of the flimsiest eyewitness identifications I had ever encountered. For nine months Sandra Barnes had no memory of seeing a man at the bank; twice, she told investigating detectives that she had not seen anyone that morning. Many months later, when she had "regained" her memory and identified Timothy Hennis in court, she said only that "he looked like" the man she had seen, and she admitted that she was unsure whether her recognition stemmed from seeing his picture in the newspapers.

Beaver included two additional notes regarding Sandra Barnes's identification. The defense had videotaped customers at the automatic teller machine and timed their transactions. The average transaction took thirty to forty seconds to complete. The killer used the bank machine at 8:56 A.M.; would he have been likely to stick around an extra two or three minutes after he had just burglarized the bank account of a woman he had raped and murdered the day before?

The second note briefly alluded to a defense witness who would testify that she had used the automatic teller machine on the evening of May 10 and had later been interviewed by the same detective who interviewed Sandra Barnes. The detective had described Sergeant Hennis in detail; when the witness insisted she had not seen anyone resembling that description at the teller machine, he acted "skeptical" and "impatient" with her.

Assuming that Timothy Hennis was innocent, what happened to Sandra Barnes to make her think that it was Hennis whom she saw at the bank machine? How could she have concocted an entire imaginary scenario and then agreed to swear under oath that it was the truth? A fairly simple explanation exists for "created" memories. In my laboratory, using subtle, suggestive questions, I can get people to remember a stop sign or a yield sign when in fact there was nothing there but a bare pole. Once the person says "Yes, I saw a stop sign," I then ask them to describe the sign for me. "Well, you know," someone might say, "it was like all stop signs, red and white and octagonal in shape . . ." In one experiment, a subject described a nonexistent tape recorder that I implanted in her mind as "small, black, in a case, with no visible antenna."

I've been able to create memories in the most benign and antiseptic of situations, just by asking a question that suggests the idea that there might have been a tape recorder or a stop sign in a particular scene. There is no pressure in my laboratory to be "right"; I don't offer a better grade or a twenty-dollar bill to students who give me a detailed description of nonexistent objects. The graduate students who help run my experiments are well-mannered and polite; they don't wear badges, they don't frown or curse or drum their fingers on the table when they get an answer they don't like, and they don't have files of information on their witnesses. And, of course, when I conduct my experiments, an accused murderer is not standing off in the wings, human bodies are not lying in the morgue, and criminal trials are not taking place. Even so, I can create memories, just by planting an idea in my subjects' minds.

Based on my research with "created memories," I think I can explain what happened to Sandra Barnes. She had a picture in her mind, a memory of the automatic teller machine on the morning of May 11, 1985. For nine months, that picture did not include the murderer. But a month before Timothy Hennis's trial began—after his picture had been in the newspaper dozens of times—Mrs. Barnes suddenly remembered that she had seen someone who looked like Hennis at the bank machine that morning. The static picture in her mind started moving, changing shape, coming alive, and into that picture she began splicing the newspaper photographs of Timothy Hennis. She could see the bank, she could see the automatic teller machine, and suddenly, with just a brief bit of fancy mental editing, she could "see" the man. He was tall and well-built, and his hair was blond. She could even see wispy strands of hair falling over his eyes as he walked to his car, opened the door, and drove away.

Sandra Barnes undoubtedly felt pressure to alter her memory. She was pressured by the fact that she was at the bank that morning, that she was perhaps the only person who could have seen the murderer, the only one who could recognize him now and help to put him behind bars. But was there a more sinister sort of pressure? Did the police intimidate Sandra Barnes, using their power and influence to force her to change her memory? From my research on memory, it's clear that the police didn't need to use coercive measures. Simply by asking her questions, by repeating the same question several times over a period of several months, they would have exerted a subtle but profound pressure on her to remember the man at the bank. If their questions were suggestive, or if the interviewer acted impatient or skeptical, as the other bank customer was willing to testify, then the pressure could be characterized as intense and could be pinpointed as a possible source of the "created" memory. In this situation, we can see the power of suggestion to induce a memory of something that never actually occurred.

The prosecution would argue that Sandra Barnes's memory was always there, repressed, buried beneath more recent memories, waiting like a big fish at the bottom of a deep pond. But if the "fish" were there, why did it take so long to surface? Based on Mrs. Barnes's initial statements that she hadn't seen anyone at the bank, and that eight months later, she suddenly remembered a man who looked "just like" Timothy Hennis, I would argue that the waters of her memory were originally empty and that the "fish" was planted in her mind by the photographs in the newspaper; it began wriggling around when the investigating detective started asking questions, and as the detective continued throwing out the hooks, frothing the water trying to get a bite, the fish leaped up, and swallowed the hook. Once the memory was "hooked," it became real. There was no doubt in my mind that Sandra Barnes truly believed now that she saw someone who looked like Timothy Hennis at the bank the morning after the Eastburns were murdered.

In my studies, a subject's reported confidence for suggested or imagined memories is often as great as that reported for memories based on actual perceptions. When we compare the descriptions of the two different types of memories, we find that the created memories contain slightly fewer sensory attributes, such as the color, size, or shape of the object. Subjects also tend to use more verbal hedges, such as "I think" or "I believe," when describing imagined memories. But when asked to describe their distorted memories, subjects were often quite long-winded, mentioning what they were thinking about or paying attention to when they "saw" the imagined object.

Descriptions of memories resulting from suggestions given under hypnosis can also be quite detailed and confident. In one experiment in which suggestions were given under hypnosis, the subject recalled being awakened one evening by loud noises. "I'm pretty certain I heard them," the subject reported. "As a matter of fact, I'm pretty damned certain. I'm positive I heard these noises."

These and other experiments indicate that subtle differences do exist between perceived and suggested memories, but that most people are unable to detect these differences. In other words, when people remember something, they tend to believe it's the truth. And when they describe their memories, their reports can be so realistic and detailed that someone listening (like a juror) tends to think that the memory is, in fact, real.

What distinguishes a real memory from a false, created memory? The psychologist William James once wrote about the "warmth and intimacy" of our memories. Sandra Barnes remembered the man's wispy hair, the stray strands of hair falling over his face, the creak of the car door opening. Her memory had shape, color, form, and substance—all the "warmth and intimacy" of the real thing.

Because of the intense pre-trial publicity, Timothy Hennis's second trial was moved from Fayetteville to Wilmington, North Carolina, a coastal city of forty-four thousand people just fifty miles from the South Carolina border. On Wednesday, April 12, 1989, I flew into Wilmington and was met at the airport by Billy Richardson and Les Burns, the private investigator who had been working on the case. Half an hour later we met Gerry Beaver at a seafood restaurant located at the inlet waterway, one of those glass and oak structures with the ficus plants strategically located in the corners and a blackboard announcing the daily wine specials. Billy, Gerry, and Les ordered the full dinner with salad bar, but I was still on Pacific Standard Time and too full of the carbohydrates that had been passed to me every two hours on the plane. I ordered a shrimp cocktail and a glass of Chardonnay.

"Tell me about Hennis," I said. "What makes you so convinced that he's innocent?"

I suddenly had the feeling that I was a game-show host facing contestants who were frantically pressing their answer buttons. All four of us burst out laughing.

"Me first!" Gerry called out. As the older member of the law firm, he was claiming executive privilege. "I'd have to start off with the absolute lack of physical evidence linking Tim Hennis to the crime. There were numerous head and pubic hairs found in the living room and bedroom and not one of those hairs matched Tim Hennis. *Not one.* In a crime of this magnitude, you would expect to find some physical evidence linking the accused to the crime, but in this case, there was absolutely nothing. In fact, a great deal of evidence, like the bloody shoeprints, pointed away from Hennis."

Billy Richardson interrupted. Round-faced and smooth-shaven, he looked fresh out of law school. "I think you also have to consider Hennis's absolute naiveté and gullibility. A guilty man would not have turned himself in like Tim Hennis did and then given so willingly of his body—his fingerprints, palm prints, foot prints, blood, saliva. Tim spent almost seven hours at the police station, answering every question they asked and never even thought about asking for a lawyer. In my experience, if there's one thing that distinguishes an innocent person from a guilty one, it's that gullible, trusting, unsuspecting nature, that willingness to go along with the police because you want to help, to be a good American citizen."

It was Les Burns's turn. Like most private detectives I've met, Burns fit into the category of "rugged individualist"—tall and lean, with a Kris Kristofferson cragginess, a beard going gray, and a fondness for straight talk. Burns reiterated Beaver's point about the lack of physical evidence. "I've been a private investigator for seventeen years, and in such a brutal crime where throats have been slashed and people have been stabbed numerous times, you'd expect to find something that would incriminate the suspect. But dozens of investigators couldn't come up with one piece of evidence that incriminated Hennis. And that's because Hennis did not commit these crimes."

Burns looked at Beaver and Richardson; it was obvious that these three men shared a "cause." "Tim Hennis is not a murderer," Burns said simply. "Think about it—what kind of person would be capable of murdering a mother and her two small children? This man has his own child, a little baby girl. Now, I'm not saying I can't be fooled, it's possible, no doubt about it. But I don't believe Tim Hennis is the murdering type.

"And then there's the walker . . ."

For the next twenty minutes, Les Burns told me how he found "the walker." When Chuck Barrett reported that he saw a man walk down the Eastburns' driveway, right into the light from a streetlight, and the man actually talked to him, saying, "Leaving kind of early this morning," Burns knew something fishy was going on. Would someone who had just brutally murdered a mother and her two children waltz down the driveway, into a circle of light, and hold a mundane conversation with a stranger? Burns didn't think so. He theorized that the person who Barrett saw had no connection to the crime whatsoever; he just happened to be walking near the Eastburn house in the early morning hours.

Before the first trial, Billy Richardson went from door to door on Summer Hill Drive and questioned the neighbors. Had they seen someone walking around the neighborhood, between 2:00 and 5:00

A.M.? Several people answered yes, there was someone who roamed the neighborhood at night. They even had a name for him; they called him "the walker." He always carried a bag over his shoulder, he wore a dark jacket and dark hat pulled down over his hair, and he was tall and well-built—just like the man Chuck Barrett had originally described.

Every night for four weeks, Billy Richardson staked out the neighborhood, arriving around 3:00 A.M., waiting, watching, hoping to catch "the walker." Les looked at Billy and Gerry and shook his head with admiration. "In seventeen years in this business, I've never had the privilege of working with attorneys so devoted to a case. Gerry was constantly digging through the law books, and Billy was out in the field every day, weekends, evenings, early mornings. They lived with this case, pursuing every lead they could find. I've never seen anything like it."

But "the walker" had disappeared, and the defense team was forced to go into the first trial with only the word of the neighbors that such a man existed. After Hennis was convicted and the appeal process had started, Burns knew he had to find "the walker" if Hennis stood any chance at all of being acquitted. He started out on Yadkin Road, the main thoroughfare that connects with Summer Hill Road, stopping at one store after another, asking if anyone had seen a guy who fit the description of "the walker."

At a small neighborhood grocery store, the manager started nodding his head. "Yeah, sure," he said. "That sounds like *Joe Polzin*. He used to work here as a stockboy. He'd stock up late at night, after we closed."

Polzin. The name rang a bell. Shortly after the first trial, one of the Eastburns' neighbors called Beaver. There was a young man in the neighborhood, she said, who bore a startling resemblance to Timothy Hennis. He was tall, blond, wore dark clothing and often walked the neighborhood at night. Beaver wrote a note to Burns to check the man out. His name was Joe Polzin.

"What did Polzin do after he got off work?" Burns asked.

"He went to school during the day," the store manager explained, "and he'd come to work with his books and a change of clothes in a backpack. After work, he'd walk around the neighborhoods, carrying the bag over one shoulder by the straps."

"Where is he now?" Burns asked.

"He left the state a while ago," the manager answered. "He went to college somewhere up north."

After a month of steady searching, Burns and Richardson found Joe Polzin at a small college several hundred miles from Fayetteville. They introduced themselves and explained that they were looking for a man who used to walk around Summer Hill Road in Fayetteville, late at night, wearing blue jeans, a dark jacket, and a hat pulled down over his head, carrying a bag over his shoulder.

"Yeah, that's me," Polzin said. "I carried my books and a change of clothes in the bag. After work I'd walk around the neighborhoods; it was just a habit with me."

Polzin told Burns and Richardson that during the first trial, after one of the Eastburns' neighbors testified that she had seen "the walker," detectives from the sheriff's department contacted him. In fact, a detective took his jacket and bag and stashed them in the trunk of his car. When his things were returned, Polzin said the clothes were all on hangers and covered with plastic bags—just like they'd been dry-cleaned. *Luminol*, Burns thought; the cops were looking for blood. They sprayed the stuff with Luminol, and when they didn't find anything, they had the clothes dry-cleaned.

I interrupted Burns' story. "Do you mean, then, that the police and the prosecutor knew about 'the walker' at the first trial?"

"That's right," Burns said.

"But they didn't tell the defense that they had located him?" I asked in amazement.

"That's right, too," Burns said.

"We have very limited discovery laws in North Carolina," Gerry Beaver interjected. "The defense is only entitled to scientific evidence and/or evidence that could be considered exculpatory. The prosecutor told us later that because Polzin wasn't a suspect in the murders, he saw no reason to hand him over to the defense. By law, the state is only required to release evidence that would tend to absolve a defendant, but they claim there was nothing about Polzin that would exonerate Hennis."

"Could they be considered look-alikes?" I asked.

"I was shocked by the resemblance," Les said. "I have artist sketches of both Hennis and Polzin, and I drew a hat on them to see if they looked alike with their hair and foreheads covered up. I showed the photos to people who told me they thought they were different photos of the same person."

"But even if they didn't look alike, there could be other reasons why Chuck Barrett got the two men mixed up," Gerry Beaver said, leaning across the table and speaking in a low voice. "Barrett apparently has a drinking problem. We have a witness, a bakery salesman who makes early morning deliveries to convenience stores on Yadkin Road, who will testify that he often saw Barrett walking around in the early morning hours, drunk as a skunk. And a policeman will testify that in 1987, after the first trial, he charged Barrett with drunk and disorderly conduct. When Barrett failed to show up for court, the state dismissed that case but reserved the right to reopen it."

Beaver raised his eyebrows and grinned at me. "We discovered one additional little pressure point that the state may have used to keep Mr. Barrett on its side. A month ago, sheriff's deputies served Mr. Barrett with a warrant for a three-year-old charge of credit-card fraud. Barrett allegedly tried to withdraw money from an automatic teller machine using a stolen credit card."

"And that's the state's star witness," I said, shaking my head. "It's hard for me to believe that Hennis was convicted based on Barrett's and Barnes's identifications. These are two of the shabbiest eyewitness accounts I have ever encountered."

It's odd, but I can remember that conversation as clearly as if it happened yesterday. I remember where each of us was sitting around the oak table, I remember the gray flecks in Les Burns's beard, I remember the intense, earnest expression on Gerry Beaver's face, and Billy Richardson's round-faced eagerness. These details are fresh and clear and colorful in my memory. But from the next day when I testified in court, I can pull out only vague impressions.

I remember that it was a new courthouse, but stately and formal, with a long steep flight of marble stairs. I remember it was a warm, spring day with butterflies and bees and women dressed in sheer, sleeveless dresses. I remember that the witness stand was carved out of dark wood, polished to a high sheen, and there was a red cushion on the seat.

On the stand, I remember talking about the power of suggestion and the ways in which unintentional information can be communicated to a witness. When police officers question a witness, I testified, they can actually impart information to the witness at the same time that they are trying to obtain information from the witness. This is particularly dangerous when the police have a suspect in mind, or when they have a theory about the case, for their ideas can be transmitted to the witness and can affect the witness's memory. Suggestive questioning, I continued, can actually induce a memory of something that never occurred. Witnesses will change their accounts out of an honest desire to cooperate with authorities.

I remember testifying that a witness's initial account will invariably be more accurate than later recollections, for time and intervening events tend to cause distortions in memory. Sandra Barnes initially told investigators that she didn't see anyone at the bank—only later, after questioning by the police and exposure to newspaper reports, did she remember seeing a man who looked like Tim Hennis. Chuck Barrett initially described a man six feet tall, weighing 167 pounds with light brown hair. Only later, after several face-to-face confrontations with Hennis, did he add four inches and forty pounds and change the hair color to blond to make the description conform to Hennis.

I remember discussing the problems inherent in cross-racial identification. Chuck Barrett is black and both Timothy Hennis and "the walker" are white. Most people are aware that whites have difficulty distinguishing between black faces, but they are often not aware that blacks have the same problem in reverse, finding it harder to distinguish features in white faces. Numerous psychological studies have shown that people of many races have greater difficulty recognizing faces of another race than faces of their own race.

After my testimony, I remember talking to Timothy Hennis for a few minutes, but I can't remember what we discussed. I must have asked him the standard question: "How are you holding up?" and he must have answered in the standard way. He was clean-cut, open-faced, shy and somewhat awkward. He kept shifting his weight from one foot to the other, back and forth, back and forth.

I remember talking with Captain Gary Eastburn, the husband and father of the murder victims. I don't know how or why I got into a conversation with him; it was probably during a recess, we were in the hallway together, and I might have felt awkward and strange, because we were supposedly on opposite sides. I remember asking him about his plans after the trial was over, and he talked for a few minutes about returning to the air force base in England with his little girl, Jana. She was five years old, he said, and would have a birthday soon. We didn't talk about the others, the older sisters and their mother, but in every word he spoke I felt his grief.

After I testified, Les Burns drove me to the airport. We had an hour to kill before my plane left, and we ordered a sandwich in the restaurant. Les talked about a famous case of mistaken identification that he had worked on several years earlier. Two brothers, eighteen-year-old Lonnie and twenty-year-old Sandy Sawyer from Mint Hill, North Carolina, were arrested for a kidnapping that took place on May 15, 1975. A department store manager positively identified them as the men who had kidnapped him at gunpoint. There was no other evidence linking them to the crimes, and both brothers had solid alibis, but the jury voted for conviction; in a subsequent interview one of the three jurors holding out for acquittal confessed that she caved into the majority because she was "tired."

After the Sawyers were convicted, the defense team hired Les Burns to investigate the case. Burns followed up on a rumor that another man had confessed to the kidnapping; he eventually discovered crucial evidence that the police had hidden from the defense, including the victim's initial description of his kidnappers and a composite sketch produced by police. Neither the description nor the composite sketch resembled the Sawyer brothers. Eventually the other man confessed to the crime and two years later, the governor of North Carolina gave the Sawyers a full pardon of innocence.

"How many cases of mistaken identification have you worked on in your career?" I asked.

Burns frowned and scratched at his beard for a moment. "I've had hundreds of cases involving faulty eyewitness accounts, and I'd estimate I've had about fourteen cases where the wrong person was accused or convicted based on a mistaken identification. Not one of those people are still in prison—except, that is, for Hennis. He's definitely one of the innocent ones."

"Will you be able to stay around for the verdict?" I asked.

"I've got another case in Charlotte," he said. "But I'll check in every day and as soon as I hear something, I'll call you."

A week later, on April 20, I flew to Chicago to give a lecture at the Northwestern University Law School. After my lecture I had dinner with the associate dean of the law school and his wife. When I got back to my room the phone was ringing. It was Les Burns.

"Not guilty on all counts!" he shouted into the phone.

The jury deliberated for only two hours and twenty minutes. After the verdict, several members of the jury told reporters that they came to a decision so quickly because the state simply hadn't proved its case. They cited the lack of physical evidence linking Hennis to the crime scene, the weakness of the eyewitness identifications, and the existence of "the walker," who proved how easy it would be to mistake one man for another. Hennis was the first Death Row inmate to win acquittal in a new trial since North Carolina reinstated the death penalty in 1977.

After Les related the details of Hennis's acquittal, he told me a disturbing story. "In July 1987 the sheriff's department received another letter from 'Mr. X,' in the same handwriting as the first," Les said. "No one mentioned this second letter to the defense. We only found out about it after we produced Joe Polzin, 'the walker,' whose testimony made the judge suspicious. What else might be hidden away in the state's filing system? So the judge ordered the state to review its files and provide the defense with any materials that might be helpful to Tim Hennis. And that's when they produced the second letter from Mr. X."

"Do you think Mr. X is the real murderer?" I asked Les.

"I don't know," Les said. "But I have a theory that whoever murdered the Eastburns has gone on to commit other murders. It turns out that there was a strikingly similar case in a tiny town about forty miles from Fayetteville, several months after the Eastburn family was murdered. A woman was raped and brutally murdered, stabbed multiple times in the chest, neck, and back, and her throat was slashed so severely that she was almost decapitated. They found her with her hands tied up with cord and a pillow covering her face—just like Kathryn Eastburn.

"But listen to this." Les spoke in a low, steady voice. "Five days before this other woman was murdered, she placed an advertisement in the classified section of the local newspaper. She had a waterbed for sale. Remember the classified ad that Kathryn Eastburn put in the paper, offering her dog to a good home? I think this is how the man picked his victims. He'd read the classifieds, make the telephone call, get the address, stake out the house, and then pick a night. The police have no suspects and no leads in either murder, but I think the same man killed the Eastburns and this woman, and I think he'll murder again."

It was late when I hung up the phone. I sat down on the queen-size bed and looked around my hotel room. The heavy floral curtains were closed, but I pulled them tighter, overlapping the edges. The heater buzzed on and off. I thought about calling someone and going down to the lounge for a drink, but it was late, and I had to give a lecture the next morning and then catch a plane back to Seattle.

I got ready for bed, climbed in, and reached for a book to read. The book stayed on my lap, unopened, as I sat and stared at the wallpaper, thinking about the Hennis case. I tried to focus only on the first part of my conversation with Les Burns, the good news about Timothy Hennis's acquittal. But I couldn't stop my mind from drifting into the last part of Les's story. I kept thinking about the murderer who chose his victims from the classified advertisements, who used the phone number listed in the advertisement to call the house and get an address, who waited outside until everyone was in bed and the lights were out. Then came the knock on the door.

OUT OF THE MOUTHS OF BABES: TONY HERREREZ

"We are a society that, every fifty years or so, is afflicted by some paroxysm of virtue—an orgy of self-cleansing through which evil of one kind or another is cast out. From the witch-hunts of Salem to the communist hunts of the McCarthy era to the current shrill fixation on child abuse, there runs a common thread of moral hysteria."

—Dorothy Rabinowitz, *Harper's Magazine*, May 1990

On July 5, 1984, at 4:15 P.M. in a suburb of Chicago, Illinois, five-year-old *Katie Davenport* jumped out of the yellow station wagon and yelled, "Thanks!" She laughed at *Paige Becker*, her best friend who was making faces at her from the backseat, and made a funny face back. Waving good-bye, she ran to her mother and gave her a big hug and kiss.

"What did you do at camp today, honey?" *Lenore Davenport* asked as they walked hand in hand into the kitchen. Katie shrugged. "Did you play with Paige? Did you make a drawing for me, or learn any new games?" Mrs. Davenport was accustomed to asking her daughter detailed questions and receiving one-word answers. Five-year-olds are so active, their attention spans so short, she thought, regarding her daughter with affection.

"We watched movies." Katie finally offered some information.

"That's nice. What kind of movies?"

Katie stared at the linoleum floor. "Funny movies."

"Funny movies?"

"Yeah, cartoons. Rabbits, elves. Funny movies." Katie giggled. "Mommy?"

"Yes?" Mrs. Davenport stroked her daughter's long brown hair.

"Did you know that 'dick' is another word for 'penis'?"

Lenore Davenport dropped to her knees and put her hands on Katie's shoulders. She looked her straight in the eye and struggled to keep her voice calm. "Sweetheart," she said, "where did you hear that?"

Katie smiled slightly and looked at her mother out of the corner of her eye.

"This is not funny, Katie. Tell me where you heard those words."

Katie began to cry. Her mother lifted her up, carried her to the living-room sofa, and sat down with the child on her lap. "Honey," she said after a moment. "What happened today? What did you do at day camp?"

"Mommy, I'm hungry. Can I have some cookies?"

"Talk to me first and then we can have some cookies. What did you see in the movies, Katie?"

"A girl with long blond hair flying through the air. And a man with something funny on his head."

"Funny?" Mrs. Davenport frowned.

"Funny. Funny bad."

"Bad? Do you mean scary? What do you mean by *bad*, Katie?"

"Just bad. Like a penis." Katie giggled again. "A penis on his head."

"Who told you it was a penis?" Mrs. Davenport's tone was sharp.

"The kids said it. And Tony."

Tony. Mrs. Davenport concentrated, trying to remember who Tony was. Oh yes, he was the new camp counselor, a pre-med student at—where was it? Northwestern? A nice-looking boy, Mexican or Puerto Rican, very sweet and polite and so loving with the kids. He was always picking up the smaller children, playing with them, giving them hugs.

"Did Tony touch you, Katie? Has Tony ever touched you in a bad place?"

Katie frowned. "No," she said.

"Are you sure?"

"Yes. I think so."

That evening after Katie went to sleep, Lenore Davenport called Paige's mother, *Margaret Becker*. Had Paige mentioned anything unusual that happened at day camp? No, Mrs. Becker answered, Paige didn't mention anything out of the ordinary. Lenore Davenport related what Katie had said about the bad movies and the penis on the head. Shocked, Mrs. Becker agreed to question Paige again the next day. Every day for the next two weeks the mothers talked to each other, and every day they talked to their children, gently reassuring them that there was nothing to be ashamed of, nothing bad would happen if they told the truth, no one would ever hurt them again.

Toward the end of July, Katie Davenport and her mother had another talk.

"Honey, remember that day several weeks ago when you told me that Tony showed you bad movies?"

Katie blushed. "Yes."

"Were you ever alone with Tony?"

"No."

"Are you sure, Katie? Are you very, very sure?"

"Honest, Mommy, all we did was go to the bathroom."

"The bathroom." Mrs. Davenport couldn't hide her anxiety. "What were you doing in the bathroom with Tony?"

"I was putting my bathing suit on. He was helping me."

"Did he touch you?"

"No."

"Katie, he must have touched you if he was helping you with your bathing suit."

"I don't know. He was helping me."

"Where did he touch you?"

"On my arm. My back. My head."

"Did he ever touch you down there, on your private place?"

"No."

"Are you sure?"

"Yes. I think so."

Approximately three weeks later, in the middle of August, Mrs.

Davenport was giving her daughter a bath. Katie turned bright red when her mother began to soap her buttocks. "Only you can touch my private parts," she said.

"That's right, Katie."

"Nobody else can. Tony can't."

"Did Tony ever touch your private parts?"

"No." Katie shook her head.

"Katie, if you don't tell me the truth, I can't help you."

"Well, maybe." Katie hesitated and then added, "Yes."

"Where, Katie . . . where were you when this happened?"

"In the bathroom."

"Did Tony do anything else? Did he ask you to touch him?"

"No," Katie said.

Her mother stroked her hair. "Are you sure?"

"Yeah."

"Yes, meaning he did touch you or didn't touch you?"

"Yeah." Mrs. Davenport lifted her daughter out of the bath and began drying her with a towel. She struggled to keep her voice calm. "Where did he touch you, Katie?"

"Dick is another word for penis," Katie said inexplicably.

"What did Tony do, Katie?"

"He put his penis on my head," Katie said. "Then he put it in my mouth."

Mrs. Davenport called the police.

On August 23, 1984, *Detective Yancey* of the Chicago police department asked Mrs. Davenport and Mrs. Becker to bring their daughters to the police department for a talk. The children were questioned for more than two hours by Detective Yancey and *Martha Sanderson*, a child psychologist. Paige admitted that she didn't like Tony because he was "unfair." She said she saw the film that Katie had seen, the one with a man who had a penis on his head.

"Was that man someone you knew?" the psychologist asked.

"It was Tony," Paige answered.

On September 15 Mrs. Becker and Mrs. Davenport took Katie and Paige to the hospital to be checked for possible sexual abuse. The doctor found no physical evidence that would allow him to state with certainty that abuse had occurred. But, he explained to the anxious mothers, it had been two months since the alleged incident occurred and if the abuse had involved oral sex, as the mothers seemed to believe, there would be no physical evidence.

Less than a week later, Mrs. Becker called Detective Yancey in tears. "Paige remembers a movie with naked bodies. And she says that Tony touched her in 'bad places.'" Detective Yancey added another page to a growing file.

Another month went by. On October 25 Mrs. Becker placed another call to Detective Yancey. After spending the afternoon with Katie Davenport, Paige remembered something else. Sometime last summer, she said that she was taken into the bathroom by Tony Herrerez, her clothes were removed, and she was photographed in the nude. Then he asked her to "kiss" his penis.

That was enough for Detective Yancey, who took his file to the prosecutor's office. In April 1985 a grand jury charged Tony Herrerez on three counts:

"On an undetermined date from June 18th to July 4th in the year 1984, Tony Herrerez engaged in sexual conduct, to-wit: fellatio with Katie Davenport, five years old, purposely compelling her to submit to such conduct by force or threat of force; fellatio with Paige Becker, five years old; and knowing that an unidentified movie was obscene or harmful, recklessly furnished such material to Katie Davenport and Paige Becker."

A trial date was set for the first week in August 1985. Early in May, Tony Herrerez hired criminal defense attorney Marc Kurzman, a Minnesota attorney who had presented a brilliant defense for two clients in the Jordan, Minnesota, sexual abuse cases.

And on June 3, 1985, Marc Kurzman called me.

"Let me tell you a story," Kurzman said after introducing himself and briefly describing the case against Tony Herrerez. Kurzman's accent was native New York City, and he had the New Yorker's habit of running one sentence into the next, the hell with the grammatical niceties. "About seven months ago, right after the Jordan, Minnesota, cases, when emotions were raw—like the old days of a communist under every bush, now there was a child abuser under every bush—I got a call about another sex-abuse case in Wisconsin. These cases, you have to understand, are popping up all over the place, like those ducks in the amusement park that you shoot with the popgun and then they bounce right back again.

"Anyway, in this particular case, a five-year-old boy—let's call him *Randy*—allegedly accuses his father, let's call him *Sam*, of abusing him. That's the top layer of facts. Sam is divorced from Randy's mother, who is living with a guy named *Maloney*. This is the second layer of facts and now we're getting into the dirt. Mom and Maloney go to Sam to ask for more child support. They want to get married but Maloney's unemployed, and they can't afford to get an apartment or buy decent food. Sam is sympathetic, but he's broke, he earns minimum wage, he doesn't have a savings account, there's no way he can afford more child support. So Mom and Maloney deny him access to the kid, and now we descend into the third and fourth layers, into the muck. For two years Sam files complaints against his wife, accusing her of mistreatment and neglect. The kid is always dirty, he has unexplained bruises and cuts on his body, the dad is sure he's getting banged around by Maloney.

"So"—Kurzman lets the word out in a quick sigh—"the next thing Sam knows, he's being accused of child abuse. And the cops have a videotape; they taped the interviews with the kid so they'd have visual proof that they did everything by the book. I sat and watched this videotape, and around the third hour of the interview, in about a ten-second spot, God, I could have missed it so easily, one of the cops asks the boy about an incident in the kitchen when Sam allegedly licked his little boy's penis.

" 'What happened?' the cop asks.

" 'I ate ice cream,' the kid answers.

" 'No, tell me about your dad,' says the cop.

" 'Dad gives me ice cream.'

" 'Does your dad lick you?'

" 'Dad didn't do that,' the kid says, 'Maloney did.' "

"Here we have a moment of truth sunk down in the mud and muck of this terrible situation. I took that little scene to the judge, who threw the case out and gave Sam full custody of the boy. There's another truly horrifying case in Oregon where a mother noticed some strange burns on her two-year-old's leg. She took him to the doctor who notified the social workers, who notified the police detectives, who brought in the child psychologists and anatomically correct dolls, and suddenly accusations of abuse were getting hurled around so hard and fast it made you dizzy. Maybe a baby-sitter burned him, they thought; or maybe, somebody suggested, it was the mother. At that point they took the child away from the mother and put her in a foster home. Then, during one of the doctor's visits, a sharp-eyed nurse raised the question: Could these 'burns' be a staphylococcus infection? And sure enough, that's what they were.

"Now I'm not saying all these accusations are garbage. I think maybe eighty-five to ninety percent of the defendants in these sex abuse cases are guilty. But Tony Herrerez is one of the innocent ones."

"How do you know?" I asked the standard question, but in this case it had a slightly different twist. This was a crime without any adult witnesses, without weapons, without any physical evidence. Thus the burden of proof had subtly shifted to the accused—Tony Herrerez, and his lawyer would have to prove that he did *not* abuse these two little girls. And how do you prove you did *not* do something?

Kurzman didn't hesitate for an instant. "First of all we've got the polygraph, voice stress, and psychological test results. Half a dozen psychologists and psychiatrists worked Tony over, and it was their independent but unanimous decision that he didn't do it. Second, we've got a disclosure by one of the little girls in this case—Katie Davenport—who claims that nothing happened with Tony. Her mother, she told the judge in a private hearing, put the idea in her head and told her what to say. Third, we discovered that the mother kept a diary. We had to fight like hell to get it—the judge read it and claimed there was no exculpatory evidence in there, nothing that would help the defense—but we kept battling to see it and finally we got it. And what did we find? Verbatim conversations where the mother described her talks with Katie. When Katie denied that anything had happened with Tony, she was sent to her room. When she admitted that Tony had abused her, she got a cookie or a pat on the head. Little Katie Davenport was coerced—if she said what her mother wanted her to say, she got a hug, or a smile, or a cookie, but if she denied anything happened, she was punished and sent to her room. Classic behavioral conditioning, am I right? The stuff of Pavlov and his dogs."

"Not really," I said, smiling to myself at the thought of this lawyer sitting in an introductory psychology class. I explained that Pavlovian, or classical, conditioning involves the repeated pairing of a neutral stimulus (the ringing of a bell, for example) with a stimulus (food) that evokes a reflex response (salivation). Eventually the neutral stimulus used alone is capable of evoking the responses; Pavlov, in his classic study, was able to make his dogs salivate just by ringing a bell.

"In the example you've given me," I said, "a person is rewarded or punished and the behavior is changed as a result. The response results from the learned association between a particular action and a desired result. B. F. Skinner developed this concept back in the nineteen thirties and forties. He proposed that positive and negative consequences mold our behavior and that the principle of reinforcement—receiving a reward for a certain behavior—is the basic mechanism for controlling behavior. When Katie Davenport said yes, admitting that she was abused, and then received a cookie or a hug from her mother, that was positive reinforcement, which will increase the frequency of the behavior. When she denied that anything was happening and was sent to her room, that was a form of punishment, which would tend to suppress or decrease that particular response."

As I explained these psychological terms to Kurzman, something kept nagging at me. This wasn't the classic eyewitness case in which the victim has only a fleeting exposure to the person they accused. These children *knew* Tony Herrerez, they spent whole days with them, he read stories to them, put Band-Aids on their hurt fingers, mediated their fights, laughed at their jokes, comforted their fears. Why would they point a finger at this man and accuse him of such horrible crimes?

If he was indeed innocent, I could think of only one explanation for their accusations. The children had been pressured, presumably by their mothers and later by police officers and therapists. But why would a mother push her child to make such horrible accusations?

"Tell me about the mothers," I said to Kurzman.

Kurzman sighed. "We've got two mothers who love their children very, very deeply. And we have to ask ourselves: Is there a stronger impulse than a mother's need to protect her child? Let me tell you what I think happened. I think the kids at the camp were engaging in bathroom talk—you know, Johnny says, Hey, I've got a penis and you don't, and then Joey says, Hey, did you know that dick is another word for penis?"

"But talking about the word penis and then saying you were sexually abused is a big leap," I interrupted.

"That's right. And I think that space was filled in by the mothers who heard their children talking about dicks and penises; who immediately became alarmed, understandably alarmed; who asked hundreds of questions; who called each other repeatedly over the next several months; who talked to the police, took their children to the hospital, and through this whole ordeal communicated their fear and even their thoughts to their children."

Kurzman paused for a breath of air. "There is no evidence in these cases—none—of sexual molestation," he said. "There is no evidence of any pornographic movies. If they showed porno movies, where did the movies go? We have only the word of the children."

Only the word of the children. My mind grabbed that phrase and settled on it, circling, sniffing, poking. *Believe the children* has become the rallying cry of child-abuse specialists and investigators. People who don't believe the children are considered guilty of betraying them. I forced myself to tune back into Kurzman's monologue.

". . . and then there are all these conversations between the mothers. They must have talked to each other a hundred times, getting more and more worked up, trading information, convincing each other, getting hysterical. After they talked on the phone, they'd sit down with their kids and try to elicit some more information. 'Are you sure he didn't touch you? Don't be ashamed, you can tell me. If anything happened, tell Mommy.' Over and over and over again, gently but surely leading the children where they wanted them to go.

"Then we've got the movies," Kurzman continued. "Wait until you see these allegedly pornographic movies. *The Little Prince. The Velveteen Rabbit. Millions and Trillions of Cats. The Giving Tree.* In *The Velveteen Rabbit,* I found the lady with the long blond hair who flew through the air. She's the 'nursery magic fairy' who gathers up the little rabbit in her arms and flies with him into the woods where she changes him into 'Real.' And in one of the cartoons there's a little figure of an elderly man wearing a big top hat that sticks way up on his head. It's a pretty phallic-looking hat. I think this is where the whole penis issue came up. Assume that during the showing of these movies, this little man appears and a kid yells out, 'Hey, that looks like a penis on his head.' And then the kids start tittering and somebody says, 'Did you know that "dick" is another word for "penis"?' And off they go. Pretty soon these words are put in Tony Herrerez's mouth and like the old telephone game, the story gets told and retold, the rumors and accusations start flying, and suddenly we're dealing with a foul-mouthed sex fiend."

"Tell me about Tony Herrerez," I said.

"He's a sweet kid, big smile, happy, emotions all on the surface, engaged to be married, pre-med, straight-A student. In our first interview he broke down, sobbing about how much he loves these little kids, he can't believe this has happened, how could they accuse him of doing something he didn't do? He cried for two hours, non-stop. That kind of agony is just not staged. We talked about racial prejudice—he's the only Hispanic on the staff, and most of the kids are upper-class WASP types. He told me about a conversation he had with the director of the day camp the day he was hired. 'You can expect to hear some accusations of child abuse,' she told him the day she hired him. 'It's inevitable with a male worker in a day care situation.' "

That little piece of information shocked me. I was certainly familiar with prejudices against women in the workplace, having just witnessed a battle waged by a female colleague to have her salary raised to a level comparable with our male colleagues. But to think that because you were a man working in a day care situation, certain people would automatically suspect you of being a child abuser—that was a stunning revelation.

"I understand that your research is mostly with memory distortion in adults," Kurzman said, abruptly switching the subject. "But you have also studied the impact of suggestive questioning on children, is that right?"

I briefly summarized my research studies with children. In one experiment conducted in the late 1970s with Phil Dale, an expert in developmental psychology, we showed preschool and kindergarten children four films, approximately one minute each. Afterward we interviewed the children and asked them questions, some of which were suggestive and elicited surprising responses. One child, when asked "Did you see a boat?" in the film later recalled "some boats in the water." Another child was asked "Didn't you see a bear?" and later recalled "I remember a bear." "Didn't you see some bees?" we asked a child who later recalled seeing "a bee in it." And a child who was asked "Did you see some candles start the fire?" later told us "The candle made the fire." There were no boats, bears, bees, or candles in any of the films.

"In other words," I explained to Kurzman, "we were able to alter the child's response, perhaps even creating a memory in the child's mind, simply by asking a suggestive question. Why were these children so suggestible? This is the hard stuff, the creative part of psychology. All we know is that we have a child saying he saw a bear when there was no bear. We have two possible explanations. Perhaps the child's original memory has faded, and it is relatively easy for us to make the child imagine that she has seen a bear. The bear literally *becomes* the memory. The alternative explanation is that the child doesn't really think she saw a bear but is just going along with the questioner because she thinks that she should have seen a bear. In other words, she thinks that by saying she did see a bear, she is giving the right answer."

I hesitated for a moment, trying to decide whether to tell Kurzman about an earlier experiment I'd conducted with adult subjects who watched a film clip of an automobile accident and then were interviewed and asked suggestive questions. By using the verb "smash" instead of "hit," we were able to change not only the subjects' estimate of the speed of the cars when the accident occurred but also the probability of reporting broken glass—even though there was no broken glass in the film and we never mentioned broken glass in our interviews. This particular experiment supported the theory that the subjects experienced an actual change in the original memory.

I looked at my watch—my seminar on eyewitness testimony was in fifteen minutes—and decided to spare Kurzman the details. "Mr. Kurzman, I have a class in a few minutes. But I do want you to know that my experiments with children are only a small part of my work in the field of memory distortion. There are several experts available who specialize only in children's memories and who know the literature much better than I do."

"That may be true," Kurzman said, "but they don't have the

courtroom experience you have, nor do they have your reputation as the acknowledged expert in the field of memory distortion. Can you be in Chicago in the beginning of August for the trial?"

"I'll be there," I said.

A few weeks later I was in my office reviewing the police interviews with the two children when I remembered something Kurzman had said when we talked on the telephone. "We have no evidence," he said. "We have only the word of the children."

I swiveled around in my chair and pulled a folder labeled "Child Abuse" out of the file cabinet. Right in the front of the file was an October 1984 *People* magazine article on the Jordan, Minnesota, child abuse cases. On the third page of the four-page article I found what I was looking for. The female prosecutor in the case, Kathleen Morris, was angrily discussing one of the early verdicts, in which a couple accused of sexually abusing six children, including their own three sons, was acquitted. "This doesn't mean they're innocent," Morris said. "This means we live in a society that does not believe children."

Is that what the verdict meant? I thought back to the time, not very long ago, when children were considered primitive, incomplete beings who could not distinguish truth from lies and who were banned from the courtroom unless an adult witness was available to corroborate their stories. In 1910 a famous German pediatrician argued vehemently that children's testimony should not be allowed in a court of law. "Children are the most dangerous of all witnesses," he pronounced.

Psychological studies conducted early in the century tended to support these stereotypes of children. In 1911 a Belgian physician by the name of Varendonck was asked to evaluate the information obtained from two young girls in a famous rape-murder case. After extensive interviews with the children, Varendonck concluded that children can be manipulated into saying whatever adults want them to say, and he devised a series of clever experiments to prove his point. In one experiment nineteen seven-year-old students were asked to report on the color of their teacher's beard. Sixteen students answered "black," and yet the teacher did not even have a beard. When Varendonck asked twenty eight-year-old children the same question, nineteen reported a color; only one correctly said the man had no beard.

"When are we going to give up, in all civilized nations, listening to children in courts of law?" Varendonck asked.

In 1913 a psychologist reviewed the literature on children's suggestibility and offered this summary: "First, the child does not distribute his attention in the same way as an adult . . . secondly, the child is uncritical in filling out gaps in his memory and uses freely material supplied through custom, through his own imagination, or through suggestion."

In 1926 a social scientist by the name of Brown made this outrageous statement: "It is never safe to depend either on the memory or the reason of a child," and then presented what he touted as "an excellent rule" regarding suggestibility: "Women are more suggestible than men, and children are more suggestible than adults."

These theories about the innate suggestibility of children dominated both scientific and lay thinking for the next four decades. Children continued to be viewed as incompetents who could not distinguish fantasy from reality, and in most cases their presence was banned from the courtroom. Even if a child was the victim of a crime, law-book statutes forbade prosecutors from taking the case to court unless they could find another witness—an adult witness—to substantiate the charge. Unless the abuser committed the crime in front of an adult, was caught in the act, or confessed, the child would not be believed. The old adage "A child must be seen but not heard" governed the courts as well as the household sanctum.

Then with the activism of the 1960s, intense pressure from feminists and child protective workers, and an increased concern with children's rights, age-old attitudes toward children began to change. Judges and juries started listening to children, competency standards ("Can the child tell the difference between a truth and a lie?") replaced age limits that excluded all witnesses under seven years old, and law books were gradually cleared of old statutes requiring another corroborating witness. Children over age four are now frequently admitted into our courtrooms, and their testimony is given serious consideration by judges and juries.

The presence of children in the courtroom is becoming more commonplace as reported instances of child sexual abuse skyrocket. There does indeed seem to be a pedophile around every corner, under every bush. According to *Time* magazine (January 21, 1990), in 1976, 6,000 cases of child sexual abuse were reported; in 1988, there were an estimated 350,000 annual reports, a nearly sixty-fold increase. Do these numbers represent an explosion of abuse in the last decade? Or do children in the liberalized atmosphere of the 1980s feel freer to tell someone when they are abused?

Another question must be asked, a terrifying question: How many of these reports of sexual abuse are actually false allegations? And this raises another disturbing question: If some of these cases are a result of false accusations, why would the children lie?

Psychological researchers studying children's memory and the credibility of children's testimony can be divided into two basic camps. On one side are those researchers who theorize that children can be led by suggestive questioning into a different version of reality, sometimes adopting the interrogator's version of reality, even if that version is not the truth. Children, in other words, become confused as time goes on and their original memory fades.

On the other side, researchers insist that children will not deliberately lie about traumatic events. While they may be suggestible about the color of someone's eyes or the meal they ate for dinner last week, if the subject is sexual abuse, they know what happened and what didn't happen. Children, the theory goes, are not able to fantasize in graphic detail about sexual acts outside their experience, nor can they be coerced or brainwashed into making allegations against their parents, teachers, or friends. Children will not deliberately lie.

As a researcher who has spent more than two decades studying memory, perception, and the power of suggestion, I think the key word to keep in mind is not lie but *deliberately*. Changes in memory are generally unconscious, and distortions occur gradually, without our calculated interference. It's not so much a question of a child being deceptive as being confused. Just as an adult's memory can be filled with false and contradictory information, so can a child's memory.

Even if children's memories were comparable to adults' on every level, children would still have memory problems. Getting a child to remember a bear in a film that contained no bears is not as fantastic as it sounds, when I've been able in my experiments to get adult subjects to remember seeing broken glass in a film of an automobile accident that contained no broken glass. We are all, adults and children alike, suggestible beings.

Perhaps we could use a child's analogy and think of memory as a chunk of clay that we hold in our hands, allowing it to warm before we mold it into different shapes. We can't change the clay into a rock or water or cotton, but we can transform it, push it, dent it, bend it, make animals and shapes, faces and forms, designs and textures. When we have finished with our manipulations, we put the molded form into the oven of our minds where it bakes until it is hard and firm. Our distortions have become a hard reality, part fact, part fiction, but in our minds an exact representation of the way things were.

I remembered a recent conversation with Stephen Ceci, a professor at Cornell University and an important contributor to the research literature on children's suggestibility. We were discussing the current national hysteria regarding child sexual abuse, and Ceci mentioned the Salem witch trials. In the year 1692, between June 10 and September 19, twenty residents of Salem, Massachusetts, were accused, tried, and convicted of witchcraft; all were swiftly put to death. What was the evidence against the so-called witches and wizards? *The word of the children.* Children between the ages of five and sixteen were the defendants' major accusers. Children gave the key eyewitness testimony against them, claiming that they saw the "witches" turn themselves into black cats, fly on broomsticks over the pastures at night, or talk to insects that then flew into the children's bodies and implanted nails in their stomachs. And children provided the only evidence against the defendants, experiencing apoplectic fits or total paralysis at the sight of the witches or vomiting nails and pins—thirty or more at a time—in the presence of the judges, jurors, and spectators.

"We'll never know if these child accusers deliberately lied or were truly convinced that they were telling the truth," Ceci said, "but the Salem records of the actual interviews with the children vividly illustrate the use of leading questions, suggestive statements, insinuations, and blatant attempts by parents, ministers, and judges to persuade the children that they had observed evidence of witchcraft. And then we have the recantations made many years later."

Ceci read a passage to me from the book *Witchcraft in Salem Village*, written in 1892 by W. S. Nevins. It was a confession made by Ann Putnam, the most notorious of the child accusers, to her pastor in 1706, fourteen years after the Salem witch trials:

> I desire to be humbled before God for that sad and humbling providence that befell my father's family in the year 1692: that I, then being in my childhood, should by such a providence of God, be made an instrument for the accusing of several persons of a grievous crime, whereby their lives were taken away from them, whom now I have just grounds and good reason to believe they were innocent persons; and that it was a great delusion of Satan that deceived me in that sad time, whereby I justly fear that I have been instrumental, with others, though ignorantly and unwitting, to bring upon myself and this land the guilt of innocent blood; though what was said or done by me against any person I can truly say and uprightly say before God and man, I did it not out of anger, mallice or ill-will to any person, for I had no such thing against them, but what I did was ignorantly, being deluded of Satan . . . I desire to lie in the dust, and to be humbled for it, in that I was the cause, with others, of so sad a calamity to them and their families. . . . (p. 250)

On August 14, 1985, the night before I would testify in court for Tony Herrerez, Marc Kurzman and I spent three hours holed up in my Chicago hotel room watching the movies that Katie and Paige had watched at camp more than a year earlier. We were looking for details that a child's mind might misconstrue. Kurzman pointed out the flying blond lady and the little man with the pointed cap, but neither of us could find anything in any of those films that could be considered pornographic.

Later we discussed my testimony. Kurzman was relaxed and informal, dressed in all-cotton Banana Republic clothes, deep smile lines etched in his cheeks, a day's worth of dark stubble on his face. Put a whip in his hand and he'd look the perfect picture of a well-seasoned lion trainer.

"Do you still believe Tony is innocent?" I asked Kurzman.

"I'm convinced of it," he answered emphatically. "There's not a doubt in my mind."

The next morning in court, Kurzman was all dressed up in a beautifully tailored suit and muted silk tie, his face cleanly shaven. He approached the witness stand, brow furrowed, eyes holding mine, and carefully led me through the usual litany—please state your name, are you currently employed, can you describe your educational background, do you belong to any honor societies, have you authored any textbooks or professional articles—before getting into the heart of the case.

"Are you familiar with the term 'memory implant'?"

"Yes, it's a term that refers to a situation that I have studied extensively over the last ten or twelve years in my laboratory." I consciously sat up straighter, pushing my shoulders back, tilting my chin up. It's easy to get slumped over sitting on those hard wooden chairs in those narrow wooden boxes. "When somebody experiences an event, they are sometimes exposed to new information after the event is over. That new information can come in the form of leading questions or in the form of allowing a witness to overhear another witness talk about the event. In many situations, the new information becomes incorporated or implanted in the witness's memory and causes a supplementation to the memory—an alteration, transformation, contamination, or distortion in the memory."

"In this case," Kurzman said, "the jury has heard testimony from two children who are presently about six years old and who at the time the events occurred were five years old. Are you familiar with any research or studies that speak directly about children that age, five-year-olds and six-year-olds, and the relationship of memory to such children?"

"One study that was conducted in my laboratory about five years ago used four- and five-year-old children," I said, looking over at the jury. "I was interested in the extent to which children who had seen films would be susceptible to leading questions. By a 'leading question,' I mean a question that suggests what the answer is supposed to be. For example, the question 'Did you see the bear?' suggests to the child that there was a bear and asks the child if he saw it.

"We found that children were quite susceptible to leading questions. If a question was asked with the use of a definite article, for example, many children would say yes, they did see this object, when in fact it did not exist."

"Can you tell the jury generally about the malleability or suggestibility of the memory implantation process as it occurs with five- and six-year-old children?" Kurzman asked.

"Let me step back and tell you briefly the procedure that is used in these studies." I was concerned that we might be jumping in too quickly with the results of the studies without first explaining to the jury how the experiments were conducted. "We can talk for a minute about an experiment with adults because even adults are susceptible to influence on some occasions. We present a film or an event to our subjects. Later we might ask a leading question, such as: 'How fast were the cars going when they smashed into each other?' And then we test the subjects for their own memory of the event and we look to examine the effects of the leading question or the suggestive information.

"We have found that it is very easy to suggest information to people, and, under certain conditions, they will succumb to these suggestions and come to believe that they actually witnessed these details. We have gotten people to tell us that they saw broken glass, if we ask a question about cars smashing into each other. We've gotten people to tell us red lights were green lights, if we ask a leading question that suggested that the light was green. We've gotten people to tell us that an individual has curly hair when in fact he had straight hair.

"It's now been demonstrated that under certain conditions children can be even more suggestible than adults. I'm referring now to children three, four, and five years old. When you ask leading questions that suggest what the answer is to be, children will pick up that information and incorporate it into their memories, and they will then come to believe that they have actually experienced these details when, in fact, they've only been suggested to them."

Kurzman went back to the defense table, picked up some notes, and then delivered one of those pregnant pauses that inform the jury that something important is about to be said. It's a simple but fascinating legal technique, calculated to make the prosecutor squirm and push the jurors to the edge of their seats.

"Dr. Loftus," Kurzman began, "I would like you to make some assumptions. Assume that on July fifth, nineteen eighty-four, at a place called *Echo Lake Day Camp*, two five-year-old girls named Katie Davenport and Paige Becker, together with approximately fifty other children of the same age group and ten to twelve counselors, were in a room watching the movies that you and I and the jury have seen.

"Assume that in one of these movies a drawing appears of an

Seven eyewitnesses swore under oath that Roman Catholic priest Father Bernard Pagano *(below)* was the man who committed a series of armed robberies. Charges were dropped when Robert Clouser *(above)* confessed to the crimes. Clouser said he had not confessed sooner because he was certain Father Pagano would be acquitted. *(UPI/Bettmann)*

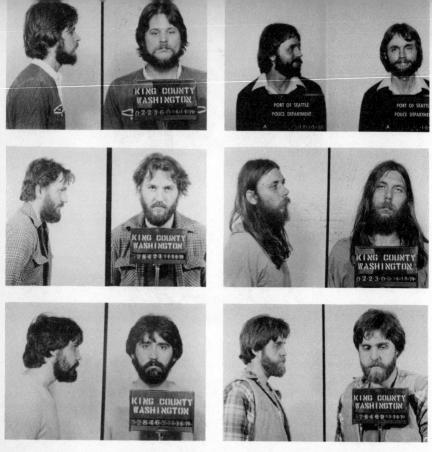

Lineup photos arranged by Detective Ronald Parker and seen by seventeen-year-old Nancy Van Roper, who was raped on October 12, 1980, in Seattle. "This one is the closest," she said, pointing to Steve Titus (*upper right-hand corner*). "It has to be this one." Titus was convicted, but charges were later dropped when another man confessed.

Steven Gary Titus in 1981. (*Greg Gilbert/Seattle Times*)

Accused serial killer Ted Bundy, presenting his own motions in the Miami courtroom where he was on trial for the clubbing deaths of two Florida State University coeds in January 1978. Eleven years later, Bundy was put to death in the electric chair. (*AP/Wide World*)

Sgt. Timothy B. Hennis, who was sentenced to death for the murder of a mother and her two children in 1985. In 1989, Sgt. Hennis went on trial for a second time. His lawyers uncovered two "Mr. X" letters and produced a surprise witness. On April 19, 1989, Timothy Hennis was acquitted. *(Photo courtesy Angela Hennis)*

DEAR MR HENNIS,
        I DID THE CRIME,
I MURDERED THE
EASTBURNS.
SORRY YOU'RE DOIN
THE TIME.
I'll BE SAFELY OUT OF
NORTH CAROLINA WHEN YOU
READ THIS. THANKS,
        MR X

The first of two "Mr. X" letters, received by Timothy Hennis in March 1987. A second letter was mailed to the Cumberland County sheriff's department in July 1987: *"I'm passing thru Fayetteville on my way to New Jersey. I murdered the Eastburns. I did the crime, Hennis is doing the time. Thanks again. Mr. X."*

Howard Haupt, charged with first-degree murder and kidnapping in the death of
seven-year-old Billy Chambers, in front of the Clark County Courthouse in Las
Vegas, Nevada. He was acquitted of the crime.

Clarence Von Williams (*left*), a forty-two-year-old chemical-plant worker, was sentenced to fifty years in prison for raping a woman and her teenage daughter. Williams's attorney, Louis Dugas (*right*), tears up a motion for retrial after received the news that another man confessed to the crime. (*Pete Churton*)

A photocopy of the alleged Soviet I.D. card, placing "Ivan Demjanjuk" at the Trawniki S.S. training camp in Poland in 1942. The U.S. Department of Justice stripped John Demjanjuk of his American citizenship and extradited him to Israel for trial.

John Demjanjuk listens to his defense lawyer Mark O'Connor, who accused an American documents expert of giving fraudulent testimony about an S.S. identity card allegedly issued to the defendant. *(AP/Wide World)*

Elizabeth Loftus *(left)*, Tyrone Briggs *(center)*, and Joanne Spencer in front of Briggs's Seattle home, March 1990, two months before Briggs's third trial for a series of muggings and attempted rapes. On June 14, 1990, prosecutors dropped all charges against the twenty-three-year-old former high school basketball star.

elderly man with a cap that sticks up on his head and a child yells out, 'That looks like a penis on his head.'

"Assume, then, that Katie comes home from seeing these movies, tells her mother that she saw some movies, her mother asks her questions and eventually Katie says, 'Did you know "dick" is another word for "penis"?' At which point the mother starts to question her more intensively about what she did at camp, what she saw, and Katie says she saw a girl with long blond hair flying through the air and a penis on a man's head."

Kurzman placed his notes on the defense table and walked slowly toward the witness stand. "Based on your experience and knowledge and based on the information in the movies that you saw, do you have an opinion about whether the child might have been relating an experience of reality that she had actually seen a blond lady flying through the air or a man with a penis on his head, or do you think the child might have mixed up reality and fantasy, mixing in pieces from the films and from the questions asked by the mother after the films were shown?"

"Objection!" the prosecutor called out. "Your Honor, I'd like to request a sidebar." ("Requesting a sidebar" is lawyers' jargon for "I'd like to speak to you privately, Your Honor.") The judge motioned both lawyers to the bench. I listened to the whisperings, the occasionally raised voices, and felt only slightly guilty about my eavesdropping. Sometimes during these sidebar conversations I would get flashbacks to my junior high school days when a group of girls would be huddled in a corner of the cafeteria, whispering and looking in my direction. Feeling left out and vulnerable, I'd watch them out of the corner of my eye, pretending not to notice, my cheeks flushed with the suspicion that they were talking about me, making fun of my clothes, my braces, or my new haircut.

I felt Tony Herrerez's eyes on me, but when I looked over at the defense table, he dropped his head and sat there for those long silent moments, staring down at the polished wood table. I could see his feet underneath the table, all dressed up in black leather shoes, newly polished, still as stones. He was a young man, maybe nineteen or twenty years old, slender and slightly awkward. He didn't seem to know what to do with his hands. He'd fold them, put them in his lap, place them palm down on the table, and drum his fingers against the hard wood. Suddenly he'd look guiltily at the jury and fold his hands back together again, squeezing so hard I could see the tension in his jaw muscles.

"Do you remember the question?" the judge suddenly asked me. The lawyers were walking back to their respective tables.

"Can I hear it again?" I said. The court reporter read back Kurzman's question—did I have an opinion about whether the children were relating a real experience or were mixing up fantasy and reality?

"Go ahead and answer," the judge commanded.

It was a comfort to fill that lonely courtroom with sound, to talk about my work and my laboratory, to explain the facts I understood and could control. "It's clear from looking at the movies that there was a woman with long blond hair in at least two of those movies," I said, "and it's certainly a possibility, given my work and the work of others, that one child would pick up the verbal expressions of another child. The phrase 'a penis on the head' could be picked up and integrated with other facts, and this would simply be the normal workings of memory."

"Assume, generally speaking," Kurzman said, "that a five-year-old child sees the movies that you and I and the jury have seen, and that child is not questioned about the content of those movies until seven weeks later. Would that seven-week period of time generally have any significance in that child's ability to accurately relate details of what she had seen?"

"In my opinion, that seven-week period is a significant period. In some of the studies that I referred to earlier, in which young children have been questioned about their memories, even after three days there is a significant memory loss. I can only extrapolate from that, and it would be a reasonable scientific extrapolation, that seven weeks would cause even more severe memory problems."

"Assume then," Kurzman said, "that one to two weeks after the seven weeks, or approximately during the first week of September, a five-year-old child who had been questioned for the previous nine weeks about what she saw and what happened at camp suddenly related that a man stuck his penis in her mouth. Assume that eight or nine weeks after an act allegedly occurred, a child who had been informed of the mechanisms of oral sex said that she had experienced oral sex. Would that nine-week period be significant with regard to the deterioration of an actual memory and with regard to the susceptibility of the implantation of the idea of oral sex?"

"Yes," I answered, "the nine-week period would be significant, and one would want to know about the intervening questioning and just exactly how suggestive it was and whether it could have produced the memory."

Kurzman abruptly switched the subject. "As part of your teaching experience, have you taught people the proper ways to question someone in order to determine the reality of their experience and to avoid implanting ideas in their minds as you question them?"

"Yes, I've lectured to police, state patrol, and other groups of law enforcement officers on the proper ways to question people to get the most accurate and complete answers."

"Do you have an opinion about whether a properly trained person in interviewing techniques, someone who interviewed a five-year-old child who had already been questioned for two months, would be able to determine whether the information received by the proper investigation was an accurate reflection of reality or a mix of fact and fantasy?"

"I do have an opinion." This, of course, was a crucial part of my testimony as an expert witness on memory. "Once someone's memory has been contaminated, distorted, or transformed by the processes I've been talking about, by suggestive questioning or by other kinds of postevent suggestions, it's virtually impossible to distinguish fact from fantasy because the individual witness now believes in what he or she is saying."

"And therefore," Kurzman said, "if a five- or six-year-old child was relating a story that contained contamination, fantasy, implantation, would this child be making a false accusation as the child understood it?"

"The child would not be making a false accusation," I said. "It's certainly possible that children can lie, and do lie, but we're talking here about children who honestly believe what they are saying, but they are saying it because of the suggestive influences that have been exerted either advertently or inadvertently upon them."

"Thank you," Kurzman said. "I have no further questions."

Although it was important to appear in control, the rational scientist, my heart always speeds up a little before the prosecutor's cross-examination.

The prosecutor was tall and thin, with a long, straight nose, side-

burns that looked like they were trimmed with a ruler, and fingernails neatly clipped and shiny, as if they'd been buffed.

"Good morning, Doctor," he said, his smile definitely forced. I'd
never met a prosector who was happy to see me in the courtroom.
"Ma'am, my name is *Ted Blanchard*, and I'm the prosecuting attorney in this case. Just so I understand, how much of your time or
your duties is involved in actually working with children, aged four,
five, or six, who have been sexually abused?"

"I don't work with children who have been sexually abused," I
answered. "I study memory."

"Okay. You study memory generally and then you apply what
you've learned in that area to four-, five-, and six-year-olds who may
have been sexually abused?"

"Yes, I study memory in general and I apply it to people's or
children's memory for events or experiences that occurred in their
past."

"Have you ever had any contact with female children, ages four,
five, or six, who have been sexually abused?"

The judge interrupted. "Maybe it's just a matter of curiosity, but
are you a treating psychologist or a research psychologist or some
combination thereof? Do you have patients or do you do research
or both?"

"Your Honor, I do research. I work in a laboratory, or sometimes
I do field studies of people's memories of their experiences."

The judge sat back in his chair and tapped his pencil against the
desk, nodding at the prosecutor.

"So, as far as your research, and whatever it is that you do,"
Blanchard said, his tone thin as spring ice, "your particular work
does not put you in a position where you have personal contact with
children who have been abused. Is that correct?"

"Right. I don't see children who are claiming that they've been
sexually abused." Blanchard was making a determined effort to show
that I had no business being in this courtroom, offering my "scientific" opinion in a case involving real live people. His questions
were heavy with the implication that I belonged in the laboratory
and I should stay there. Research psychologists should stick with
the rats.

"Have you ever talked with children who have been sexually
abused or are suspected of being sexually abused?" Blanchard was

doing something funny with his ear, pulling at the lobe and then running his index finger along the curve. He looked at me with obvious disdain: "You really don't know anything about five-year-old children who have been sexually abused, do you?"

The memory flew out at me, out of the blackness of the past, hitting me full force.

"Well, yes, I do," I said. "I do know something about this subject because I was abused when I was six years old."

Blanchard's finger stopped at midcurve, the thin smile disappeared from his lips, and he looked at me, his eyes wide and astonished. It took him a few seconds to find his voice. "You remember that?" he said.

"I remember. Yes, I do." My eyes held Blanchard's, but my mind wasn't registering his features. Instead I saw Howard the baby-sitter who used to sit next to me on the sofa and rub my arm, using the back of his hand against the smooth skin, his fingers following the gentle curve from wrist to elbow and up for a second, then back down. Back and forth, a gentle curve, a sweet touch, soft, comforting, lulling. I remembered that Howard told me that babies came from eggs that hatched, and I remembered him telling me never to tell anybody about the things he told me, never to tell anyone about the way he touched my arm. "It's our secret," he whispered.

One night after my younger brothers had gone to bed and after Howard had rubbed my arm for a while, he took my hand and led me into my parents' bedroom. He took his pants off, pulled my dress off over my head, and removed my underpants. He lay down on the bed and pulled me on top of him, positioning me so that our pelvises touched. His arms circled around me, I felt him pushing against me, and I knew something was wrong. Embarrassed and confused, I squirmed off him and ran out of the room. After that, there is only blackness in my memory, full and total darkness with not a pinhole of light. Howard is simply gone, vanished, sucked away. My memory took him and destroyed him.

I realized Blanchard was asking me a question, and my mind came back to the present.

"I don't want to go into a lot," Blanchard was saying, his eyes still wide. "I'm not going to ask any specific details, but do you remember the details surrounding that incident?"

"I do have some details in mind," I said. "It involved a baby-sitter. I remember some things. I can't tell you exactly how accurate they are, but I do remember."

"I hate to ask you the next question." Blanchard was regaining his composure. He tried to inject some sarcasm into his next statements, but it was obvious that he wished the whole subject would just disappear. "I'm assuming that's some period of time ago. How many years ago was that?"

"Approximately thirty-five years ago," I said.

Blanchard abruptly changed the subject. "You've testified here today that some of your time has been spent testifying on behalf of prosecutors; is that correct?"

"I didn't use the word 'testify.' I said I have done work for prosecutors."

"Done work for. I'm sorry." The thin veneer of courtesy barely concealed his contempt. "If at any time I say something that isn't accurate, let me know, and I'll rephrase it.

"Did you talk to any of the police officers involved in the case?"

"No, I didn't."

"Did you talk to any of the parents or the children who were involved in this case?"

"No."

"Did you talk to any members of the prosecutor's office?"

"I did not, no."

"So all the facts that you have are one-sided, or at least came from one side?"

"No, I would not agree to that because I read the full transcript of the April nineteen eighty-five hearing and—"

"How about the grand jury transcripts, did you ever see those?"

"No."

"Well, you're not aware of all the facts involving this particular case. It would be impossible for you to say yes to that, would it not, obviously?"

I just had to say it. "When you ask a leading question like that, I guess the answer is yes."

Blanchard's look could have killed. He fumbled with his papers and tried one more tack.

"You testified—and correct me if I'm wrong—that you can remember events when you were six years old. My question to you would be—while the passage of time may generally cause a decaying in memory, there are certain specific events that stay with us even well into our adult years. Isn't that correct?"

"There are some events that do stay with us, yes."

"And some of those events are significant and some are insignificant, wouldn't you agree with that?"

"The more significant and heavily rehearsed events would tend to be the ones that stay with us."

"Heavily rehearsed events." Blanchard started playing with his ear again. "Well, you're not saying that someone forty years old can't remember events back when the person was five or six years of age, even when these events weren't rehearsed, are you?"

"It is possible to remember," I conceded.

"By rehearsed, do you mean the person thinks about it in their own mind, or they rehearse it with some other individual?"

"Usually they either think about it repeatedly or tell other people about it."

"And again, that doesn't necessarily affect the quality of that person's ability to remember that particular incident."

"In fact, it depends on how you think about it. If you think about it on your own, without any suggestive influences, then the potential for contamination of the memory is substantially reduced."

With a lame "Thank you, ma'am," Blanchard announced the end of his questioning.

"You are free to return to wherever you're going to," the judge said, pointing with his pencil at the heavy wooden door to the courtroom. He called a recess, and Kurzman walked me down the long stone stairway of the courthouse to hail a cab to take me to the airport. As the taxi pulled up, Kurzman put his hand on my shoulder. "I can't thank you enough for being willing to share that memory," he said.

"I'm not sure I had any choice," I said.

Kurzman was quiet for a moment. "You know, those of us who defend people accused of sexually abusing children are despised and reviled right along with the defendant. People think we must be sick too. Your spontaneous disclosure will help the jury to appreciate the fact that you are sympathetic to the plight of sexually abused children. In that moment in the courtroom, you became more than an expert—you became human."

We shook hands, and I wished him luck. Ten hours later I was back in my house, looking out my window at the moon spreading silver on the lake, exhausted but sleepless, too tired to pull myself back into the present or to dream about the future, too absorbed by that scene in my parents' bedroom when Howard the baby-sitter betrayed my trust, stole my innocence, and put an indelible impression, a bad, black memory into the place where only good, warm, happy memories should be.

"Howard," I whispered out into the night, into the dozens of years that separated me from my childhood, "I hate your guts."

One morning in the middle of September, less than two weeks after I testified in Chicago, my phone rang. It was 6:30 A.M., I'd been sound asleep, and in a panic I started pushing at the alarm clock buttons, trying to make the buzzing go away. Finally realizing the source of all the noise, I reached over and picked up the telephone receiver, mumbling hello.

"Tony was acquitted this morning," Kurzman said, without even introducing himself.

"Acquitted?" I said, rubbing my eyes. "That's wonderful!"

"And lucky," Kurzman said.

"Why do you say lucky?" I asked. The facts, it seemed to me, were straightforward. The only evidence against Tony was the "word of the children," and there was striking evidence in the mother's diary that indicated that the child's accusations could have been "created" through rewards and reinforcements. The so-called pornographic movies simply did not exist; they, too, appeared to be imagined.

Kurzman told me that there was a racist on the jury who repeatedly made derogatory remarks about minorities during deliberations. An alternate juror called Kurzman after the first day of deliberations and told him about the juror's remarks. Kurzman went to the judge, the deliberations were halted, and the jurors were brought in one at a time for questioning. Four jurors admitted that one of the jurors made racist remarks. The judge was extremely upset. Before allowing deliberations to continue, he carefully instructed the jury to ignore all derogatory comments and decide the case on the evidence. The jury deliberated for three more days before returning with an acquittal.

"Believe me," Kurzman said, "after watching this case come to trial based on the flimsiest of evidence, and after witnessing the biases in the jurors—biases not only against this particular defendant who is a minority, but the inherent bias against anyone accused of molesting a child—I can't help wondering how many innocent people are locked up in prison for these crimes. Let me tell you another story."

I was sitting up in bed, the covers pulled up, one hand trying to hold my unruly hair back from my face. I looked at my alarm clock. Did Kurzman have any idea what time it was on the West Coast?

"I just got a new case. A male schoolteacher is accused of sexually abusing one of his students. I had this man go through a bunch of tests—voice stress, polygraphs, psychological profiles—believe me, I don't want to fly around the country defending guilty people any more than the next guy. After all the test results came in, I felt there was a damned good chance this man was innocent. So I went to the cops and I said, look, first give this man some tests, any test you want, but don't automatically charge him with this crime or his career is over, even if he is eventually acquitted. The cops stared at me like I was nothing, like they could see right through me. In their eyes I was smut, scum for defending a guy like this.

"I left feeling sick to my stomach, but one of the cops followed me out of the room. 'I can get in a lot of trouble for this,' he said, 'but I think you're straight, I think you really believe that this guy is innocent. I gotta tell you, though, this is not a trumped-up charge, we have proof that this kid was abused.' How do you know? I asked him. 'The kid has gonorrhea of the mouth,' the cop told me. I asked him when the tests were confirmed and he said just a few days earlier. So I hustled my client down to the hospital for a blood test, and he was absolutely clean, no gonorrhea. It was a scientific impossibility that he could have abused this little boy.

"Now I'll tell you the really scary part about this story. The prosecutor's office wanted to keep this information secret so that they could nail my client. If that cop hadn't told me about the gonorrhea, by the time of the trial it would have been too late for my client to use a blood test to exonerate himself. He would have been found guilty—ninety percent of these child-abuse cases end in convictions—he probably would have lost his career, been shut up in jail, and marked for life as a child abuser. Which, as we all know, is worse than a murderer. His life would have been over except for that one honest cop."

I heard voices in the background, heard Kurzman say "Yeah, okay, just a second," and then he came back on to say he had to get off, somebody was waiting for him, how could he ever thank me, and, meanwhile, thanks again for the Howard story. Then he was gone. I hung up the phone and smiled.

A drawer had opened up, way back in the deepest recesses of my mind, and out of that drawer like an old-fashioned jumping jack popped up a memory. It was Howard. He had no features, I couldn't tell if his hair was straight or curly, if he was fat or skinny, pimply or clear-complexioned, tall or short. But the scene was amazingly clear. Faceless, featureless Howard and I were sitting on the couch in my living room, and he was scratching my arm, gently, with just the tips of his nails, up from my hand, over the elbow, and then back down, back and forth, over and over again.

This time the memory brought no pain with it. This time the memory brought a feeling of triumph. Howard, I thought, you slimy son of a bitch. You were guilty, and no one ever found you out. But now, thirty-five years later, you've come to some good. I used that memory to help someone else, someone who was innocent.

Sitting in bed, watching the sky lighten up and the clouds turn from blue to pink to cream, I let myself imagine what Howard looked like now. He must be fifty-five years old, I figured, smiling at the unpleasant features my mind was putting on his blank face. He would have warts and age spots and prematurely balding gray hair. With that image in mind, I said good-bye to my memories of Howard. Good-bye and good riddance.

I let myself think, then, about the children. Katie Davenport and Paige Becker would believe for the rest of their lives that they had been abused on a summer day at camp in a cozy suburb of Chicago. These two little girls had spent almost one-third of their lives remembering and reciting the details of their victimization by a young man they once trusted and liked. They had internalized these details and incorporated them into their very identity.

There was no doubt in my mind that the children believed in their own stories. And thus, in the most profound sense of the word, they were telling the truth. If a memory that is false is believed to be true—if either Katie or Paige believed with all her heart that she had been molested—who could call her a liar? And so the question "do you believe the children?" is not really the right question. The crucial question, the question we should be asking is this: "Is this child's memory an original truth, or an after-the-fact truth?"

Tony Herrerez might be innocent in the eyes of the law, but in the eyes of these children, children whose memories would grow old with them, there would always and forever be the image of that summer day in July 1984 when Tony touched them in "bad places." That was their memory, the beginning of the end of their innocence, and they would live with the sight, the sound, and the touch of it for all the days of their lives.

"I COULDN'T DO THIS TO A CHILD": HOWARD HAUPT

"Justice would less often miscarry if all who are to weigh evidence were more conscious of the treachery of human memory. Yes, it can be said that, while the court makes the fullest use of all the modern scientific methods when, for instance, a drop of dried blood is to be examined in a murder case, the same court is completely satisfied with the most unscientific and haphazard methods of common prejudice and ignorance when a mental product, especially the memory report of a witness, is to be examined."
—Hugo Munsterberg, *On the Witness Stand*

Seven-year-old *Billy Chambers* waved good-bye to his parents and faced the video machine. Oh, boy, he thought, a whole hour and a pocket full of quarters! He couldn't wait to tell Jason, his best friend back in Corvallis, Oregon, about this trip. California was awesome, the Grand Canyon was amazing, but Las Vegas—well, he'd never seen so many video machines in his life.

He put a quarter in the machine—it was called Grand Prix—and watched the road grab the car like some giant super-fast escalator. He drove faster and faster, trying to beat the other cars to the finish line, swerving to avoid the hazards and obstacles along the way. He skidded on an oil slick, veered off the road, just missed a brick wall, got back on the road, hit a curve going maybe a hundred miles an hour and *boom!* crashed right into a Corvette. Crash! Burn!

Billy played two more games and then wandered around the room, watching other kids play. He stopped next to a girl—probably a fourth or fifth grader, he thought—and watched her fiddling with the controls at a machine called Hang On.

"The machine's not on," he said, looking over her shoulder. "You have to put a quarter in."

"I know," she answered, continuing to move the joysticks. He shrugged. Maybe she didn't have any quarters left.

Somebody grabbed his arm then, the fingers pressing hard against the small bones of his wrist, and Billy turned around, too surprised to voice his indignation. The hand grabbing his wrist belonged to a stranger, a man in a tan jacket. Billy tried to pull his arm away but the stranger held on tight and started to yank Billy toward the door of the video arcade. Billy was scared now. Who was this guy? Why was he holding onto him so tight? The man, sensing Billy's panic, leaned down and said, "I'm a hotel security guard. Your parents asked me to come get you."

Billy stopped resisting. Something must have happened to his parents and the man had been sent to get him. What could have happened? Thoughts just whirled around in his head, as the man led him out of the video arcade, down the hallway toward the casino. Then he turned abruptly and pulled Billy along with him up the stairs to the second floor.

Why are we going upstairs? Billy's heart was beating fast, he could feel it bumping around in his chest. "Where are we going?" Billy finally asked, his voice just barely above a whisper. He felt like crying, but he pushed the tears back. "To your mother," the man answered, his voice hoarse, as if he had a cold.

They continued walking down the second-floor hallway, passing a man with a suitcase, and then the man holding Billy's wrist turned around again, pulling the boy back down the same hallway and stairs. He was walking really fast now, and the hand gripping Billy's wrist felt slippery with sweat.

They walked through the lobby, which was crowded with hotel guests waiting to check out. At the entrance to the gift shop, a woman looked up at the stranger and said, "Hello, Tom." The man hesitated for a second, mumbled hello, and, walking even faster now, pulled the terrified boy down the long carpeted hallway and out the front door of the casino.

It was approximately 11:20 A.M. on the morning after Thanksgiving, November 27, 1987.

At 11:10 A.M. *Joan Chambers* left the slot machine where she had lost $7.50 in twenty minutes and returned to the video arcade to check on Billy. She walked into the arcade, scanning the room. Billy wasn't there. She looked again more carefully, walking from one machine to the next. No, he definitely was not there. She suppressed a momentary panic. Billy probably ran out of quarters and was looking for her right now in the crowded casino. She walked quickly back to the casino. Her husband was playing the dollar slots.

"Have you seen Billy?" she said. "I can't find him in the arcade."

Jack Chambers swung the arm down on the machine and watched in disgust as the slots registered two lemons and a cherry. Another buck down the drain. He took his wife's hand, and they hurriedly searched the crowded casino before returning to the arcade. They looked in the lobby, the first-floor restaurant, the gift shop, and the bathrooms. At 11:25 A.M. they contacted hotel security, and within ten minutes hotel security officers were searching the hotel for a seven-year-old boy with straight blond hair and thick prescription glasses, wearing Reeboks shoes and a red Polar Fleece jacket.

At 11:45 A.M a departing hotel guest noticed the commotion and stopped one of the security officers. "I saw a little boy upstairs with his father," the man said, looking at his watch, "maybe twenty minutes ago."

"His father?" The guard asked.

"Yeah, they looked a lot alike. The man was holding the boy by the wrist and sort of pulling him down the hallway. I thought the boy was being scolded for something. He looked sort of dumbfounded."

By noon the head of security had alerted the Las Vegas police department to a possible kidnap situation. For the next forty-eight hours, an extensive investigation was conducted by the Robbery/Kidnap Section of the Las Vegas police and the Las Vegas office of the FBI. Five eyewitnesses identified Billy from his first-grade photograph, which showed a smiling, gap-toothed boy with straight blondish hair combed down over his forehead and glasses so large that the edges of his sweet, slightly goofy smile almost hit the bottom rim. His right eye appeared to wander off slightly.

The descriptions of the man holding the boy's hand were not so consistent. Four adult eyewitnesses had seen the man and boy together: *Charles Crouter*, the hotel guest who passed them in the second-floor hallway; *John* and *Susan Picha*, both employees of the hotel, who had seen the man and boy in the first-floor hallway; and *Gwen Margolis*, a 21 dealer who said hello to the man by the gift shop. In general they described a white male, thirty-five to forty years old, between five feet seven and six feet tall, 160 to 180 pounds, with sandy blond to medium-brown hair, wearing thick, wire-frame glasses, a tan jacket, and blue jeans. Several of the witnesses commented that the man and boy looked like father and son. "So that's what a nerd grows up to look like," Susan Picha remembered joking to her husband as they passed the man and boy in the hallway.

Alison Martinek, the eleven-year-old who had talked briefly with Billy in the video arcade, described a tall man with dark-brown hair, a stocky build, and two birthmarks or scars on his forehead. He was wearing blue jeans, Reeboks shoes, and dark glasses, she told police.

Working from the eyewitness descriptions, an artist's composite sketch was drawn up and released to newspapers and TV stations, which featured the kidnapping as their top story. Police officers conducted lengthy interviews with the eyewitnesses, which were tape-recorded and then transcribed. Gwen Margolis, the 21 dealer, claimed that she knew the man with the boy. His name was *Tom Spendlove* and he worked in the hotel kitchen. Detectives interviewed Spendlove and included his photograph in a photo lineup, which they then showed to the other four eyewitnesses. John and Susan Picha immediately pointed to Spendlove as the man they had seen with the boy. Charles Crouter selected *José Garcia*, also a hotel employee, as the man who looked most like the man he'd seen on the second-floor hallway. Alison Martinek insisted that the man she saw with the boy wasn't in the pictures.

Airtight alibis eventually cleared Tom Spendlove and José Garcia, and the investigation continued during the month of December with little progress. Hundreds of hot tips phoned into the police department turned into hot air. One woman claimed she'd seen Billy Chambers on the street, but the boy turned out to be twelve years old. A man called to report someone who resembled the composite picture being shown on television; the man was forty-five years old and most of his front teeth were missing. An anonymous female called in to report a convicted sex offender who was out on parole; but he was eighteen years old and had a solid alibi.

On December 30, 1987, at approximately 11:00 A.M., a hotel groundskeeper was picking up litter and spotted a pair of glasses near the trailer occupied by the hotel manager, about two hundred yards from the hotel. He bent down to pick up the glasses and saw the body of a young boy lying face down under the rear portion of the trailer. He immediately notified his supervisor, who notified hotel security, who in turn notified Las Vegas police. Billy's mother and father, who were staying with relatives in Las Vegas, were brought to the scene. Yes, they said, tears streaming down their grief-stricken faces, that was Billy.

Responsibility for the case was turned over to the Homicide Section of the Las Vegas police. An autopsy was conducted, and after scientific testing, pathologists concluded that Billy Chambers died from mechanical blockage of the airway resulting in suffocation. The condition of the body, the pathologist reported, appeared to be consistent with the date of the disappearance. There was no evidence of sexual assault.

Homicide detectives obtained a complete computer printout of all guests at the hotel on the day of Billy's disappearance. They were particularly interested in guests registered on the second floor, since that's where Charles Crouter, the departing hotel guest, saw Billy and the man. Driver's license photos and identifying information of male hotel guests registered on the second floor were obtained from the Nevada and California departments of motor vehicles.

Only one photograph bore any significant resemblance to the descriptions given by the eyewitnesses. Howard Haupt was thirty-seven years old, six feet tall, 145 pounds, and had blond hair and blue eyes. The accompanying photo showed that he parted his hair on the left and wore wire-frame eyeglasses. Mr. Haupt registered at the hotel on November 25, 1987 and checked out on November 28. His room number was 229, located on the second floor of the south wing in close proximity to the area where Charles Crouter saw an adult male holding Billy Chambers's hand and pulling him down the hallway.

On January 13, 1988, homicide detectives sent Howard Haupt a letter, asking that he voluntarily submit to being photographed and fingerprinted for the purpose of aiding detectives in their investigation into the death of Billy Chambers. The detectives worded the letter in such a way that Mr. Haupt would believe that all guests of the hotel and casino were being asked to cooperate with authorities, and that he was not considered a suspect. In the meantime, police received a Polaroid copy of a color photograph of Howard Haupt from his employer, San Diego Data Processing Center. A photographic lineup was prepared, using five additional photographs, which were rephotographed on Polaroid film to appear similar to Haupt's photograph.

On January 15, 1988, John and Susan Picha were interviewed separately and shown the photo lineup. Susan Picha was unable to make an identification. After intensive questioning, John Picha stated that he thought number 3—Howard Haupt—was the closest, but he could not be certain. "I've seen so many photographs," he said, referring to the hundreds of mug shots he'd been shown in the seven weeks since Billy Chambers's disappearance, "that it's starting to get foggy."

On January 18, Gwen Margolis, the 21 dealer, was shown the same photo lineup. She selected number 3—Howard Haupt—and when asked to characterize her identification on a scale of 1 (uncertain) to 10 (certain), replied "I would say an eight."

On January 21, Charles Crouter was flown to San Diego and taken to Howard Haupt's workplace. The purpose of the visit was to see if he could make an in-person identification. When Mr. Haupt walked by on his way into work from the parking lot, Mr. Crouter said, "I want to see him again." Later, when asked if he recognized anyone, Charles Crouter said, "The man in the tan jacket is the man I saw with the young boy at the hotel." The man in the tan jacket was Howard Haupt.

Mr. Crouter was then shown the photo lineup. He selected number 3—Howard Haupt—as the man he had identified from his visit to the bank. Asked to characterize the certainty of his identification on a scale of 1 to 10, he stated "Seven and a half to eight."

On February 5 detectives accompanied Gwen Margolis to the data processing center. She recognized Mr. Haupt as the individual she had seen with the child. Now she was even more certain, she said, characterizing her identification on a 1–10 scale by stating "I would say probably about a nine."

On February 3 another certified letter, return receipt requested, was sent to Mr. Haupt, who had not responded to the first letter. Six days later, on February 9, Howard Haupt called the San Diego Sheriff's Office and made an appointment to meet with detectives on February 11 at 5:30 P.M. The deputy sheriff casually asked Mr. Haupt why he hadn't responded to the first letter. "I didn't think they needed me," Haupt replied. "The letter wasn't really for me."

On February 11, at approximately 7:30 A.M., John and Susan Picha were flown from Las Vegas to San Diego and taken to Mr. Haupt's workplace, where they identified him as the man they had seen with the boy. They rated their identification as "between a nine and a ten." Later, when they were again shown the color lineup, John Picha pointed to number 3 and said, "This is the man I saw. Seeing him in person fits more than the picture does."

On February 16, 1988, a formal criminal complaint was filed in the justice court, *The State of Nevada, Plaintiff, vs. Howard Haupt, Defendant*. The crimes were counted out with all the flourishes and formalities that mark our legal language:

The Defendant above named, has committed the crimes of FIRST DEGREE KIDNAPPING and MURDER in the manner following, to wit:
COUNT I—FIRST DEGREE KIDNAPPING
did willfully, unlawfully, feloniously, and without authority of law, lead, take, entice, carry away, or detain WILLIAM FENNO CHAMBERS, a minor, with the intent to keep, imprison, or confine said WILLIAM FENNO CHAMBERS from his parents, guardians, or other person or persons having lawful custody of said minor, or with the intent to hold said minor to unlawful service, or perpetrate upon the person of said minor any unlawful act, to wit: sexual gratification.
COUNT II—MURDER
did then and there, without authority of law and with malice aforethought, willfully and feloniously kill WILLIAM FENNO CHAMBERS, a human being, by mechanical blockage of the airway resulting in the suffocation of the said WILLIAM FENNO CHAMBERS.
All of which is contrary to the form, force, and effect of Statutes in such cases made and provided and against the peace and dignity of the State of Nevada.

In layman's language, Howard Haupt was being charged with first-degree kidnapping and murder in the state of Nevada. If convicted, he could face the death penalty.

Steve Stein was a man with a mission. I put him on the speaker phone so I could take notes while he talked, but I had to keep fighting the urge to put my hands over my ears as his baritone filled the airspace in my tiny office. File cabinets seemed to squeeze in on me from all sides, the steel custodians of my history at the University of Washington. Each year, as more files were added, the space for walking, talking, and breathing gradually diminished. Soon I would be squeezed out, like that scene in *Star Wars* when the walls begin to move inward, an efficient but merciless garbage compactor. Sometimes, sitting in my swivel chair, I'd put my feet against the metal file cabinets, keeping up a gentle but steady push. It made me feel like I was in control.

"This man is innocent!" Stein thundered. "I'm one hundred thousand percent convinced, there's absolutely no doubt in my mind. No physical evidence whatsoever links Howard Haupt to this crime. It's an eyewitness case, pure and simple, and the eyewitness stories change so many times, it will make your head spin. Haupt is a scapegoat for the Las Vegas police, who were under so much heat for their molasseslike investigation that they arrested the first suspect they could find who fit the general description.

"Dr. Loftus," Stein continued, "I don't take cases involving child abuse or child kidnapping, because these are abominable crimes, the most heinous crimes a human being can commit. But when this case came up and I read all the news accounts, I said to myself, 'This doesn't sound like a verifiable case.' My partners told me I was crazy. We don't need a case like this, they said. But when Haupt was extradited from California, I went to the jail to see him. And I believed him, I believe he's innocent. I have twenty years' experience in criminal defense law, and in those twenty years I've had maybe five innocent clients. And let me tell you, after twenty years in this business you know whether or not a person is telling the truth. The body language, the eye contact, the background, the way the police built their case . . ."

A picture came into my mind of Steve Stein, a young, rather

reckless figure in a cowboy hat and leather chaps thrashing a foaming horse on a wild ride to save an innocent man from a bloodthirsty mob. I suppressed a desire to yell out "Whoa!" and instead interrupted his monologue by saying "Mr. Stein?"

"Yes?" He seemed relieved, actually. Time for a breather.

"Tell me about the eyewitness identification. The chief eyewitness—the little boy—is dead. Who are the others?"

Stein briefly outlined the five eyewitness accounts. "Howard Haupt was the only hotel guest who even remotely fit the description," he concluded. "And yet the description keeps changing over time, and not so subtly, I might add. A few days after Billy Chambers's disappearance, two of the eyewitnesses claimed the man had brown hair and was between 170 and 180 pounds. Haupt is blond and weighs 145 pounds. The little girl in the video arcade who saw the man grab the boy's hand described him as kind of 'stocky' and 'muscular' with two dark spots on his forehead, either sores or scars. Haupt is slender and has no scars or birthmarks on his face. One of the adult witnesses insisted the man had a full head of hair—and yet Haupt has a pronounced bald spot. Haupt has alibi witnesses—he was at a land sailing convention—but nobody is paying any attention to them. He has no criminal record, but the cops searched his apartment, found a copy of *Playboy*, and are now holding it up as evidence that he's a child molester. You get the idea. They find a suspect who looks good, and they subtly twist what little evidence they have to make him look even better."

Stein wasn't finished. "I put Haupt on three of the most rigorous polygraphs I could find, administered by tough-minded technicians who have been in the business a long time and are known to be suspicious of defendants. He passed every one. That's when I first thought, Hey, this guy might be innocent. So then I started digging and finding these little clues that the police were leading the eyewitnesses to their only suspect. Every single eyewitness picked out someone else and then in their interviews with police they were led by the nose, straight to Haupt.

"Meanwhile, here Haupt sits, like a bump on a log. He should be outraged, he should be yelling and screaming and exploding with wrath and indignation, and he just sits there cool as a cucumber and says, 'I didn't do it, I don't know what you're talking about.' I couldn't figure out what was going on with this guy. He was holding back his emotions; he had this solid wall around him. So one night in my office I broke him down. We were going through my direct examination, and I showed him the pictures of the little boy's dead body. He looked at the pictures, one after the other after the other, and suddenly his shoulders start to shake and he begins to cry. 'I didn't do this,' he said, 'I couldn't do this to a child. Take the pictures away.' I knew then and I'm telling you now that a guilty person confronted with these pictures would not react that way. Howard Haupt did not kill this little boy."

I felt that familiar flutter of excitement. "Mr. Stein," I said, "if you would send me everything you've got on the case—police reports, transcripts of eyewitness interviews, preliminary hearing transcripts—I'll review them immediately and let you know my decision about testifying."

"You got it," Stein said, and less than a day later, via a smiling Federal Express man who actually hummed "Twinkle, Twinkle Little Star" while I signed the receipt, I did.

I skimmed through each of the documents, sorting them into various piles—useful, semiuseful, and not very useful. Nothing is useless in this sort of work, where I sift through all the facts, looking for subtle clues, delicate word twists, innuendos, inferences, implications. Stacked on my desk were the voluntary eyewitness statements, handwritten memos from the Las Vegas police department, newspaper accounts, black-and-white reproductions of the photo lineups, Xeroxed full-page photos of Billy Chambers's school photo, so on and so on, ad infinitum. I estimated that Stein mailed me more than five hundred pages of information.

In the very last group of papers was the typed postmortem examination report. I threw it in the not-so-useful pile, but a grim sense of duty compelled me to pick it back up again. The first page gave a short history of Billy's disappearance, the discovery of the body, identification by relatives, and fingerprint confirmation. The next four pages, single spaced, typed, went into great detail on the external and internal state of the dead body. I read the entire report, and when I was finished, gently placed it back in the file.

The autopsy report had its intended effect, reminding me that a real person was dead, a healthy little boy who had a family, friends, classmates, a whole world that had been destroyed by a stranger with a deadly grip. Sometimes in the courtroom, taking our sides in the central argument over a defendant's guilt or innocence, we forget about the victim, and this is most likely to happen when the crime is murder and the victim is not there to remind us of his pain and agony. I filed the details of Billy's death in a back corner of my brain and vowed to myself that I wouldn't forget him.

Pushing my glasses back up my nose, I began reading the voluntary eyewitness statements. Three hours later I had twenty pages of handwritten notes, which I read over again, scribbling in the margins. Referring constantly to my notes and the witnesses' voluntary statements, I turned to my computer and typed up a short chronological list of each eyewitness identification.

SUSAN PICHA *(hotel chambermaid)*

11/29: Photo-identified another man as possibly being the subject.
12/4: Photo-identified a different man (still not Haupt) as closest to suspect.
1/15: Viewed photo lineup with Haupt in #3 position, did not ID Haupt; identified another unknown subject as being closest to suspect.
2/11: Walk-through of data processing center and review of photo lineup: identified Howard Haupt.

JOHN PICHA *(unemployed)*

11/29: Photo-identified another man as possibly being the suspect.
12/4: Photo-identified a different man, "90% sure."
1/15: Photo-identified Howard Haupt as closest to suspect. Admits to detectives, "I've seen so many, it's starting to get foggy."
2/11: Walk-through to Haupt's workplace and review of photo lineup: ID of Haupt, "9" on scale of 1–10. Told detectives, "He was in the picture I saw."

CHARLES CROUTER *(hotel guest)*

11/27: Described suspect as 5'7" to 5'9".
12/24: Described suspect as having light brown hair combed forward and tailored hairline not receding.

1/8: Described suspect as having full head of hair, no bald spot, 5'8" tall.

1/22: Walk-through of Haupt's workplace: identified him as the "individual that meets the description." On scale of 1–10, gives a "7–8" based on glasses and tan jacket worn by Haupt.

GWEN MARGOLIS (*21 dealer*)

12/3: Identified the man with the boy as "Tom Spendlove," a friend who works in the hotel kitchen. Estimates she saw the man with the boy for 3–4 minutes.

1/18: Described suspect as having light brown hair, 5'7–5'8" tall, slender build. Shown photo lineup, identified Haupt (#3): "3 is the closest, but I can't be sure." Gave her identification an "8" on a scale of 1–10.

2/5: Walk-through of Haupt's workplace; identified Haupt. "I recognize him from his photograph and from my original memory." Rates her identification a "9."

ALISON MARTINEK (*11-year-old in video arcade*)

12/3/87: Describes man in video arcade as tall, "kinda muscular," in his late thirties, wearing sunglasses, and with dark hair. "I'm pretty sure he had dark hair. It was dark brown."

1/9/88: Remembers seeing two dark red, almost black spots on the man's forehead, like "sores or a birthmark."

1/13/88: Showed the photo lineup. Did not identify Haupt (#3).

2/10/88: Identifies Haupt in in-person lineup. Rates her identification "9" on scale of 10.

I read through the lists again and again, and with each review, I became more confident. I couldn't state with absolute certainty that Howard Haupt was innocent—that wasn't my job, after all—but this case was chock full of eyewitness identification problems. I started a file on my computer—Stein/Haupt/Las Vegas/1989—and typed in the words "postevent information."

The crime occurred on November 27, 1987. All positive identifications of Howard Haupt occurred between mid-January and mid-February, seven to twelve weeks after the eyewitnesses saw the man with the boy. This is a reasonably long time during which memories for faces can fade, but more important, all of the eyewitnesses were exposed to a number of sources of postevent information that could have affected their original memory of the man and the boy. They studied artist sketches, they were shown numerous photos, mug shots, and photo lineups, and they were exposed to extensive television and newspaper coverage of the kidnapping and murder. The original memory, decimated by the passage of time, had become increasingly vulnerable to these postevent information sources.

Most people are unaware that new information can influence their original recollection of an event. They don't know that as we take new information in, it is gradually incorporated into our original memory. Believing that this metamorphosed memory is and always has been the *real* memory, the true, unalterable, indivisible copy of our primary experience all those months or years ago, we become fiercely committed to it.

I referred to the transcript of the conversation on November 27 between Charles Crouter and a detective from the Las Vegas police department.

DETECTIVE: You don't remember the hair being sparse on top?
CROUTER: No, sir.
DETECTIVE: You have no recollection of a bald spot?
CROUTER: I don't recollect any bald spot on this gentleman.
DETECTIVE: So your recollection is a full head of hair?
CROUTER: A full head of hair.

This interview was conducted on the day Billy disappeared, just hours after Charles Crouter had seen the man and boy together in the hotel hallway. Yet almost two months later, on January 22, Mr. Crouter identified Howard Haupt, who had a pronounced bald spot. What happened in those two months to change Crouter's mind? He'd seen pictures of Mr. Haupt, he'd read descriptions of the suspect, and he knew that he was looking for a man with a pronounced bald spot. His original memory of a full head of hair was wiped out, erased, by this new information, and the bald spot nestled comfortably into his memory, becoming in his mind the real and original memory.

Alison Martinek, the little girl in the video arcade, told the police on November 27 that the man she'd seen with the boy was stocky, muscular, had dark hair, and wore Reeboks. In the preliminary hearing held six months later, Steve Stein asked Alison these questions:

STEIN: Do you remember telling police officers that he was wearing low-top Reeboks?
ALISON: No.
STEIN: Do you remember telling them that he had dark-brown hair?
ALISON: No.
STEIN: Do you remember telling the police that the man was muscular and had a stocky build?
ALISON: No.

What, Stein asked, was Alison's memory *now*—now, the question implied, that she had been exposed to six months of questions, photos, mug shots, lineups and artist's composites?

ALISON: He was tall, had blond hair, was skinny, and he had a bony chin.

Which was, of course, a precise, detailed description of the defendant Howard Haupt.

I hit the return key on my computer three times and typed in the words *photo-biased identification.* Each of the eyewitnesses was exposed to a photograph of Howard Haupt before he or she made the in-person identification. It is conceivable, perhaps even likely, that Haupt was identified because his face looked familiar from viewing the other photographs and not because he was the man the witnesses had seen with the boy. Why would Susan Picha pass over Haupt's photograph on January 15 and then identify him on February 11? Why did Alison Martinek pass over Haupt's photograph on January 13 and then identify him on February 10? When Steve Picha positively identified Haupt at his workplace on February 11, why did he tell police, "He was in the pictures I saw"? It was at least a possibility that these eyewitnesses recognized Howard Haupt from the photographs they had been shown.

Unconscious transference was the third item on my list. Howard Haupt was a guest at the hotel on the day that Billy Chambers disappeared. All five eyewitnesses were either registered guests or employed at the hotel at the same time, and there were numerous opportunities for them to have seen Haupt in and around the premises. This exposure could have contributed to the sense of familiarity the witnesses experienced when they identified Haupt several months later.

Next on my list was *time estimates*. Jurors are aware that memory is better when you have a longer time to look at something, but they are often not aware that later, when a witness tries to estimate how long a particular event lasted, there is a strong tendency to overestimate its duration. In my own experiments, people who watched a thirty-second simulation of a bank robbery later remembered that it had lasted much longer; several people gave a time estimation of eight to ten minutes.

Gwen Margolis, the 21 dealer, told police that she observed the man with the boy for "three or four minutes." If she testified to this at the trial, the typical juror would take her testimony at face value, unaware of the strong tendency for people to overestimate the duration of events. Jurors would believe that she did indeed see the man and boy together for several minutes—a fairly significant amount of time in which to study them and make an accurate identification—and they would tend to give her identification of Howard Haupt more weight.

Confidence. Like most people, jurors tend to believe there is a strong relationship between how confident a witness is and how accurate he or she is. A witness who says "Yes, that is absolutely, positively the man I saw" would clearly be more convincing than someone who says "Well, yeah, I think that's the guy." Susan Picha was interviewed in mid-February after she identified Howard Haupt at his workplace. When asked to give a number representing her level of confidence on a scale of 1 to 10, with 1 meaning "definitely not the man she saw" and 10 indicating "absolutely him," she responded with a 10.

Gwen Margolis identified Howard Haupt on January 18, rating her confidence level as an "8." On February 5, having seen Haupt in person, she upgraded her confidence rating to a "9."

John Picha identified another suspect on December 4, saying he was "90 percent sure." On January 15 he identified Haupt as "the closest," adding "I've seen so many, it's starting to get foggy." On

February 11, he again identified Haupt and gave his ID a confidence rating of "9."

Charles Crouter identified Haupt on January 22, putting his confidence level at "7–8"—based on the glasses and tan jacket Haupt was wearing.

Each witness in this case originally identified someone other than Howard Haupt. As time passed and the witnesses were exposed to more pictures of Howard Haupt, they eventually identified him as the man they had seen with the boy. With each succeeding identification, they became more certain until the in-person ID when they all rated their identifications from 7½ to 10. In the trial the prosecutor would emphasize these confidence levels, leading the jurors to believe the witnesses were always confident and thus adding greater weight to the identifications.

I had one final area to document. I typed the words "suggestive questioning" into my computer and stared for several moments at the screen and the flashing line followed by empty amber space. Suggestive questions are phrased in such a way that they suggest a specific answer or lead a witness toward a specific conclusion. Suggestive questions, in short, can produce biased answers. But of all the different ways that memory can be distorted, this is the most subjective and thus the most difficult to prove. If you have a video- or audio tape of an interview, it can be relatively easy to track down the leading questions; but in written summaries of interviews, the officer often doesn't write down the precise questions but just gives the essence of the answers.

In this case I was lucky, because the witnesses' voluntary statements were tape-recorded and transcribed. I found one particularly striking example of suggestive questioning. On January 15, 1988, the police showed John and Susan Picha the photo lineup of six different people, with Howard Haupt in the number-3 position. Susan concluded by stating that she thought number 6 was the closest.

"But you are not picking out any of them?" the detective said.

"Right," she answered.

The interviewer then turned to John Picha, asking him to go through the photos, beginning with number 1. "Definitely not," he said to numbers 1 and 2. At number 3 he hesitated and said, "I'm stuck on . . . no, that one is too old. He didn't seem to be that old."

"Well, other than that?" the interviewer said. "I mean, is it similar?"

"Yeah."

Picha looked at numbers 4 and 5. Both were definite no's." At number 6 he said, "The face has a resemblance and the glasses I think, but the hair doesn't."

"So the only two in here that kind of ring your bells are number 6 and number 3?" the interviewer asked.

"Well, actually if you put that type of a hairdo"—Picha pointed to number 3—"with that type of a face"—he pointed to number 6—"I think you would come up with a clue."

"You like number 3's hair?"

"Yea. I think that's . . ."

"How about the glasses on number 3?"

"It was more this type of glasses," Picha answered, pointing to number 6.

"You want number 6's glasses on number 3?"

"Yeah."

"Okay, and you think number 3 is too old. How old do you think number 3 is?"

"In his forties."

"What is your estimate of the age in number 6?"

"In his thirties."

"Okay. So what rules out number 3 to you is just that he looks too old?"

"And the sideburns. I don't remember because this guy was pretty much clean-shaven."

"But his hair is similar configuration?"

"The hair, yeah, from the color too."

"That's another thing about the color. What do you think about the color of number 3's hair?" the interviewer asked.

"That's what I'm saying. I can't tell from this picture."

"It's difficult I know."

"Pictures are just so hard."

"But you don't see anyone there you are positive of?"

"No. Number 1 I know is not. Number 2 I know isn't. Number 5. Number 6 . . . I've seen so many, it's starting to get foggy. It's just so foggy now that I've seen so many things and so many people."

"Okay."

"But I'd say number 3 would be the closest."

"All right. Thanks."

Most people would look at that conversation and think nothing of it. Picha took his time, looking at all the different photographs, and the investigator asked helpful questions, keeping his witness on track, bringing up the little details he may not have noticed. Eventually Picha narrowed his choice down to number 3.

But when I read that conversation, red flags went flying all over the place. The cops had a firm suspect—number 3. The eyewitness hesitated at number 3 but then rejected him as too old. At number 6 he claimed that the face has a resemblance and the glasses, but not the hair.

If the suspect had been number 6, number 3 would have been forgotten and the conversation would have focused on number 6. But instead the interviewer went back through the photos, unintentionally communicating to his witness that he was not particularly interested in number 6. He said, "So number 3 and number 6 ring your bells." And "You like number 3's hair." And "You want number 6's glasses on number 3." And "You think number 3 is too old. How old do you think he is?"

All these questions focused the eyewitness's attention on number 3. How many times did the interviewer need to repeat "number 3" before his witness got the idea that, Hey, the cops sort of like this guy number 3, maybe number 3 is the guy I'm supposed to pick, maybe if I pick number 3, I'll make them happy and get this interview over with?

I couldn't know exactly what was going on in John Picha's mind during this interview, but I did know that it is relatively easy to plant an idea in someone's mind and then have that idea take over, blur the original memory, and slowly but surely become the dominant force. I found myself wishing that I could cut into memory, as if it were some solid piece of tissue with a clearly normal and metamorphosed state. Then, perhaps, I would be able to document exactly where, when, and how these memory distortions occur.

I looked back at my computer screen and reviewed my list: Post-event information; photo-biased identification; unconscious transference; time estimates; confidence; suggestive questioning.

I had taken all the facts of this case and placed them in my special categories, arriving at an overall picture that showed serious potential weaknesses in the eyewitness testimony—the very heart of the prosecution's case against Howard Haupt. Of course, this was *my* picture. The prosecution would paint a wholly different picture from the same facts. The defense attorney would choose his facts with care too, concentrating on the defendant's lack of criminal record, the absence of any physical evidence, the alibi witnesses. It was always fascinating to watch how these different "pictures" were presented in the courtroom and to hear which version the jury accepted as the truth.

I typed up my five-page synopsis of the Howard Haupt case, stuck it in an envelope along with my curriculum vita, and Express Mailed it to Steve Stein.

Howard Haupt's trial was scheduled for October 1988 but the judge had refused to allow my testimony, claiming that it would "invade the province of the jury." In effect, the judge was saying that it was the jury's job to decide whether the witnesses were in a position to see and hear what they claimed they saw and heard. An expert, this particular judge seemed to feel, would only confuse matters.

Stein requested a three-month delay in an attempt to convince the judge to change his mind. Early in October I received a copy of a legal document Stein had filed with the District Court. Titled *Request for Order Permitting Expert Testimony*, the fourteen-page document outlined my credentials, the basic areas of my testimony, and the relevant legal arguments establishing the validity and necessity of such testimony. Stein ended his request with a thinly veiled threat:

> In conclusion, defendant contends that it will be reversible error and an abuse of discretion for this Honorable Court to exclude Dr. Loftus' testimony. As the Court of Appeals for Washington noted in State v. Moon, supra:
>> The exclusion of testimony similar to that involved here is an abuse of discretion in a very narrow range of cases: (1) where the identification of the defendant is the principal issue at trial; (2) the defendant presents an alibi defense; and (3) there is little or no other evidence linking defendant to the crime.

Courts in this country have greeted expert testimony concerning eyewitness reliability with caution and skepticism. Many judges feel little compulsion to admit such testimony because they fear "opening the floodgates" to a battle of the experts. Some judges rule against the use of expert psychological testimony on the basis that the facts about memory and perception are within the "common knowledge" of the jury; why take the time and expense to have an expert testify about issues that the jurors already know? Other judges believe that expert psychological testimony usurps the jury's basic role. "I have great reluctance to permit academia to take over the fact-finding function of the jury," one judge commented.

The Moon case that Stein mentioned in his brief was a precedent-setting case in the Washington Court of Appeals. Mark Moon and another man were charged with kidnapping a woman as she left a grocery store in Seattle. Following her release, the woman gave police a detailed description of both abductors. Several weeks later, she tentatively identified Moon's alleged accomplice in a lineup, and at the trial, she positively identified him in court. But her initial description of a brown-haired, five-foot-ten-inch, forty-year-old man with a broad, pock-marked mouth differed markedly from the twenty-eight-year-old six-foot-three-inch, black-haired, mustached, thin-lipped defendant. Expert testimony was denied, and the defendant was convicted. In 1986 the appellate court reversed Jones's conviction, ordering a new trial in which expert testimony would be permitted.

Stein's threat worked wonders. The judge relented, ruling that I would be allowed to testify.

On January 19, 1989, I flew to Las Vegas and was met at the airport by Patti Erickson, a vivacious young associate of Stein's. We drove to the hotel where I would be staying and soon settled into the thick-cushioned velvet chairs in the multichandeliered lounge. The trial had been going on for nearly two weeks. All the eyewitnesses had testified, Billy Chambers's mother had testified, and Howard Haupt had just been on the stand for two days. Things seemed to be going okay, Patti said, but a few of the jurors worried her.

"They're hard to read," she said. "Most of them are sympathetic, I think, but one or two jurors may give us a problem. During jury selection the prosecutor was kicking all the young people off the jury—he wanted older citizens, the highly authoritarian types that are known to defer to the police, to believe in the status quo and the Protestant work ethic, the ones who believe that obedience and respect for the law are the most important virtues you can teach a child.

"We were trying to exclude these people because they're known to be hostile to defendants," Patti continued, "and we were using our peremptory challenges with people who had strong religious backgrounds, military types, etcetera. We had one last challenge, and we all disagreed about who to keep and who to kick off. The choice was between an older man, a career army guy who retired at fifty and then went to work with the postal service for fifteen years, and a woman, mid-fifties, also in the army. We left the decision to the defendant, and he chose the woman. I suppose he thought that if the choice was between a man and a woman with similar backgrounds, the woman would tend to be more open-minded and sympathetic."

Patti took a sip of her white wine. "I keep thinking about that decision," she said. "I keep wondering—what if he picked the wrong person? She's a woman, sure, and maybe she'll be more sympathetic, but she's also a mother, and she's going to empathize with the boy's family. And she's an army sergeant, tough as nails." Patti shivered. "What a strange business, choosing the men and women who will decide your fate."

"Tell me about Howard Haupt," I said. "What's he like?"

She took a deep breath, letting it out slowly. "When I first met Howard I have to admit that I didn't know what to think. He was so cold and unemotional, so bottled up. He held everything inside and wouldn't let any of us see what he was feeling. Then one night, when we were trying to prepare him for the cross-examination, he just let go. The outer shell melted, and he broke down. It was like a dam that had cracked; suddenly all those feelings came out in a torrent."

She smiled at me apologetically. "Excuse me for sounding so literary about this, but I get very upset whenever I think about what is happening to Howard. How can any of us describe what is happening inside this poor man? The best I can do is to tell you what's happening inside me. I believe he is innocent. I can't articulate why. It's a collection of things. Before I met Howard, I knew from the transcripts and preliminary hearing testimony that the evidence was inconclusive and contradictory and that the eyewitness identifications were weak. I felt that this was a political persecution of sorts, because the police had screwed up so badly, not finding the boy's body for thirty-three days when it was right there on the hotel grounds. I thought Haupt *might* be innocent. Then I met him. And that's when I just *knew* that he didn't do it. As cold and aloof, as unemotional and reserved as this man was, I knew in my heart that he did not kill this little boy."

Patti was young and naive, fresh out of law school; she didn't have the long-distance perspective of the veteran defense attorneys who know all too well that most of their clients are guilty. But her belief in Howard Haupt's innocence was no less convincing for her lack of experience. As I listened to Patti talk, I found myself thinking: What if he really is innocent? The fear of losing this case, the thought of an innocent man being convicted and imprisoned, hit me full force.

Patti looked at her watch and took a final sip of her wine. It was almost midnight. "But is the jury convinced?" she asked, continuing with her line of thought. "Who knows? During the jury selection phase of the trial, the judge asked if any of the jurors would be unable to be impartial to the defendant. They all vigorously shook their heads. But what's the likelihood that a prejudiced juror would identify himself? All jurors claim that they will begin the trial with the presumption of innocence. But what are they really thinking? "If the state goes to all this trouble, he's probably guilty." I just can't help thinking that this is an uphill battle. A little boy is murdered. Five people have taken the stand and pointed their fingers at Howard Haupt. Jurors are inevitably going to be thinking, How could all five eyewitnesses be wrong? Reason would argue against it. And that's where you come in—to argue that what appears to be reasonable is not necessarily the truth.

"The truth," Patti repeated. "Before this trial I would have argued that there is such a thing as truth and justice. Now, watching Howard Haupt fight for his life in this courtroom, feeling scared to death that he might lose, I'm not so sure."

* * *

I took the stand at 9:15 A.M. on Friday, January 20, 1989. For more than two hours, Steve Stein asked me questions about the different factors that can affect the acquisition, retention, and retrieval stages of memory. I recounted the basic scientific findings, citing dozens of research studies and commenting on specific examples relevant to the eyewitness identifications of Howard Haupt.

After Stein finished his direct examination, the judge announced a lunch break, and Stein asked me to join the defense team at a little sandwich place across the street. "It's the only place where Howard feels comfortable," Patti explained to me as we all trooped down the courtroom stairs, making our way through the crowd of TV and newspaper reporters, "the only place where people don't gawk at him like he's some strange, frightening creature in a zoo."

The waiter took our lunch order. Haupt ordered a pastrami sandwich and folded his hands on the table. His fingers were long and slender, the veins appearing pale and delicate under the near-white skin. His eyes were also a pale, pale blue, the whites shot through with broken capillaries.

"How are you holding up?" I asked him after we'd finished eating. Stein and Patti were conferring, heads close together, at the other end of the table.

He raised his eyebrows, opened his mouth, and then closed it again. It was an unfair question, I realized. "It's a nightmare," he said finally. "My life is a nightmare. I wake up every morning, hoping it's all over, but it's still there. It's always there. It never goes away."

I watched him get up from the table, his movements tense and constrained, and I thought about that moment a full year ago, when he opened his mailbox to find a letter asking him to call the sheriff's office regarding the kidnapping and murder of a seven-year-old boy in Las Vegas, Nevada. In such benign circumstances, via certified mail, the horror began for Howard Haupt, and nothing would ever be the same again.

We returned to the courtroom at 1:00 P.M. and I spent another three hours on the stand being cross-examined by the prosecution. In the direct examination when the defense attorney asks me ques-

178

tions, I usually know exactly what to expect, and I feel in control of the situation. But on cross, facing a prosecutor who tries to pick apart everything I say, who asks convoluted questions in an attempt to confuse me or force me to contradict myself, who tosses statistics and research studies back at me in an attempt to trip me up, unpredictable things can happen.

This prosecutor began with the usual line of questioning, meant to belittle my research and make me look like a hired gun.

"How many times have you testified in court on the subject of eyewitness memory?"

"I've testified about a hundred times," I answered.

"And are you paid for your testimony?"

"I'm compensated for my time—my advance preparation, travel time, testimony, etcetera."

"What is your fee in this case?"

"For all my preparation, travel, and testimony, I expect to receive about thirty-five hundred dollars," I answered.

He hesitated for a moment, turning to the jury with eyebrows raised. *That's a lot of money,* those expressive eyebrows were trying to communicate. *Do you make that kind of money for offering your opinion?*

"Are you able to define what memory is?" he continued after a sufficient pause.

"Memory is the flow of information into the human mind, the storage of information there, and the retrieval of that information for the higher mental processes of remembering, thinking, judgment, and decision-making."

"Is it true that in your field psychologists disagree as to just what memory is?"

"There are a number of scientific disagreements about memory, yes."

"And there is disagreement in the field as to how it works?"

"There is some disagreement, yes."

"Aren't there in fact some noted psychologists who believe that expert testimony in the field is inappropriate?"

"There are a few of those, yes." He was referring to Michael McCloskey and Howard Egeth, two highly respected experimental psychologists who argue tenaciously against my presence, and the presence of other research psychologists, in the courtroom. They claim that no evidence exists to support the claim that jurors are overly willing to believe eyewitness testimony, that the factors that could potentially affect the accuracy of eyewitness accounts—stress, weapon focus, cross-racial identification, post-event information, suggestive questioning—are either not well documented by research or are obvious enough to jurors, and that expert testimony can be misleading and prejudicial.

Our debate, which has been heated and at times acrimonious, reflects a strong difference of philosophies. McCloskey and Egeth seem to think that the data psychologists collect must be near completion and perfection before we should feel comfortable discussing our results in a public forum. I believe that waiting for perfection is equivalent to waiting forever, for we are never likely to achieve it. And I don't believe that psychologists should withhold knowledge simply because our knowledge is not perfect. Howard Haupt, sitting at the defense table in a Las Vegas courtroom on January 20, 1989, did not have years to wait before the research is "perfected."

The prosecutor continued to spar with me, jabbing away at my research studies—you use college students as your subjects, don't you? And these students get paid, don't they? And do you really believe that a college student in a research laboratory has the same experience as an eyewitness of a violent crime?

I calmly answered that yes, it's very common to use college students in my experiments, but by no means are they the sole subjects. I mentioned a recent experiment on memory in children and the elderly using visitors to the Exploratorium Science Museum in San Francisco as subjects. Some experimenters have used convenience-store clerks as subjects. Others use mothers and their newborn babies.

Yes, I answered, we either give our student subjects course credit or we pay them for being in the experiment, but this shouldn't affect the answers they give because they would get paid no matter how they responded. And no, I said, subjects in a psychological experiment do not have the same experience as the actual eyewitness to a true-life crime; however, the stress of a real-life event would probably have a debilitating effect on the memory.

The prosecutor wound down, taking a few more stabs but nothing with any sting. At 4:45 P.M. the judge recessed for the day, and

Steve Stein drove me to the airport for my evening flight back to Seattle.

"I watched the jury carefully during your testimony," he said as we pulled into the airport. "I feel sure you made a difference. The only reason Howard Haupt is in this courtroom, fighting for his life, is because of the eyewitnesses' identifications, and you cast genuine doubt on the accuracy of those IDs.

"You know," he continued, his voice filled with feeling, "this is the kind of case a criminal defense lawyer gets once in a lifetime. It's everything I ever hoped for, a fantasy that I've had ever since law school, to have a client that you know is innocent, you know it in your mind and in your gut. Right now I'm living out this fantasy. I have this sneaking suspicion that the rest of my career will be an anticlimax—I'll probably spend the next thirty years waiting for another case like this one."

Stein parked outside the United terminal and apologized for not being able to accompany me inside. "I've got a long night of work ahead," he said. "I'll call you as soon as the jury reaches a verdict."

"What's your gut feeling?" I asked. "Will you win this one?"

"We can't lose," Stein said, but I knew from the forceful way he said it that he was terrified he might.

On the plane I took my seat by the window and stared for a while at the first page of a best-seller I'd bought in the airport gift shop. But I couldn't take my mind off the courtroom I had just left, the man who was on trial for his life, and the jury of twelve people who would decide his fate. I closed my eyes and Howard Haupt's face appeared in my mind, going in and out of focus. I concentrated and gradually it came, an image of a man with blond, thinning hair and pale-blue eyes, wearing clear prescription glasses with metal frames. In my mind I saw him sitting at the defense table, shoulders slightly slumped, a finger raised to his chin, listening, watching, holding himself together.

Was he innocent? I believed he was, but my opinion meant nothing at this point. I said what I'd come to say, and now it was up to the carefully selected members of the jury who would have to look into their own hearts and souls and decide, with one mind, a man's fate.

I let the picture of Howard Haupt recede and picked up my book, determined to read in order to forget.

On February 16, 1989, after nearly twenty hours of deliberation spanning three days, Howard Haupt was acquitted. A jubilant Steve Stein called to give me the details of the emotional scene in the courtroom.

"It was standing-room only," he said, talking a mile a minute, "and to tell you the truth, I was worried. We found out later that the first poll ended with nine jurors voting for innocence, two for guilt, and one unsure. Then it switched to ten for innocence and two for guilt, and the jury held there for almost six hours. Finally, after three days and twenty hours of deliberation, they filed in and handed the verdict to the judge. On the kidnapping charge—not guilty. We were all holding our breath. On the murder charge— not guilty. It was pandemonium, people yelling and screaming, falling all over each other. Howard Haupt threw his arms around me and started to cry. Patti Erickson was going through five Klee-nexes a minute. Haupt's mother and father were hanging onto their handkerchiefs, tears streaming down their faces. Everybody was crying."

Stein hesitated for a moment, then sighed. "Billy's parents were sitting in the front row. When the verdict was read, they put their heads in their hands and sobbed. That poor family."

"Will the police reopen the investigation?" I asked.

"I hope so," Stein said forcefully. "The killer is still out there, and if the police profile is right, he's abusing little boys. I think the cops were right on that one. The killer took Billy upstairs, intending to sexually molest him. But when he encountered Charles Crouter, the guest in the hallway, he panicked. I don't think he planned to kill Billy, but once he knew a search was on, he probably felt he didn't have any choice. Now it's been over a year since Billy was murdered, and all the leads are cold as ice. I have a feeling this case will never get solved. It'll just hang there in the books, labeled 'case pending,' and every year it will get pushed farther back. In a few years hardly anybody will even remember that Billy Chambers was murdered in Las Vegas."

The tone of Stein's voice shifted. "I've got some juror comments that might interest you. Three jurors told us that they originally believed Haupt might be guilty, but that your testimony persuaded them otherwise. 'We took Loftus seriously,' they told us. How does that make you feel?"

"Wonderful," I said. "Unbelievably, absolutely, positively wonderful." Howard Haupt was a free man, an innocent man in the eyes of the law, and Steve Stein had just told me that my testimony was crucial to the jury's final decision. If I hadn't testified, Howard Haupt might have been found guilty, he might have been sentenced to die.

How did that make me feel? I lead a different life from most academic psychologists, and I often feel the pressure to give up this flashy, nontraditional line of work. But Steve Stein had just told me that my presence in the courtroom made a difference. Howard Haupt was a free man, in part, his lawyer believed, because of the expert testimony regarding the fallibility of memory and eyewitness accounts. Now, perhaps, the Las Vegas police and the FBI would resume their search for the real killer. Perhaps they would find him and prevent him from killing again.

I thought about the other cases where my testimony was not allowed. Just a few months before I testified for Howard Haupt, I'd flown to Pennsylvania to testify for a man accused of murdering an elderly couple. The defense attorney was convinced his client was innocent, and after spending six hours with the defendant, I believed his story too.

But at the last minute the judge decided to exclude my testimony. The defendant was eventually convicted. Was *he* innocent too? The defendant was sentenced to two consecutive terms of life imprisonment without the possibility of parole. His lawyer, who called this "the most tragic case I've had in twenty years of practice," plans to appeal.

I thought about the cases where the defendant is poor and unable to afford a high-class defense. Howard Haupt's defense cost him more than $250,000, half of which came from his savings and half from his parents' savings. What if Haupt didn't have a substantial savings account, what if he didn't have wealthy parents, what if he were black and destitute, one of the typical cases that crowd the public defender's schedule?

And then I thought about little Billy Chambers. A series of pictures came into my mind, as I remembered the pathologist's description of Billy's fully clothed body lying face down under a trailer just two hundred yards from the entrance to the hotel. His palms were face up, his feet crossed, his left arm askew.

I remembered, too, the mother's description of her lost boy, given the day of Billy's disappearance. "Billy's shirttail was out," she told the police. "His red Polar Fleece jacket with the white snowflake design was unzipped. Oh, yes," she said, "I almost forgot—his shoes were tied in double knots."

Those are the minor details, inconsequential to my work, that come back later to disturb my sleep. Those are the facts, typed on clean white paper, stapled into lengthy reports, placed in folders and shut up in files labeled "case pending," that break the heart.

"SHEER, STARK TERROR": CLARENCE VON WILLIAMS

"Whilst part of what we perceive comes from the object before us, another part (and it may be the larger part) always comes out of our mind."

—William James

I was sitting on a queen-size bed in a bland, beige hotel room in Orange, Texas, feeling hot, homesick, and unhappy. I'd just had dinner with Louis Dugas, a young, energetic defense attorney representing Clarence Von Williams, accused of raping a mother and her teenage daughter. Dugas and I had been discussing the questions he would ask me in court the next day when a blonde in a tight dress and heavy makeup walked up to our table and stuck out a hand with long, scarlet fingernails. "Mr. Dugas?" she said, a Texas drawl dripping over her words. "I recognize you from your picture in the paper. I'm sure hoping you get Mr. Williams off the hook, because I'm going on vacation in two weeks, and I'd like to take that man with me!"

She sauntered out of the restaurant while an acutely embarrassed Dugas apologized profusely. "Emotions are running high over this case," he said. "Either people make sick jokes about the rapist's incredible stamina, or they write letters to the newspaper calling for a lynch mob." I told him not to worry, things like this happen, and we quickly changed the subject. But later, sitting with my back propped up against the headboard, glasses on, alarm clock reading 11:15 P.M., a headache beginning behind my left eye, and a stack of papers a foot high on the night table, I was not feeling very charitable toward the blonde.

How could someone make fun of a rape, any rape, but particularly a rape as cruel and inhuman as this one, where a masked man held a gun to a woman's head and proceeded to systematically rape and sodomize the woman and her daughter? That was the basis for the blonde's obscene joke: whoever had committed this crime had somehow been able to go back and forth between the mother and daughter for more than an hour.

I adjusted my glasses, picked up the top file on the nightstand and started reading. "Oral Deposition. Identification of *Sally Blackwell*." The deposition consisted of ninety-eight onion-skin pages bound in a cheap plastic folder. Page 1 was very official looking, with "No. D-10, 102" at top center and "The State of Texas vs. Clarence Von Williams" typed in the top left corner.

BE IT REMEMBERED that on the 14th day of February, 1980, the aforestyled and numbered cause of action came on for hearing before the Honorable Don Burgess, Judge, 260th District Court of Orange County, Texas, wherein the following proceedings were had . . .

The rape occurred in the early-morning hours of April 30, 1979. Sally Blackwell, forty years old, divorced with two teenage children, was awakened at approximately 2:30 in the morning by an intruder. She looked up from her bed, confused, trying to determine who was standing there. For a moment, she thought it was her son, *Nate*, but in the darkness she could see a man with what looked like a ski mask pulled down over his face.

PROSECUTOR: What happened after you were awakened by this individual?

SALLY BLACKWELL: I raised my head up to speak to him, but as I did, he grabbed me by the hair of the back of my head and shoved my face away from him. He put a gun to my head and told me that if I made any noise, that he would kill my kids, and did I understand that?

186

PROSECUTOR: You said you observed the individual. What type of light was present in your room at that time?

SALLY BLACKWELL: The light from the telephone and the light from the digital clock.

I had underlined her response; it would be extremely difficult to perceive facial features (even if there was no mask) by the light provided by a digital clock and the lighted dial of a telephone.

The man told her to be quiet—if she woke the kids, he would make them watch what he was going to do to her. He pulled the sheet and electric blanket off the bed, pulled up her nightgown, and began to rub her back with his hand. She tried to get away from him, there was a scuffle, and a glass was knocked off the nightstand.

The noise apparently woke the woman's son because he called out to her from the hallway. The intruder pointed the gun at the door and the mother stepped in front of him, begging him to let her take care of her son. "The man still had a gun and I feared for Nathan's life," she testified. The intruder allowed her to speak with her son, who returned to his bedroom. After the woman shut her bedroom door, the man grabbed her, threw her back on the bed, and climbed on top of her. At that point, her daughter called out.

PROSECUTOR: What was the intruder's reaction to *Janet* speaking out?

SALLY BLACKWELL: It made him extremely nervous. He was close to me, and I could feel him begin to breathe heavier. His voice became a little uncertain and he said, *"Well, we're just going to have to get you all in here together."*

They walked down the hallway to her son's room. The masked man flipped on the light, waved the gun at the boy, and then put it to the side of the woman's head. "Don't try anything funny," he said, "or I'll blow her brains out." They went to the girl's bedroom, told her to get out of bed, and the four of them went back to the bedroom with the man still holding the gun to the woman's head. He instructed the mother and her two children to lie down crossways on the bed, tied their hands behind their backs, blindfolded them, and then began the systematic, back-and-forth rape of the mother and daughter.

This was the third time I'd read the transcript giving the details of the rape, but I still cringed at the horror hidden in the black words on the white onion-skin pages. I flipped ahead to page 18, where the victim was being questioned about the blindfold. It was a very narrow strip of cloth, she testified, and it kept slipping loose. The rapist had to stop several times to retie it. At one point she said she saw the man without his mask on, when he was raping her daughter. The prosecutor asked if she could actually see his face at that time.

SALLY BLACKWELL: Yes. I saw a white male, dark complected, dark-brown curly hair, a mustache, dark eyebrows that were fairly thick. I could see him quite clearly and I concentrated on what I was seeing and, as I watched him, I knew then that I knew who that man was.
PROSECUTOR: Is that man present in the courtroom today?
SALLY BLACKWELL: Yes, he certainly is.
PROSECUTOR: Would you point him out, please, for the record?
SALLY BLACKWELL: Yes, he's sitting on the first row with the tan suit on, wearing glasses.

I looked at the clock. It was almost midnight, and I still had work to do. I put my glasses back on, took a deep breath, and looked at my notes.

Sally Blackwell had been in the same room with the rapist, according to her testimony, for almost two hours. Her children had been in the room with him for almost that long. They all swore, under oath, that Clarence Von Williams was the rapist. And yet. And yet . . .

I turned to page 55 of the transcript. Sally Blackwell was being cross-examined by Louis Dugas, the defense attorney, who was solicitous and gentle with his witness. Bullying victims does not win you any friends in the courtroom.

DUGAS: Now, your first emotion when you woke and realized it was not a member of your family was terror?
SALLY BLACKWELL: Sheer, stark terror.
DUGAS: And your second emotion was what?
SALLY BLACKWELL: Probably more sheer terror; fear and ter-

ror . . . I'd have to say fear and more fear and terror were my
emotions.

"Sheer, stark terror . . . fear and more fear and terror."
Many people mistakenly believe that under conditions of high
stress, the details of an event will be "stamped into" a person's
memory. It's true that extraordinary events are often rehearsed over
and over in a person's mind; but because extreme stress is detri-
mental to mental functioning, the ability to receive and remember
details is impaired. Thus, as the event is constantly recalled, the
erroneous and inaccurate details are also recalled and "stamped into"
the person's memory. The more the event is rehearsed, the more
confident the person becomes that what she remembers is the absolute and unequivocal truth.

Put another way, the brain simply doesn't work very well when
a lightning bolt of terror shudders through, screwing up the neu-
rotransmitters, shutting down electrical signals, scrambling the
memory drawers. The defense would emphasize the possibility that
Sally Blackwell was so terrified, her brain so numbed and paralyzed,
that she literally could not remember the details of what had happened to her.

And yet in the trial transcript Sally Blackwell told Dugas that she
knew exactly who her rapist was. It came to her on Monday morning,
just a few hours after the rape. At 8:00 A.M. she called *Lois Williams*,
her coworker, to explain that she wouldn't be coming to work that
day. But Lois wasn't at work either, and so Sally called her at home.
The two women talked for several minutes. Approximately two hours
later, Sally's boyfriend was urging her to come up with a name for
the man who had raped her. He kept telling her, over and over
again, to think, that this was somebody she knew—it had to be, he
said, because the man was always so careful not to let her see his
face.

SALLY BLACKWELL: *Bob* kept saying "It's got to be somebody you
    know. You've seen him in the neighborhood, you've seen him
    somewhere before. Just think where you've seen him. You saw
    him at the grocery store or at church; you've seen him some-
    where. You've seen him at a party somewhere . . ." When he

said "party" the name flashed with the face. I knew what name went with that face.

The name that flashed into her mind when her boyfriend said the word "party" was Clarence Von Williams. Several weeks earlier, Sally and her boyfriend picked up Lois and Clarence Von Williams and drove them to a dinner party, where the two couples spent several hours together. The women were friends, but this was the first time Sally had met Lois's husband, who was introduced simply as "Von."

I closed my eyes and concentrated, trying to push my way into Sally Blackwell's mind. The rapist, she testified, was "adamant" about not letting her see him. She concluded that he was afraid to let her see his face because she knew him and might recognize him. The more she thought about it, the more convinced she became. She figured that she *must* know him. But it was not a face she knew well; it had to be an acquaintance, someone she had met only once or twice before.

Just a few hours after the rape, she spoke with Lois Williams. It must have been an emotional conversation. Was it possible that Lois Williams might have mentioned the fact that her husband had been out drinking until three or four that morning—was that the reason she didn't go to work that day? Would that stray comment have planted an idea in Sally Blackwell's mind?

An hour later the victim's boyfriend entered the picture. "It's got to be somebody you know," he told her. "Just think . . . you've seen him somewhere . . . at a party somewhere . . ."

The disconnected facts circled madly in Sally's mind. Circled faster, gaining speed and momentum, becoming a swirling mass. *The rapist—I must know him. Lois Williams—Familiar. Think—you met him somewhere. Think—Party. Lois Williams. Party. Lois Williams's husband.* And suddenly Von Williams's face appears in her mind, like the image in a Polaroid picture that gradually emerges from a flat gray background. His face seems to match the features she remembers of her rapist. *That's him,* she thinks, seeing Von Williams's face in her mind, overlapping it onto the memory of the man who raped her. The features gradually becoming clearer and more distinct. *That's the man who raped me.*

And it might be true, Clarence Von Williams might be the rapist.

But in a stressed mind, under intense pressure to come up with someone who could be blamed for this horrible crime, those connections could have been created, welded together by fear and pain and a desire to be done with it all, to stop thinking, to find an answer, a solution.

I wondered . . . would Clarence Von Williams's face have appeared in the victim's mind if she hadn't called his wife that morning? Would she have believed it was someone she knew if her boyfriend hadn't said, "Just think. You've seen him somewhere . . . at a party somewhere . . ." What if her boyfriend had never mentioned the word "party"?

I didn't know if Von Williams was the man who raped Sally Blackwell. Nobody knew, of course, except for Williams. And perhaps one other person. If Williams wasn't the rapist, someone else was roaming around out there, someone who might rape again.

The next morning, January 22, 1981, dawned clear and beautiful. I took a quick shower, got dressed, and rode the elevator down to the coffee shop. I ordered a cup of coffee and wheat toast and pulled my notes out of my briefcase. My coffee arrived at about the same time Louis Dugas pulled out a chair and sat down across from me.

"Unconscious transference," he said, not bothering to say hello. "Weapon focus. Severe stress."

I laughed. Dugas seemed so confident and eager. "She's an extremely positive witness, Louis," I said. "She's convinced that Von Williams is the man who raped her and her daughter. 'I know what I saw in my mind,' she says, over and over again."

Dugas nodded, sighed. "But as your research shows so convincingly, confidence and accuracy aren't always associated."

"That's right," I said, "but it's a tough point to get across to a jury when they've watched an eyewitness point her finger at the defendant and state under penalty of perjury that he's the man who raped her." I switched the subject and turned to a flagged page toward the end of the identification testimony transcript. "You make a nice point in your cross-examination," I said, reading from the transcript. " '. . . an experience in terror like this, you don't forget, do you?' " you asked the witness. And she answered, 'You make a great effort to try and block out as much of it as you can so that you can get on with living.' That's a fascinating quote about memory."

"So tell me," Dugas said, leaning forward across the table, "is that what happened in this case? Do you think she was so traumatized by the rape that significant details were wiped out of her memory?"

I thought for a moment. "It's impossible to know exactly what happened in her mind. I can only make general conclusions from her testimony and the known facts of the case. It was dark in the room. The man wore a mask. He had a gun which he repeatedly held to her head, threatening her. She feared for her life and the lives of her children. All these factors could affect the accuracy of the memories that were stored in her brain. But from my reading of the transcript and police reports, I think the major problem with her memory may have occurred in the retrieval stage. She had this dim, blurred memory of the rapist, which was just several hours old, and she had another memory, several weeks old, of Clarence Von Williams. These two memories may have gotten mixed up, shuffled together by stress and fear and the incessant questioning from her boyfriend to *think*, to come up with a name."

I took a sip of coffee and a quick bite of toast. "There's another case," I said, "similar to this one, which occurred in Australia. A psychologist appeared on a local television show. Within a short time of his TV appearance, he was arrested and accused of rape, and the victim immediately and positively identified him from a lineup. The accused pressed the police for details about the rape and discovered that it had occurred at precisely the same time as his television appearance. Further investigation into the case revealed that the woman had been raped while watching the television program and that she had apparently merged the TV image with her memory of the rapist."

"What a bizarre story," Dugas said, shaking his head.

"If Williams is innocent, this story is almost as bizarre," I said. "Tell me, Louis. What's your gut feeling about Williams—do you think he raped this woman and her daughter?"

"I'm convinced he's innocent," he said. "You probably hear that all the time from lawyers, but I believe in every cell of my body that Williams did not commit this crime. No physical evidence whatsoever links him to these rapes—no hairs, fingerprints, semen, or clothing fibers. If this man was in the house for almost two hours, as the victim testified, he would certainly have left some evidence of himself behind. He has no criminal record. He's a kind, gentle man who is totally distraught, completely devastated by these accusations. I've watched him with his wife and children, and I just don't think he is the type of person who could have raped these two women."

I thought about that for a minute, drawing circles on the vinyl tablecloth with my finger. "You know, an attorney once told me that you can't tell if a man is guilty of rape. He claims it's the only crime you can't read in a man's face."

Dugas smiled slightly. "Yes, I'd agree with that. But I've got a feeling about this one. I believe him."

"Why?" I asked, pushing him on this, one of my favorite subjects.

"First you take the facts and they just don't add up. You weigh them, measure them, turn them inside out, and they still don't spell the word 'guilt.' Then you get a feeling. I work with these defendants day in and day out, and most of them are guilty. A case doesn't come to trial unless evidence is sufficient to at least suggest guilt, and most of these defendants are guilty as hell. But every once in a while you get one that just, somehow, doesn't fit. Maybe he *looks* guilty, maybe he acts guilty, maybe an eyewitness says he's the one—but deep down, you just don't believe he did it. That's how I feel about Williams. It's pure gut instinct, but I think he's innocent."

The Orange County courthouse was a zoo. People were crowded together on the outside steps, trying to push their way into the courtroom. Reporters and photographers were elbow to elbow with white-haired old ladies and mothers holding babies with pacifiers stuck in their mouths.

We made our way through the crowd and into the hallway, where Dugas continued into the courtroom and I took a seat on the bench facing the closed doors with the sign "Witnesses excluded." I watched the people milling around, looking at their watches, waiting for the show to begin.

At 9:15 A.M. the doors opened and Dugas motioned me into the courtroom. I walked down the short aisle through the waist-high, swinging doors separating the spectators from the judge and jury, and stopped in front of the witness-box where the clerk was waiting for me. "Do you solemnly swear that the testimony you are about to give will be the truth, the whole truth, and nothing but the truth, so help you God?"

"I do," I answered. I took my seat in the witness box and looked out at the packed courtroom, so quiet now you could hear the prosecutor's pen scratching across his yellow legal pad. A hushed courtroom always reminds me of a church just moments before the service begins. The same smell of sweet cologne and deodorant permeates the dusty, uncirculated air, and a look of self-righteousness settles on the faces of the onlookers.

I glanced for the first time at Clarence Von Williams. He was attractive in a swarthy sort of way, with dark, curly, collar-length hair and heavy-lidded eyes. A thick mustache covered his upper lip, then dipped dramatically at the corners.

I remembered the original description Sally Blackwell had given the police. *"A white male with very dark brown to black hair; thick hair, curly; had a mustache; dark eyebrows, thick; weight, about 180 to 200."* The description fit except for the fact that Williams weighed 160 pounds. And there was another interesting discrepancy. Before Sally Blackwell remembered Clarence Von Williams's face as the face of her rapist, she told police that her assailant was approximately twenty years old. Williams was forty-two.

Louis Dugas approached the witness stand and asked the standard, preliminary questions intended to establish my credentials and expertise. Then he asked me to explain for the jury how memory works. I described for the court the three major stages—acquisition, retention, and retrieval—in the memory process.

"It's important to note," I concluded, "that there are factors that come into play in each of these three stages that influence the quality of the memory."

"What are these factors that can influence the memory?" Dugas asked.

"One of the most critical factors, when it comes to a crime situation, is the amount of stress that a person is experiencing." I turned to the judge. "If I could have the use of the blackboard, I could show you very easily, if you wouldn't mind, your Honor."

"Certainly," the judge answered.

I approached the blackboard located in front of the jury box and with a piece of chalk drew the upside-down U shape that represented the relationship between stress and memory known to psychologists as the Yerkes-Dodson law.

"To reiterate the important point here," I said, indicating the right-hand portion of the curve, "high levels of arousal or stress cause a steep decline in our ability to process information and store it in memory. Many people mistakenly believe that extreme stress enhances memory, a misconception that is captured in the statement: 'Oh, my God, I was so frightened, I'll never forget that face.' But in reality, extreme stress can be debilitating to memory."

I described a study conducted in my laboratory at the University of Washington from 1977 to 1978. Over five hundred subjects, all students who were registered voters, were questioned about their knowledge of the factors affecting eyewitness testimony. When asked about the effects of extreme stress and arousal on the ability to process information, fully one-third of these subjects did not believe that extreme stress reduces the ability to perceive and recall the

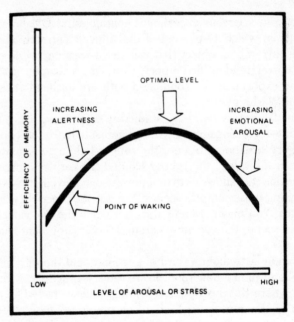

The Yerkes-Dodson law.

details of an event. Particularly curious was the fact that 18 percent of the subjects felt that the ability to recall the details of the event would be enhanced while the ability to perceive details would be reduced. If poor information gets into memory in the first place, it is hard to imagine how good information can be pulled out.

I returned to the witness stand and took my seat.

"Is the presence of a weapon a factor that's involved in how good or how bad an eyewitness's identification is?" Dugas asked.

"Yes," I answered. "We've identified a factor called 'weapon focus.' When there is a weapon involved in a crime, witnesses have a tendency—a strong tendency—to stare at the weapon. This takes time and processing away from other aspects of the situation, resulting in a reduced ability to remember other details, including the face of the person holding the weapon."

"Tell us what happens when someone points a gun at your head," Dugas said. "What happens to your later ability to identify that person?"

I discussed a famous experiment conducted at Oklahoma State University in which 49 percent of the subjects correctly identified a person carrying an object that was not a weapon, while only 33 percent correctly identified a person carrying a weapon. I also discussed an experiment I'd conducted with my husband at the University of Washington.

"In our laboratory, we have studied weapon focus using an eye-movement–recording apparatus. Our subjects looked at two different robbery situations. In one, the robber held a gun pointed at a cashier. In the other, the robber handed the cashier a check. We have a device that allows us to monitor the eye movements as people are watching these complex scenes. We can see precisely where the eye fixates. You may not know this, but when the eye is looking at a complex scene, the eye moves around the environment in a series of fixations.

"A fixation lasts about a third of a second, and then it jumps to a new spot and then a new spot. So we can see precisely, with a spot of light, where these people are fixating, and we have found more fixations on the gun, fewer fixations on the nonweapon object, and a corresponding reduced ability to remember details other than the weapon. This is the phenomenon of weapon focus. A weapon captures your attention. It's very hard to resist it."

"Dr. Loftus," Dugas said after returning to the defense table and consulting his notes, "could you tell the courtroom about any studies that have been conducted on the effects of disguises and the ability to recognize someone's face?"

The rapist had worn a mask and Dugas was hoping to establish the fact that the mask might have confused the witness. I looked quickly at Williams, who was wearing glasses. I didn't remember anything about glasses in the police report or transcript. Did Williams need the glasses, I found myself wondering, or was this a disguise of sorts? I remembered that Ted Bundy had switched the part on his hair several times during his trial. Sometimes he would change his clothes during the lunch recess, causing Judge Hanson to refer to him as "a changeling." Charles Manson was another quick-change artist, according to his biographer Vincent Bugliosi, who claimed that even a slight change in Manson's mood could dramatically affect his appearance.

I brought my mind back to the case at hand and described an ingenious research project on disguises that was published in 1977 by three British psychologists. Subjects were divided into two groups; one group participated in an ongoing training course designed to improve the ability to recognize faces. In the first experiment, subjects were presented with twenty-four photographs differing by various poses, expressions, and disguises, such as a change in hairstyle or the addition of a beard, mustache, or glasses. The twenty-four faces were shown one at a time, for ten seconds each. All subjects were urged to take "a good hard look" at each face because later on they would be asked to remember the faces they had seen. They were also warned that certain faces might later appear in disguise. About fifteen minutes after the first set of pictures were shown, a larger set of seventy-two faces was presented. For each face the subject had to indicate whether it was a "new face" or one that had been "seen before."

Three days later the subjects were tested again on their ability to recognize previously seen faces. The results were striking. For both groups of subjects, changes in appearance of a previously seen face made a tremendous difference. For unchanged faces, recognition was quite good—approximately 80 to 90 percent of the time, a subject said yes to a face that had actually been seen before. When the faces assumed a change in either pose or expression, recognition dropped off to about 60 to 70 percent, and when the faces were disguised, performance was extremely poor, at about 30 percent. Comparisons between the two groups of subjects showed absolutely no evidence that the training course helped people to remember faces.

Dugas's next question concerned the problem of photo-biased lineups. "Can the effect of showing a photographic lineup have an impact on a subsequent identification?" he asked.

"Yes," I answered. I explained the usual procedure when a crime has been committed and the police have an available eyewitness. First, the witness is shown an array of photographs; if an identification is made, an in-person lineup usually follows. Such a lineup identification has serious problems, however, since almost invariably only one person is seen in both the photographs and the lineup, and it is highly unlikely that a witness will identify in the lineup anyone other than the person who was chosen from the photographs. The chances of a mistaken identification rise dramatically in these situations, which psychologists refer to as photo-biased lineups.

Because this is such a confusing concept for most laypeople, I decided to elaborate by telling the court about the experiment conducted at the University of Nebraska in 1977. Subject witnesses viewed two groups of five "criminals" (total strangers) for twenty-five seconds each. The subjects were told to scrutinize the criminals carefully because they might have to pick them out from mug shots later that evening and from a lineup the following week. About an hour and a half later the subjects viewed fifteen mug shots, including some people who were "criminals" and some who were not. One week later several lineups were staged and the subjects were asked to indicate whether anyone in the lineup was a "criminal."

The results were dramatic. Of the people in the lineup who had never been seen before, 8 percent were mistakenly "identified" as criminals. However, if a person's mug shot had been seen earlier, his chances of being falsely identified as one of the criminals rose to 20 percent. None of these people had committed a crime or had ever been seen in person before, but were now "recognized" in the lineup because their photograph had been seen.

"Now, you can see what is happening here," I said. "A photograph can produce a strong element of familiarity, so that when the individual is subsequently seen in person, he or she looks familiar.

But that familiarity is due to the photograph rather than to a prior in-person viewing. That's the danger of the intervening photographic lineup."

"Would the makeup of the lineup have a bearing on the identification?"

"Yes, it would. It's very important that the photographic lineup, after an actual event, be as fair a lineup as possible. This means that someone who had no involvement whatsoever in the incident could be given a description of the suspect, look at the lineup of six different people, and identify the suspect with only one-sixth probability. The participants in the lineup sufficiently resemble each other so that the lineup is fair and not suggestive or biased."

"I have two photographic lineups here," Dugas said. "One is State's Exhibit Number 3; one is Defendant's Exhibit Number 2. Would you examine State's Exhibit Number 3?" Dugas handed me the lineup photos, consisting of six head-and-shoulder photos of six different men. "Do you have an opinion as to whether or not that is a photo-biased lineup?"

The prosecutor was immediately on his feet, shouting objections to the judge. "I believe that's invading the ultimate province of the jury, as to whether or not that's a fair lineup," he said, his finger stabbing at the air. "That's for the jury to determine, and I know of no science that allows her to render a legal opinion on whether a lineup meets the legal test of suggestibility or not."

"Overruled," the judge announced.

To which the prosecutor replied, "All right, your Honor."

I continued with my general comments. "When I examine photographic lineups, as I have done on many, many occasions, I usually compare the people in the photographic lineups to any description that was initially given by the witnesses."

"Assume that the identification was that of a person around five foot ten," Dugas said, "from 180 to 200 pounds, with wavy black hair, a mustache, and hair reaching down to collar length." That, of course, was the description Sally Blackwell had given the police just several hours after she was raped.

"The problem with this particular photographic composition, then, is that there are people who can be immediately eliminated because they don't bear any resemblance to that description. For example, number 6, who doesn't have dark, curly hair, but straight and light-colored hair, could be immediately eliminated as not even resembling the description. Similarly, number 5 seems to have quite short hair. And there are other peculiarities about this particular composition, such as the fact that number 1 is in a profile view, while all the others are full face. I could do tests with this particular photographic lineup and probably determine that many of these people could be easily eliminated as not matching the description."

"Dr. Loftus," Dugas lowered his voice to emphasize the importance of his next point. "Assume someone has seen a person and then they call from their memory the identity of this person; have you done any studies in that area?"

Dugas was referring to the sudden appearance of Clarence Von Williams's face in Sally Blackwell's memory and her automatic assumption that this was the face of her rapist.

"When a frightening event occurs," I said, "and afterward a particular name or person comes to mind, there is a possibility that you could come to believe that the face you have in mind is the face of the person who was involved in the frightening incident, even when that might not be the case."

"Do you have a study on that type of incident—I know you have a study on unconscious transference. Is that involved in this area?"

"This may be a kind of unconscious transference," I said. "Unconscious transference is the mistaken recollection or confusion of a person seen in one situation with a person who has been seen in a different situation. But what is happening here is the merging of an image of a person seen in one situation with a totally different incident. And that is an important phenomenon. Many people do not realize how easy it is for an 'unconscious transference' to occur, to take a person that you have seen in one context and integrate that person with your memory of an experience that happened at a different time."

Dugas nodded his head and looked briefly at the jury. He wanted that information to sink in. "I have one last question," he said after a moment. "When people perceive a situation, they'll say it lasted so many seconds or so many minutes or so many hours. Along with their eyewitness identification, is that also a phenomenon that perhaps they overestimate?"

"One of the most pervasive findings in the eyewitness area is that people invariably overestimate how long some event lasted," I said.

"We've shown people a simulated bank robbery that lasts for half a minute and they will say it lasted for five minutes, eight minutes, even ten minutes. In one experiment people saw an event that lasted four minutes and they said it lasted ten minutes; some said twenty minutes. There is a very strong tendency in the memory to enlarge these complex and stressful events so that they appear to have occurred over a longer period of time than they really did."

"If a person is placed in great fear of bodily harm," Dugas continued, "does this affect their perception or their ability to identify?"

"Yes, that strongly relates to the stress factor that we talked about. Fear of bodily harm is an extreme form of stress, or, phrased in another way, it can lead to an extreme form of stress."

"And it would have an effect on the identification that's made, or could have?"

"It would have a strong effect on the quality of that stored information, or what gets into memory precisely at that point. Of course, if you have poor information coming in, you have poor information coming out later when you try to remember."

"I pass the witness," Mr. Dugas said.

"No questions," the prosecutor said. That took me by surprise, and I could tell from the expression on Dugas's face that he was also taken aback. It doesn't often happen that a prosecutor won't welcome the opportunity to take a few jabs at me, but sometimes, particularly in a case that rests wholly on eyewitness testimony, the attorney might feel that to tangle with an expert where the expert knows so much more about the subject is to tread in dangerous water. Or by "passing the witness," he might have been trying to communicate to the jury that I wasn't *worth* questioning, that he didn't want to dignify this so-called expert with his time.

"Very well, you may step down," the judge instructed me.

I quickly glanced at my watch. I'd been on the witness stand for just an hour; it seemed like four. My plane didn't leave for several hours, so I walked to the back of the courtroom and took a seat in the last row. Lois Williams was the next witness. I watched her run her hands down her dress, smoothing, and walk down the aisle to the clerk, raise her hand, say "I do," and take a seat in the witness box.

Dugas asked about her whereabouts on the night of the rapes— could she pinpoint the exact time when her husband returned home, how did she know what time it was, was there a clock in the bedroom, did they discuss how late it was, etcetera, etcetera. She answered in short, stiff sentences. The questions and answers tried to circle in on the truth, but where was the truth? Could it, in fact, be located, pinpointed, understood?

I wondered what Lois Williams was thinking as she sat on the stand and looked down at her husband, sitting at the defense table. Was there any doubt in her mind, any thought at all, that he might be guilty? I remembered reading in the preliminary hearing transcript that Williams had been drinking at several taverns the night and morning of the rape, returning home around 4:00 A.M. The rapes allegedly began around 2:30 A.M. and ended around 4:00 or 4:30 A.M.

How deep a sleeper was Lois Williams? Did she really know the exact time that her husband came home? Did it matter to her that he stayed out drinking until nearly dawn? I wondered at the strange coincidence that Von Williams was out that particular night, drinking by himself, and not one person could be located who could say for sure what time he left the bar and returned home.

After her testimony, I used a pay phone in the hallway to call a taxi and then walked outside to wait. It was hot and muggy and the air tasted like dust. I took off my suit jacket and glanced up at the sun, hazy in the pale-yellow February sky.

Was Von Williams innocent or guilty? I remembered how he sat at the defense table, leaning forward, hands tightly folded with the thumbs up, pressing and flexing against each other. How does a defendant endure the tension of this legal inquisition? Even for the guilty, the strain must be unbearable. "Will they find me out?" he would be wondering. "What will they do to me? How will I survive prison? How can I bear to be separated from my wife and children?"

But if he was innocent. To sit there and feel the cold stares of people who immediately presume your guilt. To be forced to participate in the anguish of the victims, to know that your face is the face in their nightmares, the face they have come to hate. To feel helpless as you watch your life begin to come apart. To know, with sudden force and clarity, that no one will believe your side of the story because their minds are already made up. Guilty as charged.

* * *

I flew back to Seattle late that afternoon and immersed myself in my work. Students crowded into my office, colleagues tossed committee reports at me, secretaries handed me stacks of phone messages. Caught up once again in the midst of it all, I tried not to think too much about Clarence Von Williams.

Early in March, about two weeks after I testified, I received a letter and several newspaper clippings from Louis Dugas. "The jury was hung 9 to 3," Dugas wrote, "and the three who voted against conviction said they did so because of your testimony."

The *Beaumont Enterprise* presented the facts, as newspapers do, in clipped, unemotional prose.

HUNG JURY BRINGS MISTRIAL IN ORANGE RAPE CASE

A HUNG JURY TUESDAY RESULTED IN A MISTRIAL FOR CLARENCE VON WILLIAMS, ACCUSED OF RAPING A BRIDGE CITY WOMAN AND HER DAUGHTER. NINE JURORS VOTED TO FIND WILLIAMS GUILTY AND THREE TO FIND HIM INNOCENT.

THE JURY, WHICH MONDAY NIGHT HAD BEEN SEQUESTERED AT THE ORANGE HOUSE INN, DELIBERATED A TOTAL OF MORE THAN 12 HOURS BEFORE RETURNING WITHOUT A VERDICT.

THROUGHOUT WILLIAMS' SIX-DAY TRIAL, SPECTATORS JAMMED THE COURTROOM. AT 10:30 P.M. MONDAY, WHEN IT WAS ANNOUNCED THE JURY WOULD BE SEQUESTERED, SPECTATORS WERE STILL MINGLING IN THE COURTHOUSE HALLWAYS MANY OF THEM HAVING BEEN THERE SINCE EARLY THAT MORNING.

ON FRIDAY, A NATIONALLY KNOWN "MEMORY" EXPERT TESTIFIED, MAKING A STRONG CASE AGAINST THE RELIABILITY OF COURT WITNESSES.

I grimaced at the description. The term "memory expert" made me think of those old-time traveling "doctors" hawking their secret cures for everything from cold sores to bunions.

Reading through the different articles, I noted that the prosecution intended to retry the case.

. . . THE STATE WILL TRY VON WILLIAMS ON THE SAME CHARGE OF AGGRAVATED RAPE WHEN THE CASE IS RESET. AGGRAVATED RAPE IS PUNISHABLE BY A MAXIMUM 5–99 YEAR PRISON SENTENCE, AND A MAXIMUM $10,000 FINE.

I put the letter and articles in the front of the file marked "Dugas."
While lawyers arrange their files by client name, I always arrange
my files according to the name of the person I have the most contact
with—the lawyer. The drawer made a satisfying metal *click* when
I pushed it shut.

Seven months later, on October 9, 1981, I flew down to Orange,
Texas, to testify in Von Williams's second trial. A decidedly wearier
Louis Dugas met me at the airport and handed me a copy of that
morning's paper.

"Accused rapist denies rap in emotional court outburst," the headline read.

"He lost it," Dugas said, shaking his head and pressing his lips
tightly together. "The poor man is at the breaking point."

I quickly read the first two paragraphs of the article.

CLARENCE VON WILLIAMS, ON TRIAL FOR THE SECOND TIME ON
CHARGES HE RAPED A BRIDGE CITY MOTHER AND HER DAUGHTER,
TESTIFIED THURSDAY IN AN EMOTIONAL OUTBURST THAT THE FALSE
ACCUSATIONS AGAINST HIM HAVE RUINED HIS LIFE.

"I DIDN'T DO THIS . . . I WAS NEVER IN THEIR (THE VICTIMS')
HOUSE. IT WAS A TERRIBLE THING THAT HAPPENED TO THEM, BUT
I'M BEING PUNISHED JUST AS THEY ARE BECAUSE OF THE FALSE ACCUSA-
TIONS AGAINST ME. I HAVE LOST EVERYTHING I HAVE HAD . . ."

In court I could see the change in Von Williams. His body was
rigid, tensed with anger. Before, in the first trial, I'd seen a slump-
shouldered, wide-eyed, clearly terrified human being, but the fear
had apparently hardened into anger. Fear turns inward; it eats at
your soul. Anger can be directed outward, toward others. It occurred
to me that if Von Williams were innocent, he needed his anger;
perhaps it would protect him from the fear and frustration that would
otherwise eat him alive.

On the stand, I offered the same facts in the same controlled,
professional manner, and a few hours later I was on my way back
to Seattle. It was Friday, I remember, because I was looking forward
to working all day Saturday and Sunday without the constant inter-
ruptions from students. That night my husband, Geoff, and I dined
at a new Italian restaurant, and I told him about the Williams case.

"Do you think he's innocent?" Geoff asked me.

"Dugas thinks he's innocent," I said. "I think he might be innocent." I recalled what Dugas told me at breakfast the morning before I testified. "I've been practicing law now for twenty-five years. And in all that time I've had two clients who were innocent beyond a shadow of a doubt. Von Williams is one of them."

When I arrived at work Monday morning there was a message from Louis Dugas. "Von Williams convicted," it read. "Sentenced to 50 years. We'll appeal."

"Oh." I groaned out loud. Geraldine, the psychology department office manager, looked up at me and frowned. "Are you okay, Beth?"

"Yeah. Yeah, thanks, I'm okay." I walked down the hallway, put my key in my office door, threw my briefcase on the floor, hung up my raincoat. I opened the file cabinet, stuck the message in the Dugas file, closed the drawer, noted the *click*, sighed. Then I faced the truth—I hadn't expected a guilty verdict. The three jurors who had held out for acquittal in the first trial gave me confidence. What happened in this second trial to make Von Williams appear guilty? Was the prosecutor more confident? Was my testimony less convincing? Did Williams's hot-tempered outbursts turn the jurors against him?

I pictured Williams in my mind, sitting at the defense table, hearing the guilty verdict, then walking out of the courtroom, guards at his elbows. Williams was guilty in the eyes of the law. He would go to prison. He had lost his freedom.

But was he guilty? I slapped my hand against the closed file drawer. *Give it up, Beth. It's over.* I knew I had to put the case out of my mind, I had to convince myself that justice was done. How could I believe otherwise? Twenty-four jurors in two separate trials had listened to the facts of this case. Twenty-four minds had sifted through the evidence, searching for the truth. The first jury couldn't come to a unanimous decision, but nine of twelve jurors believed Williams was guilty. All twelve members of the second jury voted for conviction. Twenty-one of twenty-four people who had heard every shred of evidence in this case believed that Von Williams was guilty. I had no business arguing with those percentages, not if I wanted to stay sane.

* * *

Two months later, on December 3, 1981, there was another message waiting for me from Louis Dugas: "8:45 A.M. New man has confessed. Von Williams a free man."

I immediately dialed Dugas's number. "Louis, what happened?" I screamed into the phone. I didn't even think to introduce myself.

"Elizabeth? You're not going to believe this. You're just not going to believe this." Dugas took a deep breath, then laughed. "I'm sorry, I just can't stop laughing. Laughing and crying." He told me then about the events of the previous week. The Louisiana State Police, responding to a hot tip, picked up thirty-year-old Jon Simonis on suspicion of being the infamous "ski mask rapist" who had raped dozens of women in Louisiana and neighboring states. Simonis confessed to seventy-seven crimes in seven different states—including the rapes for which Clarence Von Williams was convicted.

"They videotaped Simonis," Dugas was saying, "they have his entire confession on tape. The Orange County prosecutors watched the videotape and immediately dismissed the charges against Williams. This is unbelievable, simply unbelievable."

The wire services immediately picked up on this bizarre story with the shocker of a twist at the end. On December 6 the Seattle *Times* featured this Associated Press story:

ACCUSED GETS FREEDOM, NOT PRISON

ORANGE, TEX.—(AP)—A 42-YEAR-OLD CHEMICAL-PLANT WORKER SENTENCED TO 50 YEARS IN PRISON FOR RAPE RODE OFF TO FREEDOM IN A LIMOUSINE TO THE CHEERS OF HIS FRIENDS AFTER ANOTHER MAN CONFESSED TO THE CRIME.

"I DIDN'T WANT TO BE FOUND INNOCENT, BECAUSE EVERYONE WOULD HAVE ALWAYS THOUGHT I HAD JUST HIRED A GOOD LAWYER," SAID CLARENCE VON WILLIAMS AFTER CHARGES AGAINST HIM WERE DISMISSED AT A SPECIAL COURT HEARING FRIDAY.

"I WANTED THE MAN TO BE CAUGHT AND CONFESS. I WAS SO SCARED HE WAS GOING TO BE KILLED . . . AND NOBODY WOULD EVER KNOW."

The story continued for several paragraphs, but it was those words—"and nobody would ever know"—that haunted me for weeks afterward. One person would know—Clarence Von Williams. Williams would be sitting in a jail cell right now, staring at the concrete walls, aching for his wife and children, if the Louisiana state police hadn't gotten lucky and found Simonis. I couldn't imagine a more anguished loneliness, a deeper despair, than knowing the truth and yet, at the same time, being unable to convince others of it.

I didn't like to think about what that could do to the soul of a human being, to have to sit in a prison cell day after day for a crime you had not committed. And nothing to look forward to at the end of a day but the knowledge of hundreds more days like the one you just endured.

In August 1988, more than six years after Von Williams was declared innocent and given back his freedom, I gave a speech to several hundred attorneys gathered for a symposium at Northwestern Law School in Chicago. After my talk, a member of the audience approached me, shook my hand, and introduced himself.

"I was one of the prosecutors involved in the Williams case in Texas back in 1981," he said. "I've got an interesting postscript to that case, if you have a minute." We sat down in the front row of the empty lecture hall, and he described what happened on the day that Sally Blackwell and her two children came to the district attorney's office to watch Simonis's videotaped confession.

"They didn't know at that point that Simonis had confessed," the attorney told me. "We brought them into a small room, turned the lights off, and played the videotape. After a few minutes, the two teenage children looked at their mother. It was clear from the shocked expressions on their faces that they recognized this man. But the mother refused to look at them. She continued to stare at the man on the tape, and then she slowly began to shake her head back and forth. 'No,' she said, her voice rising over the sound of the videotape, 'no, no, no, *no, no.*'

"Simonis confessed to details that only the rapist could have known, details that nobody outside the prosecutors' office knew anything about," the attorney said. "And yet the victim couldn't accept the fact that she had made a mistaken ID. She couldn't bring herself to admit that someone other than Von Williams might have committed this crime."

Here was real, living proof that people can become so attached to their memories that even when obvious contradictions and discrepancies are raised, they refuse to change their minds. I remembered something Judge Jerome Franks wrote in his book *Not Guilty*. "As a witness you will resent any doubt about your memory as an assault on your basic integrity, a presumptuous intrusion on your personality" (p. 210). Our memories are so valuable because they are literally a part of us—they tell us who we are, what we have experienced, and how we should feel.

I told the prosecutor about a recent study conducted at Yale. Subjects viewed a crime and were then asked to pick out the "criminal" from a series of twelve photographs, none of which was of the actual criminal. Several days later the subjects were asked to choose again from six photographs, one of which was the real "criminal" and one of which was the incorrect face selected previously. Forty-four percent of the time, the subjects stuck with their original choice—even with the real "criminal" staring them in the face.

"In a way, that's similar to what happened in the Williams case," I said. "The victim made her choice—Clarence Von Williams—and later, even with the real criminal staring her in the face, confessing to the rape, and bringing up details that only he could have known, she couldn't accept it. She stayed with her original choice, the erroneous choice of Clarence Von Williams. Once Von Williams's face merged with her memory of the rapist's face, and once she committed herself to that memory by stating in court that Von Williams was her rapist, it became impossible to separate the two memories. They were, in a very real sense, permanently fused together."

I thought about that conversation for a long time afterward. Research and laboratory studies have proven, over and over again, that memory is fallible. The facts are published in prestigious journals, the language is scholarly and precise, and the methodology is faultless. But what happened to Clarence Von Williams put a face on those facts, a heart and soul in those words. The Williams case brought the research out of the laboratory and made it *real*.

Sally Blackwell's testimony almost sent Von Williams to jail for fifty years. She couldn't face the enormity of that mistake. When she committed herself, in court, in written testimony, under penalty of perjury, to the choice of this face, this man called Clarence Von Williams, that choice became the memory against which all other information would be matched. Confronted with a different face, she had to reject it because it simply didn't fit what she had stored in her mind.

Sally Blackwell's memory, though persistent and powerful, was harmless now as far as Von Williams was concerned. But imagine a different ending, where the ski-mask rapist was not apprehended by the Louisiana police. Imagine that his videotaped confession did not exist. In this ending, the power of Sally Blackwell's memory would be enough by itself to keep Clarence Von Williams in prison for many years to come.

IVAN THE TERRIBLE:
JOHN DEMJANJUK

"This doubt of identification, it produces a shudder in the heart
that, God forbid, this whole thing will end in a terrible farce."
—Israeli author Chaim Guri

I t was a cold, rainy January day. The beginning of 1987, the year
in which one case would become an obsession. It all began with
a phone call from New York.

"Dr. Loftus? Dr. Elizabeth Loftus?" It was a bad connection, and
the line crackled in my ear.

"Yes, this is Elizabeth Loftus," I said, raising my voice above the
static.

"This is Mark O'Connor calling from New York City. I'm representing John Demjanjuk." He pronounced the name very slowly—
Dem-yan-yuk. "Mr. Demjanjuk is a former American citizen who
has been charged with war crimes and extradited to Israel for trial.
Five surviving witnesses of Treblinka claim that he is a Ukrainian
guard who committed horrendous atrocities at the death camp."

"Ivan the Terrible," I said the words slowly. "I've heard of him."

"We need your help," O'Connor said. "This entire case against
Mr. Demjanjuk hinges on the memories of these five eyewitnesses—
memories that are now thirty-five years old."

I didn't hesitate. "I appreciate your call, Mr. O'Connor, but I'm sorry. I can't take this case."

"Why not?" Those two simple words housed such a complicated question.

"I'm very busy," I said. "I have three other cases right now, I have classes to teach. And I'm Jewish." There now, I thought—leave me alone.

"You're also the world's expert on eyewitness memory, and without your testimony it's conceivable that an innocent man will be sentenced to die. Dr. Loftus, please, listen to me, that's all I ask. Listen and keep an open mind. I promise you—I swear to you that John Demjanjuk is innocent. He is not the vicious maniac known as Ivan the Terrible." O'Connor was talking fast, filling up the airspace in an effort to ward off any further rejections. "Several of the identifying witnesses testified right after the war that Ivan was killed in an uprising at Treblinka in August 1943. Six of the Treblinka survivors confronted with his picture did *not* recognize him. The survivors who did identify his picture did so under intensive questioning. If you will just let me meet with you, I'll give you the facts. Then you can make up your mind whether or not to take the case. But don't judge this man before he has even come to trial. He deserves a fair hearing—he is innocent until proven guilty. No matter how horrendous the crime, that is the law of our land and the law of Israel."

Even now I remember the insistent, desperate edge in O'Connor's voice. He had appealed to my curiosity—could Demjanjuk be innocent?—and to my professional ethics—how could I say no to an argument I used myself? I hesitated and O'Connor, sensing my vulnerability, pounced again.

"Let me come to Seattle and talk with you. I'll fly out this weekend."

"From New York?"

"The trial starts in a month. We don't have much time."

"I can't stop you from flying out here," I said finally. "But I won't promise anything."

"Just promise me that you'll listen," he said. "Because believe me, I will convince you that he's innocent. John Demjanjuk is not Ivan the Terrible."

*   *   *

Mark O'Connor spent two days with me, talking nonstop from early in the morning until late in the evening, pacing up and down my living room, pulling document after document from his briefcase, lecturing, pleading, shouting, using all his powers of persuasion to try to convince me to take the case.

He talked on and on about the "incredibly emotional" nature of this trial, the most famous Nazi war crimes trial in Jerusalem since Adolf Eichmann was tried and hanged twenty-five years earlier. But Ivan wasn't like Eichmann, O'Connor said, lowering his voice. No, Ivan wasn't a bureaucrat, a technocrat who signed papers, made phone calls, attended meetings, a distant architect working on Hitler's grisly plans to exterminate the Jews. Ivan was something altogether different because *he was there,* in the camps, day after day. This man tortured and mutilated prisoners, beating them with a lead pipe as they walked down the "tube" into the gas chambers. This man was responsible for driving the diesel engines that filled the gas chambers with deadly fumes, a killing process that took approximately thirty to forty minutes. Hundreds, perhaps thousands of times Ivan ran those engines. This man could be held personally responsible for murdering nearly a million men, women, and children.

"Do you know about Treblinka?" O'Connor asked me. "Do you *know* about this camp?" I sat on my sofa, mute, unblinking. "Let me tell you about it," he said. "Treblinka was the horror of all horrors, the worst of the worst, the nightmare to end all nightmares. Treblinka was a death camp, pure and simple, a place created to mass-produce death, where bodies were 'processed' as quickly and efficiently as possible."

Most of the Jews arrived by train, O'Connor explained. The average time between the arrival of a transport and completion of the killing of every man, woman, and child on that transport was about an hour and a half. Each transport brought an average of six thousand new arrivals. In one eight-hour day it was possible for this man called Ivan to kill thousands of people.

O'Connor stopped talking for a moment and we stared at each other, ashamed of this act of translating human lives into statistics. What would we do next, take out a calculator and figure how many people could be killed in a ten-hour day, a sixty-hour week, a 365-day year, given the train schedules, time spent unloading and undressing, the capacity of the gas chambers, and so on? What kind of horror is buried in such statistics?

In 1943 there was an uprising, O'Connor went on. Two hundred men and women participated. Of those, only fifty or sixty would survive the war. Fifty people survived, then, out of nearly 1 million; one person for every twenty thousand people killed.

Imagine that. Put yourself in their place, Dr. Loftus. Imagine that you survived this death camp, that you were one of only fifty people who did survive, and that now, thirty-five years later, you discover that Ivan the Terrible may still be alive. Imagine that you are in your seventies or eighties, a grandparent, perhaps a great-grandparent, and you have this opportunity to point your finger at one of the men responsible, *physically* responsible, for torturing, mutilating, murdering your people—your friends, your parents, your wife or husband, your children. You have only a few years to live. People are forgetting the Holocaust. Some claim it never happened. Here is a chance to bring the memories alive again, to reach back into history and bring justice out of those ashes. Soon there will be no one alive to remember. If you and forty-nine others had died, no one would remember, no one would know. Think about that, Dr. Loftus.

O'Connor stopped pacing and sat down on the chair facing me. "Now think about John Demjanjuk," he said, "a Ukrainian who emigrated to the U.S. in 1952 and became a naturalized American." Demjanjuk, O'Connor told me, was a church-going family man who settled near Cleveland, a retired auto mechanic for the Ford Motor Company, a grandfather who liked to putter around in his garden. The very model of the solid citizen. Until 1976 when the U.S. government pasted Demjanjuk's 1951 immigration picture on a sheet of cardboard along with photographs of sixteen other Ukrainians suspected of war crimes and sent the sheet of photographs to the Israeli government. Until nine of seventeen eyewitnesses, all survivors of Treblinka, identified John Demjanjuk as the notorious Ivan. Until 1980 when the Soviets produced a photocopy of an old ID card that placed "Ivan Demjanjuk" at the Trawniki training camp in Poland where the SS prepared prison guards for the Sobibor and Treblinka death camps. Until February 1981 when the U.S. Justice

Department concluded a denaturalization hearing in Cleveland and stripped Demjanjuk of his American citizenship, declaring him a Nazi war criminal. Until 1986, when after five years of failed appeals and incarceration in federal prisons, Demjanjuk was extradited to Israel to be tried as a mass murderer in the most sensational Nazi war crimes trial to take place in Jerusalem since the trial of Adolf Eichmann.

"In the tortuous process of these events, John Demjanjuk's life has been destroyed," O'Connor said, his hands clasped together, his eyes holding mine. "He has been bankrupted, imprisoned, stripped of his U.S. citizenship, and extradited to Israel to stand trial as the most vicious and horrific incarnation of evil imaginable. If John Demjanjuk is Ivan the Terrible, he deserves all this. He deserves worse, much worse, for all the tortures and horrors we could inflict would never equal the agony that he caused in his twelve months at Treblinka. But if he is innocent, then a terrible injustice has been done, an injustice as horrendous, as awe-inspiring as those injustices perpetrated almost half a century ago."

O'Connor made a visible attempt to calm himself down, taking several deep breaths, lifting his shoulders, exhaling loudly. When he began talking again, his voice was calm. The subject now was "the alibi." John Demjanjuk insists he was never at the Trawniki training camp, that he never even heard of Treblinka or Sobibor until after the war. Demjanjuk claims that he was a Ukrainian conscript in the Red Army when Hitler attacked the Soviet Union in June 1941. In May 1942 he was captured by the Germans in the Crimea and sent to several POW labor camps, ending up at the huge prisoners' complex at Chelm in Poland. In mid-1944 he was transferred to Austria and began fighting in the anti-Soviet Ukrainian unit, eventually joining the "Vlasow Army." At the end of the war he went over to the Allied side in Bavaria.

The Department of Justice accepts Demjanjuk's story up until the summer of 1942, when he was imprisoned in the POW camp at Chelm. They believe that Demjanjuk was transferred from Chelm to the Trawniki training camp and then to Treblinka where he remained for almost a year, from October 1942 to September 1943.

"What about the Russian identification card placing him at Trawniki?" I asked.

"It's a KGB forgery," O'Connor said. "The card was created by the KGB in an attempt to punish Demjanjuk for joining a pro-Nazi Ukrainian unit at the end of the war."

A KGB forgery? I raised my eyebrows. Was O'Connor serious?

"The stuff of spy novels, right?" O'Connor said, smiling grimly. "Okay, let's talk about this so-called ID card. The photograph on the card does resemble John Demjanjuk as a young man, and it correctly lists his birth date, his father's name, and an identifying scar on his back. But experts who were asked to examine the card found a missing umlaut on one word—how could the spelling be wrong on an original German card? The date of issue, place of issue, and officer's signature are all missing; misaligned seals on the card make it appear as if separate documents were placed together; and the photograph appears as if it were tampered with. Staple marks on the picture indicate that it had been stapled to some other documents before being placed on the card, parts of the card are blacked out, and whoever is depicted in the picture is wearing a Russian tunic. Why," O'Connor asked, "would John Demjanjuk be wearing a Russian tunic if he were, in fact, being trained as an SS guard?

"There's more," O'Connor continued. "The card lists 'Ivan's' height as five feet nine inches; John Demjanjuk is six-feet 1-inch tall. That's a four-inch mistake. And"—O'Connor spread his hands out, palms up—"we have no card. All we have is a photocopy, because the Soviets refuse to turn over the original card to Israel. Why? Because if we get our hands on the original card and discover that it is a KGB forgery, it will blow the case against Demjanjuk to smithereens and expose the Russians as liars and frauds."

"Even if the card is a KGB forgery," I said, willing to concede that the card had its problems, "how can you explain away the eyewitnesses who claim that John Demjanjuk is Ivan?"

"The eyewitnesses," O'Connor gently nodded his head. "This is the hard part," he said after a moment, "because these people were there, and their memories are incredibly precious. But remember, we're not disputing those memories—we're not saying they weren't there, or that Ivan was a figment of their imagination. We are only seeking the answer to this question: Is John Demjanjuk the man they called Ivan the Terrible? And from there we must ask one more question—are these memories still sharp enough, clear and accurate enough to condemn a man to death? Can we hang a man based on thirty-five-year-old memories? Memories, as you know better than anyone else, are sensitive and delicate, and they can be altered, even created by intervening information. Let's talk about how these memories of Ivan the Terrible were elicited."

The questioning began in Israel early in 1976 when the Israelis received a request from the U.S. government to question survivors of Treblinka and Sobibor regarding Ukrainians suspected of Nazi war crimes. Included with the request were three photographs of Ukrainians now living in the United States. Photograph number 16 was the 1951 immigration photo of John Demjanjuk, thought to be a guard at Sobibor; pasted right next to Demjanjuk's picture was a picture of Fedor Fedorenko, allegedly a guard at Treblinka.

The Israeli police published an advertisement in the newspaper, asking Treblinka and Sobibor survivors to contact them. O'Connor pulled a sheet of paper from the file and read the advertisement to me: "The Nazi Crime Investigation Division is conducting an investigation against the Ukrainians Ivan Demjanjuk and Fedor Fedorenko."

I raised my eyebrows. "Before the hearings even began, then, the witnesses knew the names of the people to be identified."

"That's right," O'Connor said. "Now let's look closely at those IDs—keep in mind that although some of the fifty survivors worked in close proximity to Ivan, they never had any face-to-face encounters with him. They never talked to him or engaged in any joint activity. In fact, they would have deliberately stayed out of his way and avoided all eye contact with him because any encounter with the dreaded Ivan could mean death. They knew that very well.

"Also keep in mind that the photograph of John Demjanjuk used in the majority of these identifications was taken in 1951 when he emigrated to the U.S. and shows him at age thirty, nine years older than he was in 1942. Thus we have witnesses thirty-five years after the fact attempting to identify a man they had known for less than a year from a photograph taken nine years after their last encounter with him."

O'Connor recited the details of the interviews, beginning on May 9, 1976, at 10:00 A.M., when the first eyewitness was interviewed. Eugen Turowski, a Treblinka survivor, recognized photo number 17, Fedor Fedorenko, but he did not identify photograph number 16—Ivan—which was pasted right next to Fedorenko's photo on the cardboard display card. Ivan, at that point in the investigation, was thought to be a guard at the Sobibor concentration camp.

At 1:00 P.M. that same day, Treblinka survivor Abraham Goldfarb claimed that the man in picture number 16 seemed "familiar." This was the first time a relationship between Demjanjuk and Treblinka was suggested; Goldfarb, however, did not mention the name Ivan. At 2:30 P.M. that same day, Goldfarb gave a second statement. The English translation from the original Yiddish sounded stilted and awkward: "To the question: I don't remember the names of the Ukrainians—the name of Demjanjuk I don't recall," Goldfarb told the Israeli investigators. "I do remember a Ukrainian whose first name was Ivan. He may have been twenty-three to twenty-four years old, was rather tall, had a full round face. He wore a black uniform, a seaman's cap, he had no rank, I didn't see a rank insignia on him."

From this part of Goldfarb's statement, O'Connor said, it was obvious that the Israeli investigators asked Goldfarb if he remembered the name "Ivan Demjanjuk." His description of Ivan's face could have been pulled from his thirty-five-year-old memory; or he might simply have been describing the picture he saw just an hour earlier.

"I believe I recognize this Ivan on picture number 16," Goldfarb continued. "The man depicted on picture 16, I remember from the gas chambers. His function at the gas chambers was, together with a German SS-man, the 'machinist' of the gas chambers whose name I have forgotten, to release the gas from the Diesel motor into the gas chamber."

Mr. Goldfarb must have been shocked by his tentative identification of Ivan, O'Connor explained, because in a memoir published right after the war he'd written that Ivan was killed in the 1943 uprising. Goldfarb's identification must have shocked the Israeli investigators too, because they had been told by the U.S. government that Ivan was at Sobibor, not Treblinka.

The next day, May 10, Eugen Turowski was interviewed once again, presumably to verify Mr. Goldfarb's surprising statement. The investigators began the interview by asking Turowski if he remembered a man by the name of Ivan Demjanjuk. Mr. Turowski responded: "When asked if I knew an Ukrainian by the name of

Demjanjuk, Ivan, I declare as follows: I know the name Demjanjuk and even better, the first name of Ivan. To me, he was Ivan. This Ukrainian I can well remember, I knew him personally, because at times he came to the shop to have things repaired."

Mr. Turowski was again shown the seventeen photographs pasted on the three brown sheets of cardboard, and this time he immediately pointed at photo number 16. "This is Ivan," he testified. "Him, I recognize immediately and with full assurance. He was of medium build, stockily built and had a round, full face. He had a short, wide neck and even then his hair looked like here on this photograph, a high forehead with a bald pate starting. He was still a very young man, could have been twenty-three to twenty-four at the most."

Why, O'Connor asked me, did Turowski recognize Ivan *immediately* and with *full assurance* when the day before he didn't recognize him at all? Isn't it reasonable to assume that because Goldfarb and Turowski knew each other and because they testified within hours of each other, they talked about this astonishing discovery: *Ivan is still alive!*

And there's a second puzzle—why did Turowski mention the last name "Demjanjuk"? None of the survivors knew Ivan's last name. They only knew him as Ivan or Ivan Grozny—*Ivan the Terrible.* How did Turowski know the name Demjanjuk?

O'Connor answered his own question. "He knew the name from the advertisement in the paper and from the investigators' questions. They put the name in his mind so that he *thought* he remembered it. I ask you—what else did they put in his mind?"

O'Connor picked up another piece of paper that listed the details of Elijahu Rosenberg's identification of Ivan. On May 11 Mr. Rosenberg pointed at photograph number 16 and said: "I see a great resemblance to the Ukrainian Ivan, who was active in camp 2, and who was called 'Ivan Grozny' (Ivan the Terrible). It is the same face construction, he had a round full face around the eyes and forehead. He had a high forehead with the beginning of baldness, at any rate, a very high forehead and very short hair. He had a short, thick neck, stocky build, and swarthy skin. I remember that his ears were standing away from his face. I decline, however, to identify him with absolute certainty. He was very young, maybe twenty-two to twenty-three years old."

Many years earlier Rosenberg, like Goldfarb, stated that Ivan was killed in the uprising. In 1947 in Vienna, Rosenberg told an investigator, "Some of the people ran into the barracks where Ukrainian guards were sleeping, among them was Ivan, and killed them with shovels. These men had the night shift and were very tired, so that they did not wake up quickly enough."

But after identifying Ivan, Mr. Rosenberg insisted that the interviewer in Vienna had misrepresented his words, that other people had *told* him that Ivan was killed, but that he hadn't actually *seen* Ivan die. Still, why did Mr. Rosenberg positively identify John Demjanjuk as the notorious Ivan when for thirty years he had believed that Ivan was murdered in the 1943 uprising?

"The Israeli hearings continued during the summer of 1976," O'Connor said, picking up a new sheet of paper. "Two witnesses, Mr. Teigman and Mr. Kudlik, did not identify Demjanjuk as Ivan. Only July 4, 1976, Simon Greenspan identified Fedorenko but failed to ID Demjanjuk. The identification of Fedorenko proves that Greenspan was at Treblinka and also that he was able to remember faces. According to all survivors' reports, Ivan made himself much more conspicuous than Fedorenko. Why, then, did Greenspan recognize Fedorenko and not Demjanjuk?"

O'Connor was attempting to use Mr. Greenspan's identification of Fedorenko as proof of a good memory. I had to remind him that an eyewitness identification, positive or negative, doesn't actually *prove* anything. "A positive identification only tells us that the person *believes* that he recognizes a face or that he believes a certain person is guilty of certain crimes. A belief is not absolute proof."

"Yes, of course, you're right, I can't have it both ways, can I?" Still, he seemed a little peeved by my interruption.

Other witnesses interviewed at that time who did not identify Ivan were Dov Freiberg, Shalom Cohen, Sophia Engleman, and Meir Suss.

The next positive identifications were obtained in September and October 1976—at least four months after Turowski, Goldfarb, and Rosenberg testified and only a month or two after the August reunion of Treblinka survivors held every year in Tel Aviv on the anniversary of the uprising. All the witnesses who identified Demjanjuk lived in Israel and attended that reunion.

"I think it is reasonable to assume," O'Connor said, "that Turowski, Goldfarb, and Rosenberg talked with their fellow survivors about the terrible shock they received when they recognized Ivan. One can imagine their conversation. 'My God! Ivan is still alive! I saw him with my own eyes!' "

On September 21 at 1:00 P.M. Josef Czarny pointed to photograph number 16 and said: "This is Ivan, yes it is Ivan, the notorious Ivan. Thirty years have gone by, but I recognize him at first sight with complete certainty. I would know him, I believe, even in the dark. He was very tall, of sturdy frame, his face at the time was not as full and fat from gorging himself with food, as on the picture. However, it is the same face construction, the same nose, the same eyes and forehead, as he had at that time. A mistake is out of the question."

On September 30 Gustav Boraks pointed at photograph number 16 and said: "This is the likeness of Ivan . . . I recognize him with one hundred percent of certainty. I recognize him by his features. He was younger then, up to twenty-five years old, the face was not as full, but there is no doubt in my mind that he is the one."

Boraks, O'Connor explained, was shown only eight pictures while most of the other survivors were shown seventeen. Israeli law requires that witnesses be shown a minimum of ten pictures.

"Why?" I asked. In the early 1980s I'd consulted with the Law Reform Commission of Canada to develop standard procedures for eyewitness identification in criminal cases. In our report, we offered these guidelines: "The witness shall be shown an array of photographs composed of the suspect's photograph and those of at least eleven distractors." Eleven wasn't considered a magic number by any means, but the consensus of the commission was that fewer than eleven photographs did not present a fair test of the witness's ability to make an identification. The danger of showing a small number of photographs is that a witness can take a wild guess and pick out the suspect a fair percentage of the time.

O'Connor shook his head at my question, a slow, tired protest. *Who knows?*

"The next positive identification came on October 3, by Abraham Lindwasser," O'Connor continued. "By now we have six identifications ranging from extremely questionable to positive. But let's go back to September 29 and an interview with a survivor called Schlomo Helman. Mr. Helman was at Treblinka from July 1942 until August 1943—longer than any of the other survivors. He was forced to assist in the construction of the gas chambers and remained in Camp 2—Ivan's camp—the whole time. He worked right next to Ivan for many months and was able to watch him from a distance of only five or six feet.

"Helman was shown only five photographs." O'Connor spread his hands and sighed—who can figure these things out? "When he came to Fedorenko's picture, he pointed and said, 'This man I have seen in Treblinka.' But from the four remaining photographs he did not identify Ivan even though he knew, as the others did, that they were looking for a man called *Ivan* Demjanjuk. Now let's consider this for a moment."

O'Connor sat down on the sofa next to me. "We can assume that there was nothing wrong with Schlomo Helman's memory, because he remembered Fedorenko. Why, then, didn't he recognize Ivan? Why would he forget the horrible Ivan and remember the lesser known, less visible Fedorenko? He knew who he was supposed to be looking for—and still he did not recognize Demjanjuk. Why were the other survivors so certain that Demjanjuk was Ivan and yet why didn't Helman pick him out with only four remaining pictures to choose from?

"We'll never know the answers to these questions," O'Connor said, "because Helman died last year."

Schlomo Helman's death was a clear blow to Demjanjuk's defense. It would have been much more powerful to have Helman walk into court as a live witness and say "That is not him" than for O'Connor to read the words from a piece of paper.

O'Connor quickly summarized the three remaining successful identifications. On March 29, 1978, Pinchas Epstein pointed to photograph number 16 and said: "This photo reminds me very strongly of Ivan. The photo is not quite clear and also the change in age must make a difference. The shape of the face, especially the rounded forehead, strengthens my feeling that it is Ivan. The characteristic short neck on broad shoulders—that's exactly what Ivan looked like."

On December 27, 1979, Sonia Levkowitch positively identified John Demjanjuk as Ivan the Terrible, and on March 12, 1980, in a hotel room in New York City, Chil Meir Rajchman identified Demjanjuk from a stack of eight photographs.

Rajchman was the ninth and final witness over a period of almost four years who eventually identified Ivan. Three of these nine eyewitnesses—Turowski, Goldfarb, and Lindwasser—died after they made their identification; Levkowitch eventually withdrew her testimony.

At this point O'Connor reminded me that there were eight known eyewitnesses who did *not* identify Ivan and at least fifteen others whose names were not known who did not identify Ivan when questioned by the Israeli investigators. But at the trial five surviving witnesses would testify for the prosecution: Rosenberg, Czarny, Boraks, Epstein, and Rajchman.

O'Connor talked about the trial, then, and I continued to take notes, ask questions, make comments. But my mind seemed to stop, for I have no solid memory of the rest of that conversation. I remember only the sensation of names, dates, and places spinning around in my head, as I struggled to find some glue to make all the pieces stick together, some vital piece of information that would make everything come together into a pattern that made sense. Why did Rosenberg positively identify Demjanjuk after believing for thirty years that Ivan had been killed in the uprising? Why did Schlomo Helman look right at Ivan's picture and pass it over? Why did the Israeli investigators show some of the survivors seventeen pictures, one eight, and one five? What about the Trawniki ID card with Ivan's name and picture; was it possible that the KGB would manufacture this in order to embarrass the Ukrainians, or was this some sort of paranoid delusion cooked up by the emotional fervor of the case? Why were there no supporting witnesses for Demjanjuk's alibi? Who, exactly, was John Demjanjuk?

Sitting on my sofa watching O'Connor plead his case, I felt as if I were being torn apart. On the outside, assessing the facts, taking notes, asking detailed questions, was Dr. Elizabeth Loftus, professor at the University of Washington and expert witness in hundreds of court cases. She wanted to say, "Yes, of course, I'll take the case." The Israeli police interrogation practices were, indeed, questionable, and the prosecution was depending on memories that were thirty-five years old. If these memories were to be believed and John Demjanjuk was found guilty, he would be sentenced to death. It was a case that cried out for expert testimony.

But in those long hours spent listening to Mark O'Connor talking about the Treblinka death camp and the aging memories of the victims of the Holocaust, something cracked my cool, professional exterior. Inside, like one of those Russian folk toys that pull apart to reveal a slightly smaller version of the same figure, was Beth Loftus, wife of Geoffrey Loftus, best friend of Ilene Bernstein, niece of Uncle Joe Breskin. Beth Loftus feared for her friendships, for the personal price that she would pay if she testified for John Demjanjuk. Beth Loftus kept thinking about Uncle Joe, a survivor of anti-Semitic pogroms in Russia and the only relative of her parents' generation still alive. "What would Uncle Joe say if I took this case?" Beth Loftus asked herself over and over again. "What would Geoff say, what would Ilene say?"

And then the shell opened wider to reveal Beth Fishman, daughter of Rebecca and Sidney, whose grandparents were born in Russia and Rumania. Beth Fishman was the five-year-old Jewish girl who cried bitterly when the boy next door made fun of her last name. Beth Fishman was the adolescent who, fearing that her boyfriend broke up with her because she was Jewish, instructed her best friend to take him a message: "Tell him I'm only half Jewish."

The lie brought a shameful flush to my face even now, thirty years later. Which of my parents did I deny then? Which half of me did I throw away so casually and for such a cheap price?

O'Connor was watching me, waiting patiently for me to make up my mind. *What was my answer—would I take the case?*

I took a deep breath and spoke very slowly, each word measured, the emphasis the same, the intonation unchanging. "You said you would convince me that Ivan was innocent. You haven't done that. Nine people have identified him. Even after thirty-five years, these memories could be accurate. But," I said, aware of the pained expression on O'Connor's face, "you have planted some doubts in my mind. I'll need some time to research the case. Leave me your files, let me look through them, and I'll let you know my decision."

"The trial starts next month," O'Connor said. "Chances are good that you won't go on the stand until next October or November. I can give you until March—but no later."

Two months, I said to myself. Could I make up my mind in two months? "One other thing. If I do decide to take this case, I don't want any money. Not a penny. You can reimburse me for my expenses, but I do not want to be paid for my time." If I was going to testify for Demjanjuk it would be for principles, not for money.

O'Connor shook my hand at the door. "I swear to you that John

Demjanjuk is innocent," he said, squeezing my hand. "I believe that with all my heart."

Shaking his hand, watching him as he walked down the cement stairs, I wondered if there was anything left that I believed in with all my heart.

The file should have convinced me. A case that relied on thirty-five-year-old memories should have been enough by itself. Add to those decaying memories the fact that the witnesses knew before they looked at the photographs that the police had a suspect, and they were even given the suspect's first and last name—Ivan Demjanjuk. Add to that scenario the fact that the Israeli investigators asked the witnesses if they could identify John Demjanjuk, a clearly prejudicial and leading question. Add to that the fact that the witnesses almost certainly talked about their identification afterward, possibly contaminating subsequent identifications. Add to that the repeated showing of John Demjanjuk's photograph so that with each exposure, his face became more and more familiar and the witnesses became more and more confident and convincing.

Then factor into all of the above the intensely emotional nature of this particular case, for the man these people were identifying was more than a tool of the Nazis, more, even, than the dreaded Ivan who ran the diesel engines and tortured and mutilated prisoners. This man, if he was Ivan the Terrible, was personally responsible for murdering their mothers, fathers, brothers, sisters, wives, children.

Dr. Loftus would have stopped with the file. She would have added up all the factors, assessed the problems, calculated the numerous possibilities for error and responded, "Yes, of course, I'll testify about the general workings of memory, and discuss how and why it can fail."

But Beth Fishman couldn't stop with the file. Thirty years earlier I had turned my back on my Jewish heritage, pretending it didn't exist, pretending it was just one of those things you're born with, like a mole or big feet or blond hair. *Pretending it didn't matter.* I had ignored the Holocaust for years, shoving it out of my mind.

Then came the phone call and the visit from O'Connor. Memories of my childhood came back to me, the stories told by my grandfather of the early twentieth-century pogroms in Russia and the stories told by my mother and father about the Holocaust. These skeletons were not all bones and fine, dry dust, but lively ghosts filled with energy and emotion and minds of their own. Faced with these haunting memories, I had no choice in the Demjanjuk matter. I had to know the facts and the faces and the events behind the facts.

It was Beth Fishman who went into the bookstores and libraries, searching for a picture or a description that would make the decision easier. I read every book I could find on Treblinka, and then I turned to the books on Auschwitz, Sobibor, Buchenwald, Bergen-Belsen. I read Anne Frank again, and Elie Wiesel, Hannah Arendt, Aaron Applefeld. I stalked the library shelves, searching for the answer to one particular question—who was Ivan and what did he do?

In *The Death Camp Treblinka,* a book of eyewitness accounts, I found some answers. Jankiel Wiernik, a Warsaw building contractor deported to Treblinka on August 23, 1942, wrote this description of Treblinka:

The machinery of the gas chambers was operated by two Ukrainians. One of them, Ivan, was tall, and though his eyes seemed kind and gentle, he was a sadist. He enjoyed torturing his victims. He would often pounce upon us while we were working; he would nail our ears to the walls or make us lie down on the floor and whip us brutally. While he did this, his face showed sadistic satisfaction and he laughed and joked. He finished off the victims according to his mood at the moment. The other Ukrainian was called Nicholas. He had a pale face and the same mentality as Ivan.

The day I first saw men, women and children being led into the house of death I almost went insane. I tore at my hair and shed bitter tears of despair. I suffered most when I looked at the children, accompanied by their mothers or walking alone, entirely ignorant of the fact that within a few minutes their lives would be snuffed out amidst horrible tortures. Their eyes glittered with fear and still more, perhaps, with amazement. It seemed as if the question, "What is this? What's it all about?" was frozen on their lips. But seeing the stony expressions on the faces of their elders, they matched their behavior to the occasion. They either stood motionless or pressed tightly against each other or against their parents, and tensely awaited their horrible end.

Suddenly, the entrance door flew open and out came Ivan, holding a heavy gas pipe, and Nicholas, brandishing a saber. At a given signal, they would begin admitting the victims, beating them savagely as they moved into the chamber. The screams of the women, the weeping of the children, cries of despair and misery, the pleas for mercy, for God's vengeance ring in my ears to this day, making it impossible for me to forget the misery I saw.

I closed my eyes for a moment, trying to stop the images set in motion by those words, to still my mind, to slow down, to *think*.

Samuel Rajzman, who lost seventy members of his family in the Holocaust, wrote these words:

We had a Ukrainian guard, a terrible man: he used to beat people to death with a rod of iron. Whoever fell into his hands—*bang*! he was dead. That was it. He used to hit them over the head. When he beat them in the face, it meant they would be taken out later on and killed.

The first thing was to torture people. They put you on a table, locked your legs and arms to the table, and gave you 25 lashes. When you had had these lashes, if you survived, you wouldn't be able to sit for four weeks. You couldn't move and you couldn't sit. One morning, they found on a prisoner some bread that hadn't originated in the camp. He had probably bought it from some Ukrainian for a lot of dollars. So another Ukrainian held his head in a pitcher of water until he drowned. I saw this with my own eyes! The tortures they invented—it's incredible!

Was that Ivan? Every time I saw the word "Ukrainian" I thought— *Ivan*? My eyes burned, but I kept searching. Having entered this particular house of horrors, I had to march through each room, looking into the eyes of all who lived there. I needed to *know* them, to touch them, to think through them. How else could I make my decision?

I searched through the survivor list at the end of the book and found the names of several of the Israeli survivors who had pointed to John Demjanjuk and said, "That's Ivan."

Gustav Boraks, born in 1901, a barber at Treblinka, now a barber in Israel: "The barber shop was located in the barrack where the women had to undress. There were five benches and 20 barbers.

226

The women disrobed in one room, stepped in through a door, had their hair cut off and then stepped out through another door into the gas chamber. We had one minute to grab the hair, make one single snip with the scissors, and that was that."

Josef Czarny, born 1927, now a trade union clerk in Israel: "I was fifteen years old and very poor. My entire family had died of starvation . . . we were placed in cattle cars like so many salted fish. We drank our own sweat and urine."

Pinchas Epstein, born 1925, now living in Israel: "I was deported from Czestochowa on September 22, 1942. I was then 18 years old. For eleven months I carried corpses in Camp 2 . . . After the revolt I escaped [and returned] to my home town, got myself Aryan papers and enrolled as a Gentile for work in Germany. I arrived in Israel in July, 1948."

Elijahu Rosenberg, now living in Israel. When asked if he still thought about Treblinka, Rosenberg replied, "I don't think about it; it's in me, like an indelible tattoo . . . I was 18 when I arrived in Treblinka with my mother and three sisters. Until the day of the revolt I saw nothing but the sky and the sand, sky and sand, and corpses on the ground."

Abraham Lindwasser, who positively identified Ivan but died before the trial, gave this description of the death camp: "They made me a 'dentist.' I could not stand it, so I tried to hang myself. I was already swinging on my belt when a Jew with a beard—I don't know his name—took me down and chided me. [He said that] someone at least should survive it all, to describe later on what was going on here."

In mid-February, just a few days before the Demjanjuk trial began in Israel, my best friend, Ilene, dropped by my office and asked me to lunch. We drove to our favorite Mexican restaurant in Ilene's car. I remember the rain pelting the windshield, the wipers working furiously, and Ilene squinting out at the dense gray fog, talking about her new research project on taste aversions in cancer patients.

Taste aversions are fascinating to psychologists because they represent one-trial learning—you eat something, you get sick, and you don't ever want to eat that particular food again. Psychologists have always viewed learning as the building up of connections, a slow process in which the reward or punishment immediately follows the behavior that it eventually shapes. Thus a rat presses a bar and gets a food pellet (reward) and learns to keep on pressing. Or the rat presses a bar and gets a shock (punishment) and learns to avoid pressing the bar again.

With taste aversions, the "punishment" is often separated from the act of eating by many hours or even days. You eat a piece of cheesecake, you go to bed, and then the next day, even the thought of cheesecake makes you want to vomit. Ilene's research is designed to test the theory that cancer patients' aversion to food is connected with the regular doses of chemotherapy. The patient eats, gets a dose of chemotherapy, gets sick, the sickness is connected to the food, and they lose their desire to eat.

As I listened to Ilene talk excitedly about her work, I couldn't help thinking, *Cancer patients—why don't I study cancer patients?*

"Ilene, I need your advice," I said when we were seated at a booth in a back corner of the restaurant. "A lawyer called a few weeks ago and asked me to testify in the John Demjanjuk trial in Israel."

"Demjanjuk," she said, looking at me. Her voice changed, becoming flat, emotionless. "You mean Ivan the Terrible."

"He is accused of being Ivan the Terrible," I said.

"Beth, please. Tell me you said no. Tell me you will not take this case."

"This lawyer came to see me. He flew out from New York and spent two days with me, trying to convince me that this is a case of mistaken identification. He believes Demjanjuk is innocent."

"He's being paid by the man, is he not?"

"I told him I'd review the file."

"How could you?" I felt the words, so heavy with contempt, settle like a stone in my heart.

"Ilene, please try to understand. This is my work. I have to look beyond the emotions, to the issues here. I can't just automatically assume he's guilty."

"He *is* guilty. People who were at the death camp, people who watched him, who *knew* him have pointed their fingers at him and said positively and with no hesitation—'*That's Ivan.*'"

"You've made up your mind that he's guilty before he's even had a trial," I said.

228

"Are you telling me that you might take the stand and call those eyewitnesses liars? Are you telling me that you would do that, Beth?"

We argued through lunch, and when we walked into the psychology building for our 1:30 P.M. classes, Ilene wasn't speaking to me. I watched her walk down the hallway, her back straight and stiff, and I knew that in her heart she believed I had betrayed her. Worse than that, much worse, I had betrayed my people, my heritage, my race. I had betrayed them all for thinking that there might be a possibility that John Demjanjuk was innocent.

I called Uncle Joe, eighty-six years old, my mother's brother, the only living relative of my parents' generation. Ever since my mother died in a drowning accident at his cabin in Pennsylvania when I was fourteen years old, Uncle Joe has been more like a father to me than an elderly relative.

On the phone I explained to Uncle Joe that I'd been asked to testify in the Demjanjuk case in Israel. I told him everything I knew about the identifications, the Trawniki training card, and O'Connor's theories about a Russian setup. Uncle Joe listened, he sighed, and when I was finished, he said, "Beth, dear. Let me think about this. I will call you back."

I received a letter from him a week later. He wrote that he had been in a quandary since our conversation, "absorbed" with the case and the upcoming trial. Many of his friends believed I should not "act as a witness," he wrote. Uncle Joe tried to be reasonable. He cautioned that I must think about Israel, for "what is good for Israel is paramount." Perhaps I should testify, he continued, for what if O'Connor hired an anti-Semite who might use "unfair practices and harrass the witnesses to discredit them"? Perhaps my testimony would be good for Israel, because I am a Jew, and my presence on the stand would speak for fairness and a balanced perspective. But perhaps not; perhaps I would be seen as a traitor, a Judas to my own people. "The decision is yours to make," he concluded.

A week later I received a message from Uncle Joe on my answering machine:

Remember, dear, this isn't a trial for just one person; it involves a whole world where these atrocities occurred. My feelings are complicated by the fact that I still feel somewhat guilty that during the Holocaust I, like so many millions of other Jews, did not do much . . . I'm so grateful that you're thinking seriously about this case, but I do feel that you have a lot more to lose than to gain if you get involved in this trial where you might say something that you would forever regret. You would be taking such a risk. Swell talking to you even through your telephone. Keep in touch, darling. Good night.

John Demjanjuk's trial began on February 18, 1987. I followed the proceedings in the newspaper. On February 23 sixty-one-year-old Pinchas Epstein testified, the first prosecution witness.

"That's him sitting over there," Epstein said, pointing at John Demjanjuk. Again I noticed the stilted translation of the Yiddish words, which gave the proceedings a formal, Old World feeling. "Age has of course changed him but not so that he would become unrecognizable. There are certain features which after so many years are marked in one's memory. I see Ivan every night. He is imprinted in my mind. I cannot rid myself of these impressions."

After Epstein pointed out Demjanjuk, many of the five hundred spectators stood up and applauded.

On February 20, sixty-five-year-old Eliyahu Rosenberg testified. Rosenberg, who spent eleven months at Treblinka, was transported to the camp from the Warsaw ghetto with his mother and sisters. He was immediately separated from his family and never saw them again. In the courtroom Rosenberg described how guards at Treblinka forced him to remove corpses of other Jews from the gas chambers. At first they buried the corpses in mass graves, but later the Nazis changed tactics and he was forced to shove the bodies into incinerators. Once, Rosenberg said, he stole some bread and received thirty lashes from the guard named Ivan, who forced him to count each lash out loud and say "Thank you" at the end of the beating.

"I remember Ivan very well," Mr. Rosenberg testified in court. "I saw him near the gas chamber with a murderous instrument, a sort of pipe or whip. I saw how he beat, shouted, and slashed at victims as they entered the gas chambers."

Prosecutors asked Mr. Rosenberg to approach Mr. Demjanjuk.

Demjanjuk was told to remove his glasses, and as he took them off, he held out his hand to Rosenberg in apparent greeting. Rosenberg drew back in horror. "Ivan!" he shouted. "I have no shadow of a hesitation or a doubt. It is Ivan from Treblinka, from the gas chambers—the man that I am looking at this very moment. I saw the eyes, the murderous eyes and the face. How dare you give me a hand, you murderer!"

On Friday, March 13, the front-page headline of *The New York Times* declared: "Treblinka Trial Becomes an Israeli Obsession." Halfway through the long article was a description of the testimony of eighty-six-year-old Gustav Boraks. O'Connor was putting the old man through a grueling cross-examination, trying to establish the fact that his memory was seriously impaired. At one point Mr. Boraks admitted that he couldn't remember the name of his youngest son, who had been killed by the Nazis. Suddenly he remembered—it was Yosef—and he turned immediately to the judge, exclaiming "I didn't forget!"

But O'Connor kept after him. Did Mr. Boraks remember the year that he testified in the United States at Demjanjuk's deportation hearing? "No," Boraks answered. How did he get to the United States from Israel? O'Connor asked. "By train," Boraks replied. His answer was followed by a gasp from the audience.

I could picture O'Connor stalking Gustav Boraks's aging memory, pouncing, holding it up like a deflated rubber ball and declaring with a victor's smile "See this old thing? It's no good anymore!" And I could picture Mr. Boraks sitting there defeated and devastated as he watched his mind being held up to ridicule, as he endured the shame of forgetting the name of his youngest son.

How can you separate a man from his memory? If you take the memories away, haven't you also stripped him of his past, of all the precious, stored events that made him who he is? Without his memories, wouldn't Gustaf Boraks fold up and die, an exterior scaffolding that has lost its inner structure and suddenly collapses in upon itself?

After reading and rereading the newspaper reports, I stared for long moments at the photographs of the survivors, seeking answers to my questions. Their pain appeared to be stamped into their anguished faces. One photograph showed Elijahu Rosenberg doubled over, his forehead pressed against the witness stand, his hand clutching a water glass. In another Pinchas Epstein held out his hand; his mouth was wide open, a howl of pain. *Listen to me*, the picture seemed to say. *You must believe me.*

And Demjanjuk. Day after day I stared at the photographs of the man in the "cage," glasses perched on the end of his nose, chin jutting out, lips tightly pressed together. Can you discover kindness or cruelty in the set of a jaw, the glint of an eye? I stared for long moments at his ears. Several of the survivors had mentioned the shape of his ears, and I kept asking myself—Is it possible that a man might be sentenced to death based on thirty-five-year-old memories of the shape of his ears?

I wonder now if I would have gone on like that for months, staring at the newspaper photographs, reading and rereading *The New York Times*, working myself into a frenzy of agonized indecision. I had less than a week to make up my mind when David Sucher, a close friend, dropped by my house for a Saturday morning visit. We were drinking coffee in my living room, and I told him about my dilemma.

"If I take the case," I explained, having talked this out with myself hundreds of times, "I would turn my back on my Jewish heritage. If I don't take the case, I would turn my back on everything I've worked for in the last fifteen years. To be true to my work, I must judge this case as I have judged every case before it. If there are problems with the eyewitness identifications, I must testify. It's the consistent thing to do."

"Do you know what Emerson said about consistency?" David asked, smiling gently at me. " 'A foolish consistency is the hobgoblin of little minds.' "

"The hobgoblin of little minds," I repeated. For two days that strange phrase became my litany. I latched onto it like a lifeline, allowing it to pull me out of the quicksand of my indecision. It was less an action than an implosion of sorts. I simply caved in upon myself. I didn't have the heart to take the case. Or perhaps I didn't have the courage.

I called Mark O'Connor at his hotel in Jerusalem and told him I couldn't take the case.

* * *

The defense team made one last-gasp attempt to change my mind. It was mid-May and I was in Brighton, England, to give a talk about expert testimony to the British Psychological Society. One evening, just before dinner, there was a knock on my hotel room door. Yoram Sheftel, Demjanjuk's chief Israeli lawyer, had flown in from Jerusalem to try to talk me into testifying. Speaking with a heavy accent and using staccato sentences that conveyed extreme urgency, he brought out all the contradictory facts, rearranging them, changing emphasis, sorting, shifting, and continually shuffling his legal deck of cards.

I was unmoved. I could not testify, I told Sheftel over and over again. After three hours of nonstop talking, he brought out his ace in the hole—Schlomo Helman. Schlomo Helman, Sheftel reminded me, had been in Treblinka for almost the entire life of the death camp. Schlomo Helman did not say "That's Ivan," he did not say "I recognize this man!" He looked at the photo spread and did not recognize John Demjanjuk. And yet Schlomo Helman had been in Treblinka for a full month longer than any of the other survivors.

I could feel myself pulling back, resisting Sheftel's heavy magnetic pull. "A month is not something I can get worked up about," I said. "The other survivors were at Treblinka for almost as long, and they did identify Demjanjuk as Ivan. One month just doesn't matter that much."

"But Helman was forced to assist in the construction of the gas chambers." Sheftel kept pushing. "He worked right next to Ivan, just a few meters' distance from him. For thirteen months he worked right next to this man! Wouldn't he recognize him? We can't fault his memory, because he did positively identify Fedorenko. Why did he remember Fedorenko and not Demjanjuk?"

"I don't know," I said. I have never spoken more truthful words.

"They showed him only five photographs," Sheftel kept after me. "Only five. He picks out Fedorenko. Now that leaves four—just four photographs left." Sheftel threw up his hands. "He could have guessed and had a 25 percent chance of being right. But he didn't guess. He didn't need to guess because he didn't *see* Ivan. Just four pictures left and he didn't see him!"

"He didn't identify Ivan," I said, "but neither did he say, 'That's *not* Ivan.' The absence of a positive does not make a negative."

Sheftel flew back to Jerusalem, leaving me with anguished

thoughts of Schlomo Helman. If only Helman were still alive! Perhaps he would be testifying in court right now, saying that John Demjanjuk could not possibly be Ivan. What reasons would he have given—his eyes were too widely spaced, his teeth too crooked, his ears too pointed?

Or perhaps Schlomo Helman would have changed his story. "I was wrong," he might be saying right now, pointing a bony finger at John Demjanjuk. "I see now that this is Ivan."

Ivan Grozny. Ivan the Terrible. Ivan the nightmare of nightmares.

I wrote an article about my decision on the Demjanjuk case that appeared in *Newsweek* magazine's "My Turn" column on June 29, 1987. That summer I received hundreds of letters, ninety percent of which were fiercely critical of my decision not to testify. One writer suggested that I should immediately surrender my degrees and leave my profession: "You have ruined your career." Another accused me of having "prostituted principle for friendship." If Demjanjuk was innocent but found guilty and executed for the crimes of Ivan the Terrible, another writer pointed out, I was no different from the real Ivan, for "to commit murder or to allow murder to be committed when you can stop it is the same whether there is one victim or one thousand."

A friend of John Demjanjuk's wrote, describing Demjanjuk's ordeal in Ayalon prison in Israel, where he was "incarcerated like a caged animal." Demjanjuk's friend then related his journey to villages in the immediate area of the Treblinka death camp to talk with other survivors of Treblinka, who were certain that John Demjanjuk and Ivan the Terrible "were absolutely *not* the same person!" These survivors remembered a very different Ivan, a six-foot, seven-inch giant with a small head, bulging eyes, an ambling shuffle, and a "grotesque, angry facial expression which could indicate a severe psychosis."

That letter fascinated me. These survivors remembered Ivan as a Frankenstein-type creature with a shuffling walk, distended eyes, a tiny head, and a hideous facial expression. Had the original memory of Ivan metamorphosed over time into this monstrous incarnation, this nightmarish depiction of evil?

There were other, more personally painful, letters filled with hatred and venom. One described me as a "supercilious, archetypal, liberal, protector-of-the-criminal-at-all-costs Jew." And another wrote that while he had no sympathy for people like Ivan the Terrible, he did have sympathy for John Demjanjuk, who was innocent until proven guilty. The letter writer concluded that if Demjanjuk was innocent and died because I chose not to testify, I should "burn in hell."

I stuffed the hundreds of letters into two big manila envelopes, walked down the basement stairs, and placed them in a heavy cardboard box in the corner of the cellar. The box was filled with my childhood diaries, scrapbooks, and other memorabilia, and I spent several minutes moving things around so that the *Newsweek* letters were at the bottom of the pile. I walked back up the stairs, shut the door, and leaned against it. I could hear the furnace rumbling and groaning; my back, pressed against the door, picked up its steady vibrations. I had this sudden feeling of horror, as if I had just taken a live body downstairs and buried it. Maybe when I could find the courage to go back downstairs and look in the cardboard box, it would be dead.

Toward the end of August 1987, I arrived home from work to find a brown package, about the size of a shoebox, on my doorstep. I picked it up and glanced at the name on the return address: The John Demjanjuk Defense Fund. It was a Federal Express label, which was puzzling because the Federal Express truck usually left packages with my next-door neighbor.

I picked it up—*God, it's heavy,* I thought—put my key in the door, and immediately put the heavy package down on the floor, near the front door. I took off my jacket, draped it over a chair, went into the kitchen, poured a glass of juice. I came back and looked at the package, all wrapped up in a wrinkled paper bag with lots of tape and black Magic Marker. The John Demjanjuk Defense Fund. What the hell was that?

I called Geoff at work. "Don't open it," he said. "I'm coming right over."

Something in his tone scared me, and I picked up the phone again and called the University of Washington police. I hurriedly described the package. "If you think it's a bomb," the officer said, "tie a string around it, walk it thirty feet away, and pull on the string."

"You want me to tie a string around the package, jerk the string, and if it's a bomb, it will go off?"

"Yes, that's right," the voice said.

"Do you really want me to do that?"

"Maybe you should call the Seattle bomb squad," he said, giving me the number.

Wanting to laugh and cry at the same time, I called the police. Within fifteen minutes two officers arrived. They listened to my story, looked at the package, and looked at each other. I retrieved the manila envelope from the basement and let them read some of the worst letters. "I'm not going near that thing," one of the men said, looking sideways at the package. "Let's call the bomb squad."

Three more policemen arrived about ten minutes later in an armored truck. They walked around the package, put their ears to it, asked me questions, whispered among themselves. Finally they decided to make their "assault" on the package. They told Geoff and me and the two regular policemen to stand behind a brick wall at the back of the house, "just in case there's an explosion." We waited, crouched behind the wall, our hands over our ears. A few minutes later a member of the bomb squad walked over and handed me a huge bundle of papers. "I don't think there's a bomb here," he said.

The John Demjanjuk Defense Fund had sent me hundreds of letters, articles, clippings, and personal pleas. Three months after I'd given my final decision to Demjanjuk's lawyers, his loyal supporters were still trying to convince me that John Demjanjuk was innocent.

In October 1987 I flew to Israel to watch my friend and colleague, Willem Wagenaar, testify at Demjanjuk's trial as the defense team's expert witness on memory. The trial was held in a huge converted theater, and I sat in one of the front rows next to Wagenaar's wife, Margreet, a pediatrician. Willem and Margreet live in Holland and have four beautiful children, two boys and two girls. I visited them once and I remember watching the family gathered together by a piano, the children in their pajamas, as each member of the family took their turn to play.

On the third day of Willem's testimony, during one of the recesses, Margreet turned to me and said in her lovely accented voice, "Why didn't you testify, Beth? You're here watching and listening, you told Willem that you'd be prepared to provide the defense with information about research on memory. Why aren't you up on the stand?"

It took me a few seconds to pull my answer together. As I looked around the audience filled with four generations of Jews—little children, their parents, grandparents, and great-grandparents—I tried to explain to Margreet that it was as if these were my relatives, and I, too, had lost someone I loved in the Treblinka death camp. With those kinds of feelings inside me, I couldn't suddenly switch roles and become a professional, an expert.

Did Margreet understand? I wasn't sure. But as I sat in that huge auditorium, I knew that only a few of the people in that audience had been there, in the concentration camps. Their memories were alive now—they were *alive!* But soon, when this older generation had died off, the memories would become secondhand, dusty remnants of the real thing. Time would march on, the memories would gradually fade, and the stories would lose their flesh and blood immediacy, becoming an allegory for the "dark time" in the middle of the twentieth century.

Maybe, I thought, looking out at those faces, I lacked the courage to testify. Maybe refusing to testify was the most courageous thing I could have done. But as I sat there and watched the tears flowing freely down the cheeks of teenage boys and girls, children who were born thirty years after the horror was over, I could only think how precious the survivors' memories were. If fifty more had died, no one would have known the true horror of Treblinka.

I could not have taken the stand and talked about the fallibility of memory without every person in that audience believing that I was indicting the specific memories of the survivors. I would have been perceived as attacking their memories. I couldn't do it. It was as simple and agonizing as that.

The recess was over and Willem was speaking into the microphone, answering the defense attorney's question. I touched Margreet's arm and leaned toward her, whispering in her ear. "Maybe it comes down to this," I said. "My head said yes. My heart said no. This time I listened to my heart."

On the last day of my visit to Israel, I participated in a panel discussion at Hebrew University on the role of the psychologist in the courtroom. Afterward, a small group of psychologists and students had lunch at a small café, and a heated discussion ensued about the possibility of a mistaken identification. I was sitting at one end of a long table, and from the other end I heard Willem Wagenaar say, "Well, you know, there were witnesses who said that John Demjanjuk was not Ivan."

"Excuse me, Willem," I said, raising my voice so I could be heard at the other end of the table. "What witnesses are you referring to?"

"Schlomo Helman, for one," Wagenaar said.

I have the greatest respect and admiration for Willem, but I felt I had to say something. "Schlomo Helman never said that John Demjanjuk wasn't Ivan."

"He looked at the photographs and didn't identify anyone," Wagenaar explained.

"Yes, but that's very different from saying that John Demjanjuk was not Ivan."

We discussed the point for a few minutes and the conversation gradually drifted into other topics. But I spent a long time thinking about the creative ways in which human beings can twist and shape facts. With just a little shove here, a slight shading there, a little deemphasis over there, we can alter the way we perceive and understand our experiences.

I knew, even as I argued the point with Willem, that if I had agreed to take the case, I might also be giving a subtle twist to the facts. Schlomo Helman would have become my crutch, my anchor, the weight to my weightlessness. *Helman didn't identify him. Helman looked right at his picture and didn't see Ivan. Helman said it wasn't him.*

Should a psychologist in a court of law act as an advocate for the defense or an impartial educator? My answer to that question, if I am completely honest, is *both*. If I believe a defendant is innocent, if I believe in his innocence with all my heart and soul, then I probably can't help but become an advocate of sorts.

If I had appeared on the stand in the John Demjanjuk case, I might have become his advocate, using my arsenal of subtle psychological tools in an attempt to get across the point that he might be innocent, a victim of mistaken identification. But I wondered—would my advocacy be generated by a wholehearted belief in his innocence or by the need to convince myself of his innocence in order to justify my presence in the courtroom?

On Monday, April 18, 1988, a panel of three Israeli judges returned with a verdict. John Demjanjuk was declared guilty of war crimes, crimes against humanity, crimes against a persecuted people, and crimes against the Jewish people. One week later, on April 25, John Demjanjuk was sentenced to death.

December 1988. Dov Eitan, one of Demjanjuk's Israeli attorneys, jumped off the top floor of a Jerusalem hotel. Friends and relatives insist he was pushed; they call it murder.

Yoram Sheftel, the attorney who visited me in England and tried to convince me to take the stand for Demjanjuk, attended Eitan's funeral. Afterward, he was approached by seventy-one-year-old Yisrael Yehezkeli, a Holocaust survivor who lost his entire family at Treblinka. Yehezkeli shouted something at Sheftel, and with an anguished cry threw acid in the attorney's face, burning the skin and severely injuring his eye.

Yehezkeli was convicted of aggravated assault, sentenced to five years in jail, with two years suspended, and ordered to pay Sheftel $6,000 for the ophthalmologist's bill and $5,300 compensation for his suffering. After the sentencing, Yehezkeli said he felt no regret for his attack. He was proud, he said, of disfiguring a "superkapo"— a Jew who betrays other Jews.

Who, then, is innocent and who is guilty? When I think about John Demjanjuk and the kaleidoscope of events surrounding his case, my mind cannot penetrate the darkness. I see only the gray area between justice and injustice, truth and lies, the past and the present.

When I think about guilt or innocence, I think of the children in the Treblinka death camp, standing in line, motionless, just moments away from their death. These were the true innocents staring at the truly guilty. Their eyes were open. They *saw*.

It is only one step farther into the horror to imagine that I could look into the dark pools of their eyes and, in their clear reflection, know once and for all if John Demjanjuk and Ivan the Terrible are one and the same.

TEN

A MOLE AND A STUTTER:
TYRONE BRIGGS

"The truth shall come out, and the truth shall set you free."
— Dorothy Harris, Tyrone Briggs's mother

"Guilt and innocence are not black and white. Sometimes we never know the truth."
— Richard Hansen, Criminal Defense Attorney

I t is a fine line I walk as a psychologist in a court of law. While the debate about guilt and innocence is waged with passion and partisan zeal, it is my task to deal with the facts. As an expert witness, the facts I must deal with extend beneath the surface, deeper than the newspaper headlines, deeper even than the confidential police reports and the court transcripts. I am privy to the defense lawyer's strategy; I've read the victims' descriptions of the accused; I know the sordid and intimate details of the crimes; I've viewed the lineups and listened to tape-recorded interviews. But still there are facts I will never hear, details that are beyond my expertise or concern. The defense attorneys tell me what they want me to know, selecting only the facts I will need in order to testify. I do not have access to the prosecutor's files. I rarely have the opportunity to talk at length with the defendant. And I don't venture into the jury room to hear their confidential and privileged conversations about guilt, innocence, and reasonable doubt.

But in the Tyrone Briggs case, I became immersed more deeply in the facts than I had ever been before. In this case I was stripped of my expert's status and forced to watch the trial from the outside . . . until a former juror approached me and led me into the passions and emotions, the dark heart of the case of the State of Washington versus Tyrone Briggs.

The attacks came one right after the other, and with each new assault the fear mounted.

On November 28, 1986, the day after Thanksgiving, a Seattle University pre-med student was taking a run around the campus track when she noticed a man standing by the public bathroom. She continued running, and as she neared him, he called out, "Wait a minute, I have a question." She hesitated while he started toward her, and suddenly he lunged at her, wrestling her to the ground. A serrated kitchen knife fell next to her and she grabbed for it; she felt a sudden, brief flash of pain, and then the man was dragging her by the wrists, toward the public restroom. "Get in there," he said, his voice stern and forceful. She wriggled out of her sweatshirt and was on her feet, running in her bra across the field toward the campus buildings. "You robbed my cousin!" he yelled after her. "I'm going to get you!"

On December 3, at approximately 8:00 A.M., an attorney with the King County Prosecutor's office was walking toward the courthouse when a man jumped out of nowhere and knocked her to the ground. "I want your purse," he said, "give me your money." He held a serrated kitchen knife in his hand. "I'm going to stab you, give me your money," he repeated over and over. He put his hand under her skirt, she reached for the knife, cutting her hand on the sharp blade. He ran off, taking her purse and gym bag.

On December 4 a social worker at Harborview Hospital parked her car near the Yesler Terrace Housing Project and began walking toward the hospital. A man came around the corner of the street, walking quickly, and when he was four to five feet away from her, pulled out a small steak knife and said, "Your purse or your money." She started screaming and the man ran away. The encounter lasted approximately twenty seconds.

On December 15, at 8:15 A.M., a Harborview social worker was

242

walking to work at the hospital when a man with a kitchen knife jumped out of the bushes, grabbed her, and in a low, conversational tone of voice said, "I'm going to stab you in your fucking head. Give me your money." She frantically searched in her purse and handed him what she had—five dollars. "That's not enough," he said, threatening again to stab her in the head. When he put his hand up her skirt, she started screaming and scratching at his arm. "Shut up and let go of my arm," he said. Kicking, scratching, and screaming, she managed to get away from him and started running down the street; the attacker ran in the other direction.

On December 18, just before 8:00 A.M., an X-ray technician at Harborview Hospital was walking to work when she saw a man standing in the darkened entrance to an alleyway. She paused for a moment and turned to look at him, but decided to keep walking. Seconds later she was lying on the ground, dazed; the man had come up behind her and hit her in the back of the head with a fence board. He hit her in the face with his fist several times, then dragged her down a series of concrete stairs and into a vacant apartment where he tore at her clothes and attempted to rape her. The door suddenly banged open and another man rushed in, yelling "Hold it! I've got a gun!"

"Man, why are you jumping on me?" the attacker said. "She jumped me first. Man, I'll even give you some money."

The man with the gun yelled up the stairs to his girlfriend to call the police. The victim began crawling toward him, and the attacker bolted through a back door.

On December 19 the Seattle police department held a community meeting at Harborview Hospital; two to three hundred people crowded into the hospital auditorium. Detective Robin Clark, who was in charge of the investigation into "the Harborview attacks"—all the attacks occurred within several blocks of each other—conceded that there was "a lot of public pressure" to apprehend a suspect and assured the audience that the police force was working hard to do just that.

The police conducted a stakeout of the neighborhood, developing a list of sixty to seventy-five suspects. The victim of the December 15 attack worked with a police artist, and on December 29 a sketch of the attacker was released to the media and published in local newspapers, shown on television, posted around Harborview, and carried door to door in an attempt to find a suspect.

On January 20, 1987, Detective Clark knocked on an apartment door in the Yesler Terrace Housing Project. She showed the artist's drawing to the woman who answered the door. "That looks something like the boy who lives down the hallway here," the woman said. "I think his name is Tyrone."

Tyrone Briggs, Detective Clark discovered, had an outstanding $56 traffic warrant. Around 1:00 P.M. that same day, she found Briggs in the Yesler Terrace indoor basketball court. "Mr. Briggs?" she called out. The nineteen-year-old youth turned, basketball in hand, and looked at her. Detective Clark explained that she was arresting him for the outstanding traffic warrant. She escorted him to the police station, booked him, took his picture, and questioned him about the Harborview attacks.

"What would you say," Detective Clark said, "if I told you that I thought you were the Harborview rapist?"

Tyrone stared at her for a moment, uncomprehending. Was she serious? "Well," Tyrone said finally, speaking with a severe stutter, "I suppose you would say that. But I'm not the one."

A few hours later Tyrone's father arrived at the police station and posted bail for his nineteen-year-old son.

That same afternoon Karl Vance, the man who held the gun on the attacker in the December 18 attack, identified Tyrone Briggs from a series of twenty-one photographs.

At 7:00 P.M. the next day, January 21, Detective Clark knocked on the door of Tyrone Briggs's apartment. His mother answered the door. Tyrone was visiting a friend, she said; if the detective would just wait a minute, she'd go get him. When Briggs returned with his parents to the apartment, Detective Clark arrested him.

At 12:30 A.M. on January 22, a team of detectives and uniformed patrolmen knocked on the Briggses' apartment door. They showed Tyrone's mother the search warrant and began a thorough search of the apartment. The Briggs family huddled together in the middle of the living room, watching the strangers search methodically through every closet, cabinet, and dresser drawer. The police were unable to locate any stolen property, knives, or distinctive clothing.

Later that same day, four of the five victims were brought down to the police station for the announced purpose of a lineup. After they were kept waiting for more than an hour, the officer in charge explained that they weren't able to get enough people together to ensure that the man they had in custody would get a fair lineup. They would have to do a photo montage instead.

All four victims pointed to photograph number 4—Tyrone Briggs. A week later the fifth victim identified Tyrone Briggs from the same photo lineup.

Several weeks later an in-person lineup was conducted. All five victims and the man with the gun identified Tyrone Briggs as their attacker. The King County Prosecutor's office charged Tyrone Briggs with seven counts of assault, robbery, and attempted rape. A trial date was set for May.

Early in March criminal defense attorney Richard Hansen called to ask if I would appear as an expert witness in the case of the State of Washington versus Tyrone Briggs.

"The police have made a grievous error," Richard said. "They were under intense pressure to find someone—a black man was out there attacking white and Asian professional women—and Tyrone happened to look something like the man in the artist's sketch. From that point on, it's been a tragedy of errors."

Tragedy of errors. I liked that.

"Tyrone is nineteen years old, a high school basketball star, living in an apartment in the Yesler Terrace Housing Project with his family. He's the sweetest kid you could imagine. And he's got a terrible stutter. It's the worst stutter I've ever heard."

Richard wouldn't be relating that little fact without a reason. I waited, enjoying the suspense.

"Not one of the victims mentioned a stutter," he continued. "Not one. In fact, from the victims' initial descriptions, it would appear that the attacker couldn't stop talking. He was calm, he didn't whisper or shout but spoke in a 'normal conversational tone.' If you could hear Tyrone speak, you would know that this could not be the same man—he's had a severe stutter ever since his parents can remember. I'm talking severe—it takes him nearly a minute to say his name and address."

Stutter, I wrote on a piece of note paper.

"But that's not the only problem with the prosecution's case. The victims' initial descriptions of the attacker are so far off the mark it's like the proverbial shotgun that can't hit the side of a barn. One victim described a man with a receding hairline, a short Afro, about 190 pounds; another described a full-grown man in his mid-twenties, between five eight and five nine. The most detailed description was given by the last victim, who described her attacker as twenty-two to twenty-five years old, five nine to five ten, with yellow crooked teeth, a space between the two front teeth, a bushy Afro tinted red, and a ski-jump nose. At the time of the attacks, Tyrone Briggs was barely nineteen years old, wore his hair in jeri curls—the Michael Jackson look—weighed about 155 pounds, had straight, white teeth, a very large nose, very large lips, and a prominent mole above his right lip. Not one of the eyewitnesses mentioned a mole. In fact, the only detail that consistently fits is the fact that Tyrone is black. I'll send this stuff to you by messenger, and we can discuss it after you've had a chance to review it. I've got to be in court in"—a slight pause while Richard cupped the receiver against his shoulder and looked at his wristwatch—"ye gods, in five minutes. Gotta run. Call me."

I spent that evening in my office going through the Briggs file, making my little checkmarks in the margins, scribbling my notes, sifting, sorting, and separating the facts into the relevant categories. Right away three things bothered me about the case. First and most obvious, five women victims and a male eyewitness had identified Tyrone Briggs as the Harborview attacker. Eyewitness testimony is problematic, but when you have six positive witnesses pointing their fingers at the same man, even a skeptic like me begins to believe there might be something to it.

The second problem had to do with the available lighting conditions when the attacks took place. In daylight or artificial lighting conditions, we process more information into memory and thus have more information to pull out of memory later, when we are asked to recall an event. Even though it was gray and rainy in Seattle and close to the shortest day of the year when these attacks took place, there was, theoretically at least, enough light available for the victims to see their attacker.

The third problem concerned the duration of the attacks. The longer a person has to look at something, the better his or her memory will be, and only one of the attacks could be considered "fleeting"; several of the women were with the attacker for at least a minute or two.

I sipped my coffee and stared at the sheets of paper covering my desk. This just wasn't one of those cases that came hurtling at me, screaming of injustice. It didn't hit me, for example, like the recent case I'd worked on in Florida, where a teenager was accused of attempted rape and attempted murder after stabbing a twenty-four-year-old woman in the stomach with an eight-inch butcher knife. On the night she was attacked, the victim told a detective that her assailant was a teenager who wore braces; later she identified eighteen-year-old Todd Neely, who had never worn braces and who had an ironclad alibi confirmed by credit card receipts that showed that he was eating dinner at a restaurant with his family when the crime occurred. Police claimed Neely left the restaurant early, although they had no proof; moreover, the victim changed her testimony about her assailant's braces. In court she said she might have seen a reflection of the indoor light off his teeth and mistaken that for braces. Neely was convicted in a nonjury trial and sentenced to fifteen years.[1]

When the Florida lawyer sent me the police reports and preliminary hearing transcripts, I became convinced that Todd Neely was a victim of mistaken identification. But with Tyrone Briggs I wasn't so sure. I kept thinking—six eyewitnesses. *Six.* I knew of cases where five, six, seven, even as many as fourteen eyewitnesses were wrong, but these were the unusual, highly publicized cases that occurred once in a blue moon. Most of the cases I work on involve just one or two eyewitnesses.

But, I reminded myself, if one person can make a mistaken identification, so can five. The odds may go up, but it can happen. It had happened before.

I began a more careful reading of the police reports, incident reports, and lineup statements, looking specifically for contamina-

1. On August 24, 1990 charges against Todd Neely were dropped and he was cleared after an appeals court ruled that prosecutors withheld crucial evidence in the case. "We can't get it through our heads that it's over," Neely's stepfather told the *Palm Beach Post.* "It's sort of like being on a battlefield when the shelling stops. The silence is deafening." The four-and-a-half-year ordeal cost the Neely family approximately $300,000.

tion. Our memories are not, as so many people believe, perfectly preserved in our brains, frozen in time. Like other organic substances, memories can go "bad" when exposed to polluting influences.

I put on my glasses and went to work.

On January 20 Tyrone Briggs was tentatively identified from the police artist's sketch by a Yesler Terrace resident. "That looks something like him," she told Detective Clark. Briggs was arrested on an outstanding traffic ticket, his picture was taken and included in a stack of twenty-one photographs that was then shown to Karl Vance, the man who held the gun on the attacker in the December 18 attack. Vance positively identified Briggs, signing this statement:

> Today Detective Clark showed me a photo montage of twenty-one pictures. I positively picked picture numbered four as the person I saw dragging a lady into an apartment and I stopped him as he was trying to rape her. As soon as I saw the picture, I picked it up and knew it was the same person. I am absolutely positive that that is the person.

A lineup was scheduled for the morning of January 23; but newspaper and TV reporters discovered that the police had arrested a suspect in the Harborview attacks and arrived en masse at the Public Safety Building, cameras loaded and ready to shoot, a hastily assembled, celluloid firing squad. Four of the five victims were brought into the lineup room, a small auditorium on the fifth floor of the building. At that time, Richard wrote in his notes, a police sergeant prepared the women for the shock of seeing their attacker in person. "It is not uncommon for a person to have an emotional reaction upon seeing a suspect again for the first time," he said. "Those feelings manifest themselves in a lot of different ways. Some people get a chill down the spine, a rumbling in the stomach, palpitations, some people sweat, some people get frightened all over again."

This was already a kind of memory contamination. The police sergeant had, in effect, told the victims that they were about to see the man who attacked them. He had set them up, communicating to them that the police had a definite suspect.

The sergeant left the room, then, and returned some time later to apologize for the delay. He explained to the victims that they couldn't get enough people together to make sure that the person they had in custody—another not-so-subtle clue that the police had a definite suspect waiting in the wings—would get a fair lineup. They would have to do a photo montage instead.

The witnesses were kept waiting while a photo montage was hastily assembled. Robin Clark, the detective in charge of the investigation, took a ball-point pen and marked a mole on every photograph, being careful to make it match in size and shape the mole above Tyrone Briggs's right lip.

Now this was tricky. It's a well-established psychological finding that unusual features or objects draw our attention. When people try to recall the details of Mikhail Gorbachev's face, for example, they might first mention the prominent birth mark on his forehead. In a photo lineup, it's standard police practice to either cover up an unusual facial feature or to make sure that everyone has it. If a suspect has a strange hairdo, the police will cover the "distractors' " heads with a hat; if the suspect wears braces, the police would ask the suspect and others in the lineup to keep their mouths closed; if the suspect has a deep scar on his face, the scar should be concealed or the distractors should have a similar scar.

When Detective Clark drew a mole on the other five faces in the montage she was actually following standard police procedure designed to protect the suspect from bias or prejudice. Nevertheless, there were two significant, potentially serious problems stemming from this act. First, not one victim ever mentioned a mole on the attacker, but since every face in the photo montage had a mole, it would not take great powers of deduction to conclude that the police had a suspect who had a mole. The eyewitnesses' original memories, exposed to this potent source of postevent information, might then undergo change and contamination. Their minds would simply use their own mental pen to draw a mole on the face in their memory. Just like that, with little or no conscious thought, the memory would change to incorporate the new information.

The second problem would come later, in the actual in-person lineup. If Tyrone Briggs was the only person in that lineup with a mole, then the whole identification procedure would be tainted. After the photo identification, the eyewitnesses would be left with the impression that the suspect had a mole. When they viewed the in-person lineup, they would notice the man with the mole. They might, then, pick him out as the attacker not necessarily because he *was* the attacker, but because he was the man with the mole.

I wanted to jump ahead and look through the in-person lineup statements and photographs, but I forced myself to proceed slowly, going step by step, inch by inch through the evidence, sifting through the facts.

I found the Xerox copies of the victims' "montage identification statements." All five victims identified Tyrone Briggs as their attacker, but in every case the victims expressed reservations and uncertainty; in their written statements, they indicated that they arrived at their choice through the process of elimination.

The Seattle University student who had been assaulted on November 28 wrote: "I picked picture number 4 as the person who looks like and could be the person that assaulted me. His lips in the front view look thick but I don't really remember the lips. Everything else about his face looks right. It is definitely not any of the other five photographs."

The victim of the December 3 robbery wrote: "I am not positive it is number 4, he could be the person. It is definitely not numbers 1, 2, 3, 5, or 6."

According to the December 4 victim: "It seems more like number 4 because number 1 is not heavy enough, and number four is lighter complected and has smoother features. However, I am not positive that it is number 4."

The December 15 assault victim wrote: "I feel that it is number 4. I don't remember a mole being there, but I don't remember it not being there."

According to the December 18 assault victim: "It is definitely not numbers 1, 2, 3, 5, and 6. I am sure that it is number 4, but I don't remember the mole on his face, but I do remember a spot on his face."

Every one of these statements reflected a response that was closer to a guess than a positive statement. Guessing can be extremely dangerous, because when a witness is uncertain, guessing may actually fill the gaps in the initial skeletal representation of the event, causing an actual change in the underlying memory. Later, when searching her memory, the witness may incorrectly recall something that had earlier been merely a guess as an entrenched part of memory. Furthermore, while an initial guess may be offered with low confidence, later, when the witness mistakes the guess for a real memory, the confidence level can rise. The witness is no longer able to distinguish the original facts from the subsequent guesses, and in her mind she "sees" the entire construction as the truth. The facts have been cemented together through guesswork.

Imagine a memory as a pile of assorted bricks (details, facts, observations, and perceptions) piled up in a big mound. Guessing is the cement slapped on the bricks, allowing them to become a solid, cohesive structure. In the beginning, the guesswork may be liquid and malleable, but it can harden over time, becoming firm and resistant to change. Each time the memory is recalled, it becomes more vivid, more colorful, more *real*, and the witness becomes more confident that this is, indeed, the way things were.

In an actual criminal identification procedure, police and prosecutors often exert a subtle but profound pressure on their witnesses to be complete and accurate; under such pressure, a guess can quickly solidify into a certainty. Witnesses will also put pressure on themselves, for it is a general characteristic of human nature that we will try to avoid looking uncertain or confused. Once we have offered a response, we tend to stick by it, becoming increasingly more confident as time goes by. Any attempt to get us to rethink or question a statement that we have offered as fact may be perceived as an assault on our honor and integrity.

One other factor may have affected the witnesses' identifications of Tyrone Briggs. Three of the victims were Caucasians, two were Asians, and the assailant was black. It's a well-established fact that people are better at recognizing faces of people of their own race than they are at recognizing people from different races. This phenomenon, known as cross-racial identification, has been observed in numerous psychological experiments, yet many people remain unaware of its effects. In 1977 and 1978 I conducted an experiment designed to test general knowledge of the factors that affect eyewitness identification. One of our hypothetical scenarios was surprisingly similar to the Briggs case.

Two women are walking to school one morning, one of them an Asian and the other white. Suddenly two men, one black and one white, jump into their path and attempt to grab their purses. Later the women are shown photographs of known purse-snatchers in the area.

Which statement best describes your view of the women's ability to identify the purse snatcher?"

(a) Both the Asian and the white woman will find the white man harder to identify than the black man.
(b) The white woman will find the black man more difficult to identify than the white man.
(c) The Asian woman will have an easier time than the white woman making an accurate identification of both men.
(d) The white woman will find the black man easier to identify than the white man.

Fifty-five percent of the subjects chose the correct answer, b— that the white woman would find the black man more difficult to identify than the white man. Sixteen percent thought both women would find the white man *harder* to identify than the black man; 16 percent felt the Asian woman would have an *easier* time accurately identifying both men; and 13 percent indicated that they thought the white woman would find the black man *easier* to identify than the white man. In other words, 45 percent of the respondents in this survey did not understand the phenomenon of cross-racial identification.

Assuming for a moment that Tyrone Briggs did not commit the crimes, then cross-racial identification might provide a partial explanation for the victims' confusion of Briggs's face with the face of the real attacker. The phenomenon of cross-racial ID could not, however, be used to explain Karl Vance's extremely positive identification of Briggs. Vance, like Briggs, is black. Why did Vance ID Briggs if the young man was indeed innocent, and why was Vance so positive of his identification? "I am absolutely positive," he said, indicating Tyrone Briggs's picture, "that that is the person."

According to Richard's notes, Karl Vance's girlfriend lived next door to the vacant apartment where the December 18 attack took place; she was the mother of Tyrone Briggs's best friend, Craig Miller. Vance visited that apartment three to five times every week for a period of three years—in other words, Richard figured, he had made over 480 visits to the apartment of Tyrone's best friend, the same apartment that Tyrone visited every day, sometimes two to three times a day, for several years. Both Craig and Tyrone remembered passing Karl repeatedly and even, on occasion, speaking to each other. Karl Vance, in other words, had seen Tyrone Briggs in the housing projects, he knew his face, and it would have looked familiar to him when it appeared in the group of twenty-one photographs shown to him by the police.

When Vance chose Briggs's photo from the group of photos and said he was "absolutely positive that that is the person," it could be because he had indeed seen his face before; it could be that this was not the face of the attacker but only the face of his girlfriend's son's best friend whom he had seen hundreds of times around the Yesler Terrace Housing Project.

I put my pencil down and stared at the papers scattered all over my desk. So far I had five headings: Weapon Focus (in every attack the man carried a knife); stress (the attacks were clearly stressful and violent); postevent information; cross-racial identification; and unconscious transference.

Now it was time to look at the in-person lineup when the five victims and Karl Vance positively identified Tyrone Briggs from a six-person lineup. After the lineup identifications, the cops knew they had a "wrap," and the prosecutors would have informed Briggs's defense counsel that they were proceeding with criminal charges against Tyrone Briggs. With six positive eyewitness identifications, the case must have looked airtight.

But I smelled something rotten. *What about that mole?* I studied the glossy eight-by-ten-inch photograph of the six men in the lineup. Even in a photograph, with Tyrone Briggs reduced to Tom Thumb size, I could see the mole above his right lip. I could also see that not one of the other men in the lineup had a mole.

This was what I had feared, a situation ready-made for disaster. From the photo identification that took place five weeks earlier, the eyewitnesses learned that the suspect had a prominent mole, because every single photograph in that montage featured a man with a mole, drawn in by a detective using a ball-point pen. But only one man in the lineup had a mole—Tyrone Briggs. And only one man from the photo ID pictures reappeared in the in-person lineup—Tyrone Briggs.

I typed "photo-biased lineup" into my computer, using capitals, bold, italics, and double underlining. When the witnesses looked at the six people in the in-person lineup, the person whose photograph was seen before would look familiar. It's possible, perhaps even probable, that this familiarity was mistakenly related back to the crime rather than back to the photographs where it properly belonged. It would not be difficult to imagine what went on in the minds of the victims when they attended the in-person lineup: "The men in the photo ID had a mole. I picked out the man in photograph number 4—the man standing up there with the mole. Nobody else has a mole. That must be the man who attacked me."

At this point, in walks the problem of confidence. With each succeeding identification and with the transformations that occurred in the original memory due to postevent information, the witnesses would become increasingly confident. By the time they got to court, after all the lineups, repeated exposures to Tyrone Briggs, and mental dress rehearsals, they would be extremely confident that Briggs was the person who had attacked them—even though he did not fit in any way, shape, or form the original description they had given to the police, even though not one of the victims originally remembered a mole, even though every one of the victims' photo identifications was tentative and uncertain.

I discovered two additional problems with the lineup. When the police sergeant conducting the lineup asked Tyrone Briggs to repeat certain phrases, the young man stuttered. One of the victims noted in her lineup statement that Briggs stuttered and the man who attacked her did not. Another noted that Briggs "seemed sort of nervous and drew attention. To speak things, it took him a while." Briggs was "fidgety and appeared to be very nervous and had difficultly speaking," wrote another.

In their original reports to the police, not one of the victims mentioned a stutter or speech impediment. But here was a man— the man with the mole, the only man who appeared in both the photo and in-person lineups—who had difficulty speaking, who seemed nervous, and who stumbled over his words. It was clear from their lineup statements that Briggs's nervousness and speech difficulties impressed the eyewitnesses—they noticed him, they commented on his nervousness, their attention was gradually focused on him.

What might have been going on in their minds? Here's a possible scenario. The victims' original memory of the attacker did not include a stutter or speech problem; in fact, several victims commented on the attacker's "conversational tone of voice." But the suspect standing in the lineup was obviously nervous and having difficulty speaking—why was he so nervous? *"Maybe because he's guilty. Maybe because he knows he's going to be identified. Maybe because he's the man who attacked me."*

After identifying Briggs in the lineup, all five witnesses were brought together by the prosecutor who told them that they had identified the same person and that he lived in the neighborhood of the attacks. In effect, the prosecutor was reinforcing their identification, "rewarding" the victims by telling them that they had picked the right man, they had done "good." Such positive feedback would tend to produce a repetition of the behavior that caused it and increase the confidence the victims felt in their identifications. By the time they appeared in court, they would feel more confident and certain that the man they had picked was indeed the man who had attacked them. This confidence would be picked up by the jurors, who would find their testimony overwhelmingly persuasive. Nothing is more convincing to a juror than a positive witness.

After this little meeting with the prosecutor, one of the witnesses said, "We all felt happy." After the meeting four of the victims said they were absolutely certain now that Briggs was their attacker. Only one victim, the attorney who was attacked on December 4, continued to express any doubts.

There was one additional problem that did not fit so neatly into my little boxes, a little rotten apple that had rolled away from the barrel. One of the victims had tentatively identified another man as her attacker, a man who fit the victims' original descriptions, who looked exactly like the man in the police artist's sketch, who had been arrested in one of the stakeouts conducted near Yesler Terrace and yet did not live in the area and had no business there.

This man's name was *Phil Widmer*. His photograph was never shown to any of the other victims who eventually identified Tyrone Briggs, nor was he included in the various lineups. Once police attention was focused on Tyrone Briggs, it seemed as if Widmer was dropped like a hot potato. Why? I could only speculate. The Seattle police obviously had developed a theory that the Harborview attacks were committed by one person—they occurred in the same area at around the same time of day, and the general description was of a black male, twenty-two to twenty-five years old, light-skinned, between 170 and 200 pounds, with a short Afro and a possible receding hairline.

While this general description fit Widmer in every respect, perhaps he had an ironclad alibi for one of the attacks. This would have eliminated him from consideration as the "Harborview attacker," whom the police had convinced themselves was responsible for all five attacks. Once Briggs was identified by Karl Vance and then by several victims, Widmer became a nonissue. The police had "a live one" who had been positively identified by six eyewitnesses—why spend time and energy pursuing someone else?

I finished typing my thoughts into the computer, closed the file, and called Richard to tell him I'd testify in the case.

"You're a shoo-in," he said. "This is an eyewitness case, pure and simple, Briggs has an alibi defense, and there is little or no corroborating evidence."

"Little or no?" I asked.

"Briggs is left-handed and some of the women claimed their attacker was left-handed. And one of the victim's purses was discovered in a trash can several doors down from Briggs's apartment. That's it."

"There's no physical evidence whatsoever—no fingerprints, footprints, saliva, semen, hairs, clothing fibers?"

"Nothing. The cops thoroughly searched Briggs's apartment and they came up with nothing, no clothing that matched, no hidden purses or wallets, not even a steak knife in a kitchen drawer. There is not one shred of evidence tying Tyrone to this crime except for the pointing fingers of the eyewitnesses."

"Six of them," I said.

There was a hesitation on the other end of the line. "You sound doubtful, Beth. What's up?"

"Just being professional"—I laughed—"trying not to jump to conclusions." But I wasn't being wholly truthful. I was bothered by the fact that since Tyrone Briggs had been arrested, not one woman had been attacked in the Harborview area—at least no attacks were being reported in the newspapers or television news. I was bothered too by the fact that I had to pick and choose among my cast of categories in order to explain away the IDs. Cross-racial identification and weapon focus were issues for the five Caucasian and Asian victims, but Karl Vance was black and Vance had held a gun on the attacker for several minutes at eight in the morning. I could only assume that Vance was watching the man carefully, and I knew from the material Richard sent me that they had a fairly lengthy conversation.

But always, always, there is another side. Vance originally described the attacker as twenty-two to twenty-five years old, with a short Afro and a receding hairline. Those facts could not be stretched to fit a nineteen-year-old with a full head of hair that he wore in long jeri curls. And Vance never mentioned a stutter or a mole.

I carefully arranged my notes, filed them away, and for the next four weeks put my mind on other things.

On May 5 Judge Donald Haley ruled that there was sufficient corroborating evidence to give him discretion to exclude my testimony. In other words, he would not allow me to appear in his court as an expert witness. The evidence he cited included the fact that Briggs generally fit the descriptions given by the victims; all five victims and an eyewitness identified him; Briggs was left-handed and several victims had testified that their assailant was left-handed; Briggs lived in the same neighborhood where the crimes occurred; and one of the victim's purses was found in a trash can four doors away from his home.

Richard Hansen was furious. "Listen to this," he said. "One piece of corroborating evidence cited by Judge Haley was the fact that when detectives searched Tyrone's apartment, they didn't find anything. He cited this lack of evidence as *evidence* that Briggs must have hidden the weapons, clothing, and other *fruits of the crime.*"

I could picture Richard stabbing a legal pad with a sharp number-2 pencil, and for some reason a memory flooded over me. I remembered a scene described in the book *Fatal Vision,* in which Jeffrey MacDonald, the Green Beret captain accused of murdering his pregnant wife and two young children, gleefully threw darts at a blow-up photograph of his prosecutor.

"Let's be up front about this," Richard was saying. "Tyrone's family lives in a housing project, they are dirt poor, they don't have any money to buy steak knives. Hell, they don't have the money to buy steaks! And yet this judge makes a ruling based, in part, on the fact that no steak knives were found, indicating that Tyrone must have hidden them!" Richard swore under his breath. "Prejudice comes in all sorts of little packages, and this neat and tidy ruling has prejudice written all over it."

The headline in the May 6, 1987, issue of the Seattle *Times* read "Judge Rebuffs UW Psychologist":

The ruling yesterday excluding the expert testimony of Dr. Elizabeth Loftus angered the defense attorney for nineteen-year-old Tyrone Briggs. The teenager is on trial for alleged sexual assaults and robbery of five victims near Harborview Medical Center last November and December.

Attorney Richard Hansen told Judge Donald Haley that he had "made a grave error" in his decision.

"I think you've taken away any chance that we have of putting on a defense in this case," Hansen said.

Hansen admonished the judge further by saying that if Briggs is innocent and is wrongly convicted "it is going to be in large part because of your honor's ruling."

The trial continued for five additional days. Closing statements were delivered in May 11, and on May 12, after seven and a half hours of deliberation, with votes ranging from eleven to one on one point and ten to two for overall acquittal, the jury informed the judge that they could not agree on a verdict. A mistrial was declared, and the prosecutor's office immediately announced plans to retry the case.

Tyrone Briggs's second trial for the Harborview assaults began on July 22, 1987. Once again Richard tried to have my testimony admitted, and once again the judge rejected his plea. The prosecution, however, was allowed to present the testimony of an expert witness—John Selmar, a speech pathologist who taught at the University of Washington. Jurors in the first trial were troubled by Tyrone Briggs's stutter—how could Briggs have been the assailant, they asked, when not one of the victims mentioned a stutter? The prosecutor hoped to solve that problem by having a stuttering expert testify about the conditions under which a stutterer might *not* stutter.

One of the prosecutors in the case questioned Selmar about specific situations in which a stutterer was demanding something from a stranger. "Would you expect a stutter?"

"If he feels in control of that situation, I would expect very little, if any, stuttering under the circumstances," Selmar answered.

The defense attempted to counter the expert witness's testimony by calling one witness after another to testify that Tyrone Briggs had a severe stutter that was obvious in every word he uttered and every conversation he held. An instructional aide who worked on a one-to-one basis with Tyrone for an hour a day for eight to ten weeks testified that Tyrone always spoke with a "very extensive, very noticeable" stutter.

A special education teacher with a master's degree and eight years of teaching experience testified that Tyrone's stutter was "very noticeable" and that "he always has trouble starting sentences, and until he can get his sentences rolling, there is a definite stutter."

Tyrone's basketball coach, Larry Whitney, testified that Tyrone "always, always stutters . . . I would say that he trips on the beginning of every sentence, uh—uh-uh-uh."

Tyrone Briggs took the stand, and when asked his age answered, "Uh-uh-uh-uh-uh-uh-uh-uh, nineteen." The next question asked for his birth date, to which he responded with ten uhs without ever completing a word. Many times during the question-and-answer process, Tyrone's stuttering prevented him from providing an answer to a question.

It was clear from the newspaper reports that the stuttering issue had become the predominant focus of the second trial. The eyewitness issues seemed all sewed up—six eyewitnesses identified him, that's all there was to it. I didn't like the feeling of sitting on the outside looking in, absolutely powerless to affect the proceedings. It also seemed patently unfair that the prosecution had been allowed to present expert testimony when the defense was denied it. At least on this issue, it seemed apparent that the court was biased in favor of the prosecution. And if the court was biased, wouldn't the jurors also be biased?

It seemed to me that the jurors were being denied the facts they would need to make a fair and just decision. I knew from my research that jurors have misconceptions about eyewitness testimony, and I knew too that in this second trial, the victims would be even more confident of their identifications. The jury would be powerfully impressed, perhaps even persuaded, by that confidence.

On August 17, after nearly three days of deliberations, the second jury to consider the case of the State of Washington against Tyrone Briggs returned with a verdict. Tyrone Briggs was pronounced guilty on two counts of first-degree robbery, two counts of first-degree attempted rape, one count of second-degree assault, and one count of attempted first-degree robbery.

Afterward the jurors were questioned by various news reporters.

One juror told reporters that there was no doubt left in any of the jurors' minds after the prosecution had finished with their closing arguments; from the very first ballot, the jury of five men and seven women agreed on almost everything.

"Six people were so positive in their identifications that Tyrone Briggs was the assailant. It was very, very convincing," another juror said. "Ten people might describe a horse in ten different ways, but we would all still recognize it as a horse."

Did the stuttering expert make the difference? they were asked. It might have had an influence, several jurors responded, but even without that testimony, they probably would have voted to convict, just on the basis of the eyewitness identification. "All the victims identified the guy, plus Karl Vance. In our minds, the girls were sure he was the one."

On December 12, 1987, Judge Faith Enyeart sentenced Tyrone Briggs to sixteen years three months in prison. Richard Hansen immediately filed a notice of appeal. One of the issues that he mentioned in the appeal brief was the judge's refusal to admit my testimony, but the heart of the appeal was a juror misconduct issue. Back in September and October a private investigator hired by the Briggs family questioned jurors in the second trial about the deliberations. He discovered that one of the jurors discussed his own speech problem—a stutter that occurred only in certain circumstances and that he was able to control—during jury deliberations. One of the other jurors gave the private investigator this sworn statement: "*Mark Perry* talked about how he was able to control his stuttering. Perry's discussion of this personal experience with stuttering and how he was able to control it helped me to understand how Tyrone Briggs might have been able to control his own stuttering problem so that none of the victims could have detected it."

Another juror gave this statement: "Mark Perry introduced this subject and his personal experience as a stutterer to the jury in order to explain how Tyrone Briggs might be unaware of his stuttering and how someone like Tyrone might be able to commit the crimes without stuttering."

During the voir dire process, when the lawyers question jurors about their background, competence, and potential biases, Richard asked if anyone in the jury panel had any prior experience or contact with stuttering or speech problems in general. Perry was silent. In the jury box, Perry never mentioned his speech impediment. After the verdict, he reluctantly admitted that he discussed his speech problem during jury deliberations in order to assist the jury in resolving the critical issue of stuttering. In a written, postverdict statement, Perry admitted that he: "offered this personal experience to the jury as an aid to understanding evidence of the stuttering issue . . . My experience as a person with this speech problem pointed out to the jury's conclusion that Tyrone did not always stutter."

In June 1988 I ran into Richard at a party in West Seattle and asked about the Briggs appeal. When did he expect the court's decision?

"Not for another six months, at least," he said. "In the meantime, Tyrone is back in jail. He'd been out on bail pending appeal, but the judge used some paltry excuse to throw him back in the King County jail until the appeal court makes their decision. Every time I drive past the jail and think of Tyrone locked up in there, I feel sick to my stomach."

"You really believe he's innocent," I said.

"It's more than a belief, it's a conviction," he said. "It's intolerable, absolutely intolerable to know that Tyrone is innocent, that a jury has found him guilty, and that he might be locked up in prison. Winning Tyrone's freedom is the most important thing in my life right now, but there's nothing I can do but wait and pray that the appellate court sees things our way. I'm confident they will, I've never been so confident. But the waiting is agony."

Six more months went by. It was the middle of March 1989 when I received the letter from Joanne Spencer.

Dear Professor Loftus:
    As a member of the first jury of Tyrone Briggs, who has been convicted in Seattle of being "the Harborview Attacker," I am writing to you on his behalf. I and countless others feel that he is innocent, a victim of mistaken identity . . .
    The point of our concern at this time is that his appeal process is about to begin. Throughout this ordeal, the media has put out so much negative publicity on him. We need to gain some media support

so that the public can hear and be open to the truth of this matter. He and his family are suffering beyond measure from his wrongful conviction. We all feel that we are up against very great odds to get justice for him.

Joanne E. Spencer
Chairperson, Justice for Tyrone Briggs Association

I read the letter twice, not quite believing my good luck. For more than ten years I'd been conducting "jury studies" in the hopes of discovering how juries work, how they "think," and how they make decisions. Since 1985 I'd worked as a consultant on an American Bar Association study of jury comprehension, analyzing and interpreting data on how juries function and how well they understand the issues in complicated cases. But there was a major problem in this and all other attempts to investigate juries—federal law makes it a crime punishable by fine or imprisonment to record, listen to, or observe federal juries while they are deliberating or voting.

Furthermore, most jurors don't want to be bothered with detailed, analytic questions—they've done their duty, and they want to put it behind them.

I'll never forget a comment by a juror in a complicated case: "Being a juror was a terrible thing. I'm not smart and I'm not educated, and I don't know if it's right to put a person like me in that position of being a judge. It was awful. I had to think like I've never thought before. I had to try to understand words like justice and truth and . . ."

But here in my hand I held a letter from a juror who had served in a complicated criminal trial, and she was seeking *me* out. If I could talk with her and pick her brain about the Tyrone Briggs trial, I could learn more in a few hours than a more formal study with uninterested jurors might uncover in months of hard work.

But what did Joanne Spencer want from me? I'd been excluded from testifying as an expert in this case in two previous trials. Unless the appellate court ruled that the trial court erred by not allowing me to testify, it was virtually a certainty that I would not be permitted to testify in any future trial. Perhaps Joanne Spencer just wanted to ask me some questions. Maybe she thought I could pull some strings, make some phone calls, add some fuel to her fire. Or maybe she just wanted me to be on her side, to believe, as she obviously did, that Tyrone Briggs was innocent.

I picked up the phone and ten minutes later had a lunch date at 11:30 A.M. the next day with former juror Joanne Spencer.

It was a windy March day, the sky filled with thick, threatening clouds that reminded me of cotton balls dipped in black ink. Sailboats by the hundreds were moored outside the Seattle Yacht Club, a flat, unpretentious building located on the cut between Lake Union and Lake Washington, just a stone's throw from the University of Washington campus. The clunk and clangor of halyards, thick as a grown man's forearm, against forty-foot aluminum masts was deafening.

Joanne Spencer was waiting for me in the foyer. She was barely five feet tall, in her mid-fifties, energetic, with a rich, smooth voice. She wore a chocolate-brown suit with a beige satin blouse, dark, patterned stockings, and two-tone brown-and-beige heels. The hostess seated us at a table by the window, and for several minutes we talked about the wind, the weather, and the fabulous view. After the preliminaries, Joanne reached into her large leather purse and placed a thick document on the table next to her butter dish.

"The brief," she said, patting the inch-thick document. "Our chance for salvation. Our last shot at justice. To tell the truth," she confided, "I feel like I just dialed 911 and I'm screaming for help. I just keep screaming, hoping that someone, somewhere will hear me."

I raised my eyebrows slightly and wondered again what she wanted from me. How could I help her?

"I simply want people to know the facts," she said. "Let me begin at the beginning, with the first trial. I'll never forget the queasy feeling in my stomach when the prosecutor named Tyrone Briggs as the Harborview attacker. Chills ran up my spine to think that I was sitting in the same courtroom with the man responsible for these horrible attacks. However, I took jury duty very seriously and reminded myself of the judge's instructions to always keep an open mind and not make a decision until I had hear *all* the facts. The judge allowed us to take notes, and mine were extensive."

Joanne paused to take a sip from her water glass. Her lipstick left a bright salmon smudge on the rim. " 'Don't make up your mind until all the arguments have been heard,' the judge kept telling us. You know, I had a very strange feeling that he was saying this man had done all these things. It looked pretty convincing to me, with all the victims pointing at him. Oh, he looked harmless enough, but then I thought of Ted Bundy who also looked pretty harmless."

Yes, I thought, I know about Ted Bundy.

"The victims told their stories," Joanne continued, "and I felt so sorry for them, because someone certainly did these things to them and it was just a horrible experience. Right from the beginning I thought I would bring in a guilty verdict. I have two granddaughters, I don't want people like that on the streets. I'm very tired of attacks on women, violence, theft, the whole scene. And I don't like to see guilty men go free. Whoever did these things should be punished, and should not be let out into society. But as this trial went on, hour after hour, day after day, I began to think, *Wait a minute, this doesn't make sense!* The initial descriptions of the attacker given directly after the attacks did not in any way resemble Tyrone Briggs; neither did an artist's sketch nor a composite drawing, which showed a receding hairline. The defendant sitting in that courtroom had prominent features that were never described by the victims. Tyrone has a very broad nose—as his mother says, 'Everyone knows my son's nose is spread all over his face!'—and he has very thick lips, and he is six-feet-one-inch tall. He had just turned nineteen years old when these attacks were taking place. His teeth were straight and white, and his long hair was processed into jeri curls. In fact, at nine-thirty A.M. on the morning of the last attack, he was sitting in his hairdresser's shop, waiting to have his hair cut and processed.

"But what do the victims have to say about their attacker, just moments after they were attacked? One of the victims said her attacker was 190 pounds, had a receding hairline, and short hair. Another said there was nothing unusual about the size or shape of his lips, that he had short, unprocessed hair and was a full-grown man in his mid-twenties. Another claimed he had average features and lips, and a short Afro."

"You know these facts cold," I complimented her.

"Oh, just wait"—she laughed—"you ain't seen nothing yet. The victim of the December 18 attack described her assailant as twenty-four years old—that's five years older than Tyrone; five nine to five ten—Tyrone is six one; he had yellow, crooked teeth, with a space between the two front teeth—Tyrone's teeth are perfectly straight and white; and she said he had 'a bushy Afro' tinted red—Tyrone's hair was processed into soft, long curls and had never been tinted. She also told police that her assailant had a turned-up nose, which she described as a 'ski-jump nose'—Tyrone's nose is large and flat. She said that her assailant's lips were 'not large for a black man'—Tyrone has very large lips."

Joanne looked at me across the white linen tablecloth. Behind her, framed by the huge picture window, I could see the sail masts swaying in the breeze. "How can that be?" she asked, softly pounding the table with her fist. "How can a description taken just minutes after an assault be so far off the mark? Not one detail fits, not one. It just didn't make sense, nothing added up. And there were two pronounced things about Tyrone that were never mentioned by any of the victims. First, he has a very prominent mole, just above his right lip. And second, he has a bad stutter, he literally stutters on every word he speaks." She smiled, and her voice lost its sharp edge. "Sometimes Tyrone jokes about his stutter. The toughest part is getting the first word out—'Trying to get the motor started,' he calls it. He's the sweetest kid. I never met a nicer kid. But I'm off the track. Let me see."

Joanne went on with her story. "When Tyrone got up to testify, I watched the victims sitting together in the front row. They were huddled together, and they looked really terrified of this young man. But when Tyrone started talking, beginning with his usual uh-uh-uh-uh-uh-uh—their mouths literally dropped open, their eyes widened, they looked at one another, they looked at him, and they looked at one another again. They couldn't believe it, they were flabbergasted. *Their assailant didn't stutter!* Sure, they had heard Tyrone stutter in the lineup, but they thought he was stuttering because he was so nervous. And they figured he was so nervous, because he was the man who attacked them. When they heard him in court, when they heard the extent of his stutter, they were simply dumbfounded. The shock was written all over their faces."

"What was the reaction of the other jurors?" I asked. I wondered, Did they see what Joanne thought she saw?

Joanne shuddered. "Oh, those deliberations," she said. "I've never been so frustrated in my life. When we went into the jury room to deliberate, there were two holdouts, both men. One man finally voted innocent on one count—Tyrone was charged with seven counts—but the other man always voted for guilt, he would not budge. We couldn't get down to more than eleven to one for acquittal on any count. But at one point we did get down to ten to two on all counts."

The waitress brought our lunch, but Joanne pushed hers to the side, set her elbows on the table, and kept on talking. "We started out seven to six, always with more of us voting for innocence than for guilt. The two men who voted guilty didn't take any notes. They just sat there with their arms folded and glared at the rest of us. It was strange, but right from the beginning we chose sides around the table. The two men who were absolutely convinced that Tyrone was guilty sat at one end; those of us who were absolutely convinced he was innocent sat at the other end of the table; and in the middle were the people who were swaying around. At one point I said to these holdouts, 'You prove to me that any one of those witnesses saw the face of Tyrone Briggs before the lineup—from all the evidence we've seen—you prove this to me.' "

"Well, one of the men just sat there and said, 'The girls said he did it, I believe the girls.' One of the jurors who was convinced Tyrone was innocent, she's an operating room nurse, a lovely woman, looked at this man and in utter disgust said, 'Oh, come on, give me a break!' We kept asking these men—why did the victims give descriptions that did not in any way fit Tyrone Briggs?" Joanne lowered her voice and leaned across the table. "Do you know that poor kid had to go up to each member of the jury and open his mouth so we could look inside and see for ourselves that his teeth are not yellow and spacey, but white and evenly spaced? But in the jury room we got into an argument about his teeth. I said to the holdout, 'What about the yellow, spacey teeth—how do you square that?' And he said, 'Well, I'm sure that his attorney had a dentist go into the jail and fix his teeth.' "

Joanne leaned across the table. "But the worst was the Boeing engineer, who just folded his arms and glared at us. Honestly, I was so frustrated and furious, I felt like I was going to have a heart attack in that room. It was as if he were saying Hey, don't confuse me with the facts, I have my mind made up. I don't care about all the rest of the testimony, the descriptions, the lack of physical evidence—

the girls said he did it and that's good enough for me. That's what we were stuck with. I was so angry when I came out of that jury room, I was just really beside myself. There was just nothing we could do with this man.

"We only deliberated seven and a half hours, which is not a long time, but believe me, we weren't going anywhere. The man who worked for Boeing was getting full pay for every day of the trial, and he said, 'Look, I don't have to go anywhere, I can stay here for the rest of my life, and nothing is going to change my mind.' So that was that. It really was a hopeless thing.

"Let me tell you what happened after we told the judge that we were deadlocked, and he announced a mistrial. Anne Bremner, the prosecutor, Robin Clark, the detective in charge of the investigation, and Richard Hansen, the defense attorney, came into the jury room and asked if we would be willing to talk with them. They wanted to know what our impressions were, what we thought of the case. All twelve of us stayed to talk. At one point Detective Clark said, 'There are several things that we couldn't tell you during the trial. One is that all the attacks stopped after we arrested Briggs.'"

"Yes," I said, "I read that in the newspapers."

"You and thousands of others," Joanne said, shaking her head in disgust. "More than anything else, that little piece of information turned the public against Tyrone Briggs. And it simply isn't true. I don't know whether Detective Clark was aware of this, but we know now that there was at least one more attack that occurred after Tyrone was in jail. I'll tell you about that in a minute, but first let me tell you about the other little piece of information that Detective Clark confided in the jury room. 'Mr. Briggs,' she told us, her voice dripping contempt, 'was accused of rape before.' But once again, Detective Clark's information was misleading. The truth of the matter is that when Tyrone was fourteen years old, he was named in a paternity suit. He had a blood test and it was determined that he was not the father. That's what the police department calls a rape."

"Legally, sex with an underage girl is statutory rape," I said. "If all Detective Clark had was a rap sheet that listed Briggs's priors, then it would look like rape to her because she wouldn't know the underlying facts."

"Yes, I understand," Joanne said. "But do you see how that information, when conveyed to a jury without the underlying facts, could sway us and make us doubt our own conclusions? The day after the trial, the juror who is an operating room nurse called me. She said she was confused because of what Detective Clark had told us in the jury room. 'Do you think we did the wrong thing yesterday when we voted not guilty?' she asked me. No, I said, absolutely not, there is no way he could have been the attacker. The descriptions the women gave never fit him, no one ever mentioned his huge mole, no one ever heard him stutter, there was absolutely no physical evidence whatsoever—how could it have been Tyrone? And she said, 'Yes, you're right, I guess we did the right thing.' But you see, the detective and prosecutor tried to sway us in that jury room, and apparently they did sway some of the other jurors; they planted a real doubt in their minds. Of course, all this is after the fact, it didn't affect our deliberations. But these are the kinds of rumors and innuendos that were being circulated about Tyrone Briggs."

Joanne's tone grew sharp. "Let me tell you about the prosecutor. In the beginning, I thought she was so charming, but she is a shark. Do you know how she started out the second trial? I watched it on TV, I have the videotape. She said that there are people who are stutterers—Marilyn Monroe, Mel Tellis, Winston Churchill—who do not stutter when they're in control of a situation. And then she said, and these are her exact words, 'Marilyn Monroe doesn't stutter when she's acting. Mel Tellis doesn't stutter when he sings. And Tyrone Briggs doesn't stutter when he rapes.'"

Joanne looked disgusted. "This was her opening statement to the jury, and the judge allowed it, even though Richard was on his feet, screaming out objections. *When he rapes*, she said, even though there was never, in fact, a rape. Right from the beginning that second trial was off to a bad start. It ended badly, too, when Bremner told the jury in closing arguments that each witness 'picked the man that everyone else picked.' It simply isn't true that everyone who viewed the lineup pointed to Tyrone Briggs as the attacker. Seven witnesses involved in similar incidents were brought to Tyrone's lineup and all seven were certain that Tyrone was not the person they saw. Seven."

"What?" I said.

"Oh, yes," Joanne said, nodding solemnly. "You didn't know that little fact, did you? That's not the kind of information the police wanted to leak out; that's the kind of information they keep under lock and key. But seven witnesses went to the lineup and did not pick out Tyrone Briggs. These witnesses were willing to testify for the defense, but the trial judge excluded all evidence about similar incidents in which witnesses would testify that Briggs was not the man they saw. Dr. Loftus, let me tell you something. If Tyrone Briggs is the Harborview attacker, I'm Jack the Ripper."

I laughed. "Joanne," I said, "you mentioned another attacker."

"Yes. Philip Widmer. The victim of the fourth attack worked with a police artist to prepare a sketch of her attacker that was then circulated throughout the community. A short time later she identified Widmer, who bore a remarkable resemblance to the artist's sketch, to the composite sketch, and to the descriptions given by the victims. Widmer is an admitted cocaine user who does not live in the Harborview area and had no apparent business there. He was stopped during one of the stakeouts, within a few blocks of four of the assaults."

Lips pursed together, forehead creased, Joanne picked up the brief and began to page through it.

"Here it is, page eighty-five." She began reading from the police report.

> By the time of the second trial, it came to light that Mr. Widmer had pled guilty and was sentenced to prison for a purse snatching robbery against a woman committed on April 11, 1987, in Seattle. . . . The defendant told [a] Detective that he had previously been to prison for robbery in another state . . .

Joanne reached for her water glass, took a sip, and then continued reading from the brief.

> For some inexplicable reason, the police never showed Widmer's photograph to any of the other victims. . . . The court would not allow any testimony about him other than the fact that one of the victims had made a tentative identification of the man and that he had been seen in the area. . . . All of this evidence was not only relevant and admissible, but was necessary to assist the jury in determining whether Tyrone Briggs was responsible for these crimes.

"I don't understand all this," Joanne said, putting the brief back in the file folder. "Isn't it justice we're concerned about! How can the police just ignore these other leads, how can they ignore the seven witnesses who did not identify Briggs, how can they ignore the absolute lack of physical evidence? When I sat through that first trial, I began to realize that this trial wasn't about justice, it was about winning. The prosecution didn't seem to care a whit whether Tyrone Briggs was innocent or not; he was on trial, they had him cornered, and they were going all out, no holds barred for a win. A win. When you're so concerned about winning, who has the time to think about justice?"

I didn't know what to say. There had been times, in other trials, when I had wondered the same thing. I looked at my watch and realized I had fifteen minutes until my one-thirty class. "Joanne, I'm sorry, but I'm afraid I've got to run," I said.

Joanne walked me to my car and surprised me by giving me a big hug. "Thank you for listening," she said. "I know you're in a rush, but just let me say one more thing. I've gotten to know Tyrone Briggs. I volunteered to be one of his monitors when he was released from jail pending his appeal. I've spent literally hundreds of hours with him. In the beginning it was justice that concerned me. That was it, period. I wanted to know in my heart that justice was done. But when I got to know Tyrone and his family, I became involved emotionally. He is the sweetest, most lovable kid you can imagine." She sighed, and for a moment I was afraid she might start to cry.

"I don't know what you can do for us," she said, still holding my hand. "I just wanted you to know all the facts, and I wanted you to hear about the rumors and the outright lies that are being spread around about Tyrone. There's just one more thing," she said, reaching into her purse and handing me a single sheet of paper. "I made a copy of a letter that Tyrone wrote me from jail. You can read it later, when you have time."

I thanked her for a wonderful lunch and rushed off to my class. Two hours later, after the last student straggled out of the classroom, I sat down on top of one of the desks and read the letter from Tyrone Briggs. It was addressed to Mr. and Mrs. Spencer.

I'm just sitting here thinking about all the things I'm going through. I catch my self drifting off into space. I'm just sitting there, can't move, my eyes are open wide like if I were hypnotised and my friends . . . ask me what's wrong, I pretend like nothing's wrong, but

I keep asking myself over and over why me? And I get down on my knees with a tear drop in my eyes and ask the good Lord, Why me? Last night I had a wonderful dream. . . . I was at home, everyone was telling me it's over, you don't have to go back. I was too frightened to close my eyes. I try to stay awake as long as I can. I heard this loud sound, and I wake up, the door was opening, it was time to eat breakfast. I didn't feel like eating, I was so upset I slowly started drifting off again. I'm hoping I'll be home soon. I will never forget the love your family has given me. May God bless you all.

From Tyrone Briggs

Love Always

After my conversation with Joanne, I felt unbalanced. I feared being biased by Joanne's emotions and her obvious affection for Tyrone Briggs, and I felt it was important to get a broader perspective in the case. I decided to call my close friend Py Bateman. There are people in the world—and Py is one of them—who believe that when victims say something happened and point to a specific individual as the person who did it, they should be believed. Six eyewitnesses had pointed to Tyrone Briggs and identified him as the Harborview Attacker. Py would identify with the victims, and I wanted to hear what she had to say about the case.

Py is the founder of Seattle's Feminist Karate Union—she has a black belt in karate—and for eighteen years has directed "Alternatives to Fear," teaching self-defense classes to women, children, and the elderly, hoping to communicate that they are not defenseless but can protect themselves in an increasingly violent world. Py knows firsthand about violence. In May 1986 she returned to her Seattle home in the early afternoon and surprised a burglar. For fifteen to twenty minutes this five-foot-two-inch, 115-pound woman fought for her life against a six-foot-three man wielding a hunting knife. He slashed at her hands and face, cutting both eyelids, and left her bleeding and semiconscious on her living-room floor.

Brain surgeons relieved the swelling and pressure in her skull, and plastic surgeons worked their magic on her face, correcting the damaged eye tissue and hiding the livid scars. But Py's anger against criminals and the "soft" system of justice runs deep. "When are you going to start working for the good guys?" she asks me. It's become a refrain, and our soft laughter just barely disguises the tension between us.

On the phone I told Py about my conversation with Joanne and my confused feelings about the Briggs case.

"What do feelings have to do with this, Beth?" she said, her anger suddenly right on the surface. "I'm surprised at you—how can you let feelings interfere with the facts? Five victims and an eyewitness identified him—the attacks occurred in the daytime, these women had a chance to see him face to face, they talked with him, for God's sake, and one after the other they said that he's the one. How can you doubt them?" Her voice lowered and took on a cynical edge. "All I hear about is the so-called Briggs Brigade, this incredible outpouring of community support for Tyrone Briggs. Tell me, who is out there fighting for the victims? Five women have been forced to sit through two trials and tell their stories over and over again. Now they may have to relive the trauma of these attacks one more time if the appellate court decides to throw out Briggs's convictions on a technicality."

The issues presented in the appeal brief were not mere technicalities, but I didn't have the heart to argue the point with Py. She kept after me. "How could you turn your back on these victims, Beth? How could you let this case work on your emotions and destroy your ability to look at the *facts?*"

I explained to Py that I was trying to look at the facts, that this phone call was an attempt to gather the facts and the feelings from the other side, her side, the victims' side. I tried to tell her that I was confused, that this case did not fit into neat little boxes, that the issues weren't black and white at all but spread out into a dense, amorphous fog that I was hoping, somehow, to penetrate. But Py felt betrayed and abandoned, and I could not reach her.

After we hung up I thought for a long time about Py's accusation that I was being swayed by the emotions in the case. Was I? Joanne's passion certainly got through to me. Richard's insistence that Tyrone was innocent got through to me too. And Tyrone's letter was so sweet, so full of pain . . .

Maybe Py was right, maybe I wasn't looking clearly at the facts. As a scientist, I couldn't afford to let emotions take over and influence the way I look at life; I had to stick with the facts. As the weeks went by, I gradually slipped into the onlooker role again. After all, there was nothing I could do to help Tyrone Briggs; a judge had denied me my professional role in this case, and it would be inappropriate for me to step out of that role. Besides, I had other cases, other concerns. I would just wait and see what happened.

Four months later, on July 31, 1989, the State Court of Appeals voted to reverse Tyrone Briggs's convictions based on the juror misconduct issue. "Appellant was prejudiced by juror misconduct because it deprived him of an impartial jury and, therefore, of a fair trial," read the ruling. A third trial was scheduled for April 1990.

On March 17, 1990, a three-page story about the Briggs case appeared in the Seattle *Times*. The first page presented a synopsis of the case, and two separate articles focused on the families of the accused and the families of the victims. I read the articles and again felt the push and pull of the facts. "I want him to tell me why he did it," one of the victims said. "I want to say, 'Look at what you've done to me!" And in the other, opposing article, Tyrone Briggs's mother described the scene when the police knocked on her apartment door and arrested her son. "Mom, don't let them take me!" Tyrone cried out to her as the police handcuffed him and led him out to the patrol car. "Don't take my son!" she called out as several officers restrained her. "Bring him back inside this house! Bring him back!"

Impulsively I picked up the phone and dialed Joanne Spencer's number. "I just got off the phone with Tyrone," she said. She sounded happy to hear from me. "He's out on bail now, but I'm so afraid they'll find some excuse to put him back in jail. Hey, I've got a great idea—would you like to meet him?"

I didn't know what to say. Yes? No? I shouldn't?

"It would only take an hour of your time," she said. "I'll pick you up and drive you over to his house."

Meet him? I thought. That wouldn't be right, I'd be stepping out of my role, taking sides. But wait a second, I argued with myself, what role was I talking about? I was not an expert witness in this case. I was just an ordinary Seattle citizen, reading the newspapers like other ordinary Seattle citizens. Why shouldn't I meet him? How often did I get the chance to meet and talk with a defendant and his family?

"I'd like to meet him," I said, and the next morning at nine o'clock Joanne Spencer and I were speeding over Capitol Hill in her red, two-door Honda, talking about the two antagonistic sides in this battle over the guilt or innocence of Tyrone Briggs. I decided to tell her about a conversation I'd had with a friend who called Joanne "a bleeding heart liberal"; too late, I realized that I'd wounded her.

"So that's what they call me," she said, cutting in and out of the slower traffic. "It's ironic, isn't it? Here I am, married to a doctor, leading a comfortable life with my children and grandchildren, and suddenly I'm doing things I never imagined I would be doing. I've been on television, arguing the case for this young man's innocence. I've served as a volunteer monitor, getting up at three A.M. to make sure that this 'convicted felon' is safe at home and not prowling around the streets. I spoke at a community meeting in a Baptist church, and every face in that audience was black. I've organized petitions, written newsletters, I even marched on the jail—why, I've never marched on anything in my life!

"So people think I've done all this because I need a cause?" She waited impatiently at a red light, her fingers tapping the steering wheel. "Well, I don't need a cause, I need a rest. My husband is sick and tired of eating dinner at odd hours so that I can run off to meetings and community rallies." Her tapping fingers had curled into a fist, which softly thudded against the plastic steering wheel. "But I will not give up. Tyrone is not a cause. He's like a child to me. My whole existence is getting Tyrone free. My whole reason for getting involved in this case is justice, from the very beginning it's been about justice." The light turned green, and she sped through, shifting fast. "I had to see this thing through, no matter how much time it took, no matter how much money I had to spend from my own pocket, no matter what it cost me in terms of friendships or personal relationships. This is bigger than Tyrone; it's much bigger than this one case, because I learned in this trial that anyone can be accused of anything. Believe me, when a defendant is brought into court, there is a presumption of guilt, not innocence. Tyrone Briggs was convicted in the newspapers before he ever got to trial. All I have to do is mention Tyrone Briggs and people start shaking in their boots and calling foul—if they only knew what a sweetheart he is. He's still a kid, just a young kid, and his life is in ruins."

She shrugged and managed a weak smile. "A bleeding heart liberal, that's a good one. But I don't care what they call me. I will not stop, I cannot stop until Tyrone is free."

We pulled into the driveway of a small house in a working-class neighborhood on Seattle's Beacon Hill, a few miles east of downtown and a few miles south of Harborview Hospital and the Yesler Terrace Housing Project. "The family moved here several months after Tyrone was arrested," Joanne explained. "They couldn't stay in that housing project with all those awful memories."

A woman wearing an apron came out onto the small cement porch and motioned us into the house. "Hello, hello!" she called out as we got out of the car. "Can I fix you some breakfast? Pancakes, sausage, orange juice?"

"Dorothy"—Joanne laughed, giving her a big hug—"this is Elizabeth Loftus. Elizabeth, this is Tyrone's mother, Dorothy Harris."

I walked up to the porch to shake her hand, but she raised her spatula in mock surrender and protested, "No, no, my hands are full of breakfast. Come in, make yourself comfortable. We'll be done in just a minute."

In the hallway we met Eric, Tyrone's oldest brother, and Felicia, his twelve-year-old sister. Sitting around the table in the cramped kitchen were several smaller children who smiled shyly, their mouths full of pancakes. We decided to go back outside and sit on the porch in the rare Seattle sunlight. Eric joined us, and we talked for a few minutes about his work with Larry Daly, a private investigator in the case. Things were starting to happen, Eric said somewhat mysteriously; they had new leads, new evidence, new witnesses.

"New witnesses?" I said.

"I can't talk about it now," he answered. "We've got to be careful."

A tall, sleepy-looking young man walked onto the porch. "Ty, this is Dr. Loftus," Eric said, putting his arm around his younger brother. Tyrone smiled and looked down at his feet. "Hi," he said. His stutter was so severe that it took him several seconds to say the word. I looked at the thick black band on his wrist with the square box on top; he noticed me staring at it.

"This is a big eyeball," he said with a smile.

"That's the electronic surveillance bracelet," Joanne explained. "It's a radio transmitter with a receiver attached to a phone in Tyrone's room. They monitor every move he makes, calling him at all times of the day and night."

"It's like a collar and chain," Eric said, looking at the bracelet with a mixture of disgust and fear. "Ty's on a 150-foot chain, and if he goes just one foot farther, a radio signal is transmitted to police headquarters and all hell breaks loose."

As if to make the point, a telephone rang and Tyrone's mother, still holding onto her spatula, came hurrying outside. "Tyrone, that's your phone, hurry up now, hurry up!" she said, waving him inside.

"You want to see how this works?" she asked me. "Come on."

I followed Tyrone into the house, down a short narrow hallway, and into the corner bedroom. He put the black box on his wrist into the phone receptacle, picked up the receiver, and stuttered his name into the phone. After a minute he put the receiver down in its cradle.

"I feel like a dog," he told me, staring at the black box. But he said he put up with it for his family, so that he could be with them; without this monitoring system, he would be in jail waiting for his third trial to begin.

We stared for several seconds at the black box on his wrist; neither of us knew what to say.

"Do you have any hope?" I suddenly blurted out.

"Hope?" He repeated the word as if he didn't quite understand it. When he spoke, all his energy was concentrated in overcoming his stutter. I found myself leaning forward, my mouth open, nodding my head as he pushed the words out, one by one.

"No," he said. His sentences were short, choppy, interrupted by the constant, never-flagging stutter. "I don't have hope. How can I have hope? I don't believe in the system. Poor people like me, what kind of hope do we have? If you're out there all alone . . ." He stopped, swallowed, took a deep breath. "Every day we struggle. Every day I go to work, and I think, how are we going to pay for this? The box, the bracelet—it costs me ten dollars a day. The trials . . . so much money . . ." He shook his head; the words didn't come.

"Tell me about prison," I said.

"Prison," he repeated. "I was lost. It was a whole different world. You can't pretend. It always hits you. When the doors shut. Every night I'd pray. I'd say, Why am I here? What's my purpose? I couldn't come up with an answer." He looked at me, his eyes so wide and white, his hands spread, palms out. Then a thin curtain of anger and fear seemed to fall, his hands dropped to his side, his shoulders slumped. "Why would someone do this to me? The police, they look at us as lower-class people, as nobodies."

I didn't know what to say. We stood in the hallway for a moment, both of us staring at the green shag carpet. "How do you keep your spirits up?" I asked him, when the silence became awkward.

"I pray," he said simply. "I ask God to end this terrible nightmare. To put it way back, like it never existed. To give my family strength, to be back as one again. I know God can hear me. I ask Him, 'How long? How much longer?' "

We walked back outside and sat on the kitchen chairs that Dorothy and Eric had carried out and placed in a semicircle on the front lawn. "Dorothy, tell Elizabeth about the time the police came to the house," Joanne said.

"Oh, that was terrible, just terrible," Dorothy said. "A few months ago the police got a tip, somebody said they saw Tyrone sitting in front of a hotel in West Seattle in the middle of the night. It was pouring rain, five-thirty A.M., when I heard the police car drive up. I looked out my window and thought, 'They're here now, they're going to take my son.' I went to the front door and said, 'Can I help you?' 'Is Tyrone Briggs here?' the man asked. 'Yes, he's here. You go in and look.' And they went in with their big flashlights and their big boots, and their raincoats dripping all over my floor. They walked into my house, and they shined their lights in Tyrone's face as he was lying there in bed. I wanted them to see my baby in his bed, right where he's supposed to be at five-thirty in the morning. He wasn't out in a car in the rain in the middle of the night."

She looked over at Tyrone. "You know," she said, leaning toward me, her voice low, "you're brought up to be a mother, you take care of your children, you feed them, you love them, you mend their clothes, you fix their hurts. But those policemen came and took Tyrone away from me, they put him in jail, they fed him oatmeal and when he put the milk in it, these little worms come floating up. 'Mom,' he says to me, 'they're feeding me oatmeal with worms in it!' And I stand here, helpless, there isn't anything I can do. I'm falling apart, my family is falling apart. And there isn't anything I can do." She looked at her hands, lying still in her lap.

"Our lives will never be the same. We're victims too, and we don't know why. We don't know why. I feel so sorry for the other victims and their families, I just feel so bad. But in the newspaper, one of the victims' sons said that if he saw Tyrone on the street, he would get a stick and bash him in the head. When I read that, I wanted to cry. Somebody is walking these streets who wants to bash my boy in the head. How do I know when this is going to happen? How can I stop it?"

She stretched a hand toward me and gently touched the hem on the sleeve of my blouse. "I could fix this hem if it was unraveling. A mother can fix things. I could feed you if you were hungry. I take care of my children, I love them, hold them, tell them what's right and what's wrong. But I can't fix what is happening to Tyrone. I can't do anything to help him, and I feel like I'm letting him down."

Sometimes you get a feeling, lawyers say to me when I ask them why they think a client is innocent. *The facts don't add up, and you just get a feeling.* I've trained myself to be wary of emotions, which can distort and twist reality, and to be as objective as possible. But sitting in the spring sunlight in the Briggs family's front yard, feeling the power of the emotions that were tearing this family apart, I was having a hard time staying detached and dispassionate.

On May 21, 1990, Tyrone Briggs took his seat at the defense table and faced his accusers for the third time in four years. His new lawyers, Jeff Robinson and Michael Iaria, seemed confident and chatted amiably with the prosecuting attorneys, Rebecca Roe and Jeff Larson. Tyrone watched them, his face registering his confusion—how could they seem so relaxed and unconcerned? This was his life on the line.

On May 30 I walked down the ninth-floor hallway of the King County Courthouse to Room 965, Judge Donald Haley's courtroom, opened the door with its handprinted sign "Witnesses excluded from this courtroom" and took a front-row seat next to Joanne Spencer. "How are things going?" I whispered. "Fabulous!" she whispered back. On a piece of paper she wrote me a note: *Jane Doe witness this morning; attacked November 24th, said it was definitely not Tyrone. And we have a bloody shoeprint!*

I listened to several defense witnesses testify about Tyrone's stutter and his physical appearance at the time of the attacks. One of the witnesses, a childhood friend of Tyrone's who had moved to

Georgia several years earlier, testified that she had known Tyrone for seven years, and he always, always stuttered. It didn't matter if he was relaxed or nervous or under stress, he always stuttered.

I watched the jurors. What were they thinking? What would they decide? I watched the bailiff sitting off in the corner of the courtroom leafing through a "daily reminder" book. The defense attorneys kept their eyes fixed on the witnesses, while the prosecutors scratched madly away on their yellow legal pads. Judge Haley leaned back in his chair, glasses in hand; this was the same judge who had excluded my testimony in the first trial. What would have happened if he had permitted me to testify . . . would it have changed anything? Would Tyrone be sitting at the defense table right now?

Joanne and I had lunch that day at a delicatessen in Pioneer Square, just a few blocks from the courthouse. She told me about the "Jane Doe" witness, who was attacked by a man holding a kitchen knife who demanded her purse. The attack occurred at 8:00 A.M. on November 24, 1986, four days before the first attack that Tyrone was accused of and just a block away from two of the Harborview attacks. On the stand "Jane Doe" testified that Tyrone Briggs bore a remarkable resemblance to the man who had attacked her; but her attacker did not have a mole, he did not wear jeri curls, he was older, and he had freckles. Tyrone Briggs, she said, was definitely not the man who had attacked her.

"How did the defense find this witness?" I asked.

"Larry Daly, a private investigator, found out about her just a month ago," Joanne said. "The defense team got a court order to look at the police computer sheets and tip books. Eric Briggs told me that when Daly arrived at the police station, he was told that he could have only fifteen minutes to look through the files, and he couldn't take any notes. He discovered this attack, and he memorized the woman's name and phone number. When he called her she said, 'I always wondered why the police never got back to me.' "

"What a stroke of luck," I said.

"And then we have the bloody shoeprint," Joanne said. "It's from the apartment where the December 18 attack took place, the one where Karl Vance ran in and held a gun on the man. The shoeprint didn't belong to either the victim or to Karl Vance, and the only other person in that room was the attacker. A man from the state crime lab testified that the shoeprint was taken from a size seven and a half to a size nine men's shoe. Tyrone wears a size eleven shoe."

"No one else was in that room?" I asked.

"It was a vacant apartment. The police were there afterward, but presumably they would know better than to go traipsing through the room, stepping in pools of blood." Joanne's lips twisted into a smile. "But even that wouldn't surprise me. The police have bungled this case from the beginning. Five crimes and they couldn't come up with one piece of physical evidence—not one fingerprint or clothing fiber!"

"Joanne," I said, choosing my words carefully, "if this jury convicts Tyrone, will it change your mind?"

"Absolutely not," she said.

"What would it take to convince you?"

She stared out the window for a moment, a manicured fingernail pressed against her lower lip. "If they had some physical evidence, some incontrovertible evidence, I would change my mind. But they have nothing; they had nothing in the first trial, and three years later they still have nothing. The prosecution is supposed to get stronger with each trial as they learn the defense strategy and have time to strengthen their case—but they have nothing. *Nothing.*"

"Do you think Tyrone will be acquitted?"

Joanne sighed. "We have the new witness, and we have the bloody shoeprint. The third victim stressed even more in this trial that she wasn't sure of her identification of Tyrone. But I look at the jury, and I see some of the same kinds of faces that I saw in our jury room . . . obstinate, fixed, automatically assuming guilt, the type who cross their arms over their chest and say, *Go ahead, convince me he's innocent!* Well, this is not the way it's supposed to be. This system is based on the concept of innocent until proven guilty. But I know for a fact that it is the other way around. A defendant walks into a courtroom and people's minds are made up already—why would he be there if he weren't guilty?" She shook her head. "I'm afraid that the most we can hope for is a hung jury."

The jury began deliberations on Monday, June 4. On June 7 at 2:00 P.M., Joanne Spencer called me with the news. After five days and twenty-two hours of deliberation, the jury deadlocked with ten jurors voting for acquittal and two voting for conviction. "The same overall count that we had in our jury," she said. Was she happy with the decision? I asked.

"It's not an acquittal," she said, "but we'll take it. The prosecutor's office won't dare to try this case a fourth time. I think they'll just sneak off and lick their wounds."

She was right. On June 14 the King County Prosecutor's Office announced its decision to drop all charges against Tyrone Briggs. Joanne sent me a copy of the motion for dismissal of charges, dated June 14, 1990, and signed by deputy prosecuting attorney Mark Larson.

This case was tried to a jury on three occasions resulting in two hung juries and a conviction which was reversed due to juror misconduct. The most recent trial ended in a mistrial with the jury apparently split 10–2 in favor of acquittal. As there is no reason to believe that a fourth trial would offer some further resolution of the case, it is in the interests of justice that the case be dismissed."

"*. . . in the interests of justice . . .*"

Was justice served in this case? The State of Washington spent hundreds of thousands of dollars and thousands of man-hours in its attempt to prove that Tyrone Briggs was guilty, and in the end, after forty-one months, it failed. Theoretically, Tyrone Briggs is innocent, because the state failed in its attempt to prove guilt. That's what our system means by "the presumption of innocence"—a defendant is innocent until proven guilty.

But Tyrone Briggs's reputation has been sullied in the three and a half years since he was first accused of being "the Harborview Attacker." A newspaper editorial written after the final verdict reminded readers that Briggs is "not innocent, mind you, but not guilty." Even if another suspect is found, even if another man confesses, there will always be people who believe that Tyrone Briggs got off on a technicality, that he slipped through the system because the system is too "kind" to criminals.

"Not innocent, mind you, but not guilty." If you are not innocent and not guilty, what are you? A double negative does not make a positive, it just makes two negatives. And where does that leave Tyrone Briggs?

There are two separate worlds here, containing two separate, contradictory truths. There is the world of Tyrone and his family, Joanne Spencer, Richard Hansen, and all the others who believe with all their hearts that Tyrone is innocent. And there's the world of the victims and their families, the prosecutors and the police who believe equally firmly that Tyrone is guilty. Each world gathers into itself its supporters, who believe just as fiercely in their version of the "truth."

Three and a half years of accusations, imprisonments, trials, and ambiguous verdicts do something to a human being. Tyrone's stomach has been bothering him; he wakes up in the morning and takes a slug of Maalox. He's been suffering from headaches and nosebleeds. In the middle of the night, he is wrenched from sleep by a nightmare—the police are knocking on the door, walking down the narrow hallway, shining their massive lights in his face. The nightmare is that his life now is a dream.

The nightmare is that the past has come into the present. On the basketball court, playing one on one with his brother Eric, Tyrone freezes when a car door slams. He waits, poised to shoot the ball in the hoop, looking over his shoulder, letting the fear fade.

Police sirens make his heart speed up. Newspaper headlines—a woman is raped; a suspect is arrested; a trial begins—bring flashbacks, vivid and horrifying. The telephone rings and he holds back, afraid to breathe. "It's nothing," his mother automatically says, gently waving him away.

He fears being alone most of all, because when you're alone, you have no witnesses, no alibis, no one to add their voice to your story. "Keep a journal," his lawyers advise. "Write down everything you do, everywhere you go, everyone you see."

Is this the life of innocence? Tyrone is beginning to feel the anger that's been forced down all these years by the heavier weight of fear. Now that he's "free," now that the state has cut its chains and he can walk more than 150 feet from his house, he has the time and space to reflect on what he has lost. His best friend will graduate soon from college; because of the accusations and the trials, Tyrone never had the chance to finish high school. He shoots hoops every day, but because of the three years he's lost from his life, he's rusty and out of shape; he wonders, with sudden, sharp fury, if it's too late for him, if that basketball scholarship will go to someone younger, someone who's been practicing all these years. He works with his father as a stevedore at the shipyard, loading and unloading cargo ships, working overtime and through the weekends in order to help pay the bills, which are literally piled high.

A few days before the verdict in the Briggs case, I came across an article in the science section of *The New York Times* about catastrophic experiences that cause permanent changes in brain chemistry. Scientists discovered that when rats are subjected to electric shocks which they cannot escape, specific brain sites actually undergo physiological changes; researchers theorized that the same alteration in brain chemistry underlies the posttraumatic stress syndrome seen in Vietnam veterans, whose brains also may have been physically altered by the catastrophic, uncontrollable stress of combat.

> A single instance of overwhelming terror can alter the chemistry of the brain, making people more sensitive to adrenaline surges even decades later . . . for the brain changes to occur, people usually have to experience the stress as catastrophic, an overwhelming threat to life or safety and one over which they have no control . . . the more intense the trauma, and the longer it lasts, the more likely it is to result in post-traumatic stress. (*The New York Times,* June 12, 1990, p. C1)

The key, of course, lies in memory. If the rat could somehow forget the repeated electric shocks, each new shock would come as a surprise, and the brain would jolt along from shock to shock without undergoing any permanent change. If the Vietnam vet could erase all memories of the war, then the sound of a car backfiring or a helicopter hovering would lose its power to trigger brain responses. If Tyrone Briggs could take the last four years and pull them out of his brain, leaving no images intact, no memories to linger, he might truly be free.

But fear, powerlessness, and catastrophic stress make their mark on the mind. Some memories are so deeply rooted, so heavily rehearsed, that they stay with us word for word, image for image, for years. I once heard a story about the Venezuelan poet Ali Lameda who was imprisoned, interrogated, and tortured for more than six years in North Korea. When he was finally released from prison, he said, "They killed everything except my memory." What did he remember? During his imprisonment he had written in his mind more than four hundred poems and three hundred sonnets; every one of them was engraved in his memory.

How long will it take for Tyrone Briggs to forget, for the memories to fade and lose their power to hurt? How long will it take for Clarence Von Williams, Howard Haupt, Timothy Hennis, and Tony Herrerez to forget? When a memory spans a year, two years, four years of a life, when the bitterness and torment go on, day after day, year after year—at what point does the memory leave a permanent scar, vivid and deep in the mind?

I will forever be haunted by my memory of the day I knelt down by Steve Titus's grave and read the words on his tombstone.

> *He fought for his day in court,*
> *he was used, deceived, betrayed*
> *and denied justice even in death.*

Titus had been dead for five years, but the bitterness and anger lived on in those words. The memory was engraved in stone, and no one reading those words would be allowed to forget his tragic story.

And so it is with the others who have been trapped on the dark side of justice. The memories may fade, but the pain and anguish live on, in all who knew them, in all who were touched by their story.

SELECTED REFERENCES

Borchard, E. M., *Convicting the Innocent* (Garden City, NY, Garden City Pub. Co., 1932).

Buckhout, R. "Eyewitness Testimony." *Scientific American*, 231 (1974), 23–31.

Ceci, S. J. "The Suggestibility of Preschoolers' Recollections." Unpublished manuscript, Cornell University.

Ceci, S. J. Toglia, M. P., and Ross, M. (eds.). *Children's Eyewitness Testimony* (New York, Springer, 1987, pp. 79–91).

Clarke-Stewart, A., Thompson W., and Lepore, S. "Manipulating Children's Interpretations Through Interrogation." Paper presented at the Society for Research in Child Development, Kansas City, MO, April 1989.

Cutler, B. L., and Penrod, S. D. "Improving the Reliability of Eyewitness Identification: Lineup Construction and Presentation." *Journal of Applied Psychology*, 73 (1988), 281–290.

Dale, P. S., Loftus, E. F., and Rathbun, L. "The Influence of the Form of the Question on the Eyewitness Testimony of Preschool Children." *Journal of Psycholinguistic Research*, vol. 7, no. 4 (1978), pp. 269–277.

Donat, A. (ed.) *The Death Camp Treblinka* (New York, Holocaust Library, 1979).

Frank, J. *Not Guilty* (New York, Doubleday, 1957).

Freedman, J. L., and Loftus, E. F. "Retrieval of Words from Long-Term Memory." *Journal of Verbal Learning and Verbal Behavior*, 10 (1971), pp. 107–115.

Goodman, G. S. "Children's Testimony in Historical Perspective." *Journal of Social Issues*, vol. 40, no. 2 (1984), pp. 9–31.

Greene, E., and Loftus, E. F. "What's New in the News? The Influence of Well-Publicized News Events on Psychological Research and Courtroom Trials." *Basic and Applied Social Psychology*, 5 (1984), pp. 211–221.

Hopkins, E. H. "Fathers on Trial." *New York*, January 11, 1988. pp. 42–49.

Israel, M. "The Hard Fall." *New Jersey Monthly*, October 1981.

Lloyd-Bostock, S., and Clifford, B. *Evaluating Witness Evidence* (Chichester, England: Wiley, 1983).

Loftus, E. F. "Experimental Psychologist as Advocate or Impartial Educator." *Law and Human Behavior*, vol. 10 (1986), pp. 63–78.

———. *Eyewitness Testimony* (Cambridge, MA: Harvard University Press, 1979).

———. "Incredible Eyewitness." *Psychology Today*, December 1974, pp. 117–119.

———. *Memory* (Reading, MA: Addison-Wesley, 1980).

———. "Ten Years in the Life of an Expert Witness." *Law and Human Behavior*, vol. 10, no. 3 (1986), pp. 241–263.

Loftus, E. F., and Davies, G. M. "Distortions in the Memory of Children." *Journal of Social Issues*, vol. 40, no. 2 (1984), pp. 51–67.

Loftus, E. F., and Doyle, J. M. *Eyewitness Testimony: Civil and Criminal* (Charlottesville, VA: The Michie Co., 1987).

Loftus, E. F., and Freedman, J. L. "Effect of Category-Name Frequency on the Speed of Naming an Instance of the Category." *Journal of Verbal Learning and Verbal Behavior*, vol. 11 (1972), pp. 343–347.

Loftus, E. F., Greene, E. L., and Doyle, J. M. "The Psychology of Eyewitness Testimony." In D.C. Raskin (ed.), *Psychological*

Methods in Criminal Investigation and Evidence (New York: Springer, 1989, pp. 3–46).

Loftus, E. F. and Loftus, G. R. (1980). "On the Permanence of Stored Information in the Human Brain." *American Psychologist*, vol. 35, pp. 409–420.

Loftus, E. F., and Schneider, N. J. "Behold with Strange Surprise: Judicial Reactions to Expert Testimony Concerning Eyewitness Reliability." *University of Missouri–Kansas City Law Review*, vol. 56, no. 1 (1987), pp. 1–45.

McCloskey, M., and Egeth, H. "Eyewitness Identification: What Can a Psychologist Tell a Jury?" *American Psychologist*, vol. 38 (1983), pp. 550–563.

Munsterberg, H. *On the Witness Stand.* (New York: Doubleday, 1908).

Nevins, W. S. *Witchcraft in Salem Village* (Salem, MA: Salem Observer Press, 1892).

Nickerson, R. S., and Adams, M. J. "Long Term Memory for a Common Object." *Cognitive Psychology*, 11 (1979), pp. 287–307.

Piaget, J. *Play, Dreams, and Imitation* (New York: Norton, 1962).

Rabinowitz, D. "From the Mouths of Babes to a Jail Cell." *Harper's*, May 1990, pp. 52–63.

Raskin, D. C. "Science, Competence and Polygraph Techniques." *Criminal Defense*, 8 (1981), pp. 11–18.

Rattner, A. "Convicted but Innocent: Wrongful Conviction and the Criminal Justice System." *Law and Human Behavior*, vol. 12, no. 3 (1988), pp. 283–293.

Rattner, A. "Convicting the Innocent: When Justice Goes Wrong." Unpublished doctoral dissertation, Ohio State University, Columbus, OH, 1983.

Rodgers, J. E. "The Malleable Memory of Eyewitnesses." *Science 82*, June 1982, pp. 32–35.

Ryan, A. A., Jr. *Quiet Neighbors: Prosecuting Nazi War Criminals in America* (New York: Harcourt Brace Jovanovich, 1984).

Schooler, J. W., Gernard, D., and Loftus, E. F. "Qualities of the Unreal." *Journal of Experimental Psychology*, vol. 12, no. 2 (1986), pp. 171–181.

Sereny, Gitta. "How Guilty is Ivan?" *The Sunday Correspondent*, May 13, 1990.

Severance, L. J., and Loftus, E. F. "Improving the Ability of Jurors to Comprehend and Apply Criminal Jury Instructions." *Law and Society Review*, vol. 17, no. 1 (1982), pp. 154–197.

Sheehan, P. W. "Confidence, Memory and Hypnosis." In H. M. Pettinati (ed.), *Hypnosis and Memory* (New York: Guilford Press, 1988, pp. 95–127).

Varendonck, J. *"Les témoignages d'enfants dans un procès retentissant."* Archives de Psychologie, 11, 129–171.

Wagenaar, W. *Identifying Ivan* (Cambridge, MA: Harvard University Press, 1988).

Wells, G. L., and Loftus, E. F. (eds.). *Eyewitness Testimony: Psychological Perspectives* (Cambridge, Cambridge University Press, 1984).

Wells, G. L., and Turtle, J. W. "Eyewitness Testimony Research: Current Knowledge and Emergent Controversies." *Canadian Journal of Behavioral Science*, 19 (1987), pp. 363–388.